30p

A Guide to Learning Independently

A Guide to Learning Independently

Lorraine A. Marshall   Frances Rowland

The Open University Press

Milton Keynes

First published in this edition 1983
Reprinted 1989

Open University Press
12 Cofferidge Close
Stony Stratford
Milton Keynes MK11 1BY, England

British Library Cataloguing in Publication Data

Marshall, Lorraine A.
  A guide to learning independently.
  1. Independent study   2. Education, Higher
  I. Title   II. Rowland, Frances
  378' .17943   LB1049

ISBN 0-335-10117-8

Printed and bound by Butler & Tanner Ltd, Frome and London

Contents

List of Tables

Acknowledgements

We would like to thank the following for permission to reproduce illustrative material: Dennis Dobson, Publishers, London, for two drawings by Gerard Hoffnung from *Hoffnung's Constant Readers*, published by Dobson Books Ltd, and United Press International for six Peanuts cartoons by Charles M. Schulz © United Feature Syndicate, Inc. Sources for textual quotations are acknowledged in the Notes on pages 208–15.

Thanks

We would like to thank the people who have given us encouragement and advice, especially those who put time into reading the manuscript — Simon Avenell, Michael Booth, Mary Dale, Patsy Hallen, Richard Jakob-Hoff, Jim Macbeth, John Raser and John Webb. For comments on the section on using libraries, thanks to Tricia Cawley, Nancy Lane and Hugh Webb. We'd also like to thank our typists/secretaries Anne Francis, Leonie Pimm, Annette Ritchie, and especially Meredith Beevers for burning the midnight oil. For the use of a word processor, thanks to Bruce Kirkby and Churchlands College of Advanced Education, and for patient advice to two new authors, thanks to Christopher Roering and Juan Bailey of Longman Cheshire.

Thanks to my parents for their encouragement — to my father who gave so much and would have been so proud to have his copy of this book, and to my mother for her continuing support. Thanks to Al for the spark that led to this book. And last, but in fact first, special thanks to Jim for his patience and support throughout, for his endless reading of the drafts and for saving my sanity at sea.

Lorraine Marshall

My personal thanks to John Holt, who reminded me of what I believe about teaching; to Ann, who taught me about learning; and to Ann's babysitters, without whom I wouldn't have written this book. And to John — thank you.

Frances Rowland

Read This First!

If you're looking for a book which does more than describe techniques to help you succeed in your formal education, **A Guide to Learning Independently** is the book for you. It will help you with learning skills such as writing assignments, reading textbooks, taking notes and concentrating when you study, and it does present a range of techniques to help you meet the requirements of your teachers and courses. However, **A Guide to Learning Independently** is also designed to help you discover your own learning purposes and style. It doesn't set out to prescribe how you should learn, but offers a range of ideas and techniques from which you can choose. These alternatives are presented in the context of encouraging you to use tertiary institutions for your own purposes. To set the ideas and techniques in a broader framework, the book also discusses learning in general and tertiary education in particular.

This book focuses on you — who you are and what you bring to your learning. Throughout the book you are encouraged to examine your purposes and what you want to learn. You are also encouraged to look at how you learn informally, and to build on this self-knowledge in your formal learning. Implicit in this approach are the beliefs that there is no one way of learning which suits everyone and that it is your right and responsibility to shape your own learning.

So the *first five chapters* of the book concentrate on you — those aspects of your self and your lifestyle which affect your learning, when and how you study, and the decisions and adjustments you make when beginning tertiary studies. The importance of asking your own questions in your learning is emphasised, as is learning in ways that suit you so that you remember what you learn. The *next four chapters* look at how you can find, take in and evaluate information and ideas when pursuing your own and other people's questions. These chapters deal with defining and researching a topic, finding and using a range of information sources, reading and listening to lectures. The *last six chapters* look at communicating, using and evaluating what you learn. They deal with tutorials, seminars and informal discussion groups, with developing your writing style, and with writing and presenting assignments and reports.

Within each chapter you'll find questions and ideas about you as a learner. These are intended to centre the book on you and to help you discover your own purposes and methods for learning. Because the questions are based on the premise that only you can answer them, we don't prescribe one 'best' way of learning, but instead suggest alternative study techniques. We give reasons for these techniques so you can decide how useful they are for your purposes, and we encourage you to try them as you actually learn and study to find those which suit you. Often these techniques are presented in the framework of 'before', 'during' and 'after' stages of a learning activity, such as researching a topic and reading.

This book contains frequent *cross references* to other sections of the book. These direct you to another section within the chapter you're using [see '........'], to a section within another chapter [see '........' Ch. X], or to another whole chapter [see Ch. X].

In case you wish to go into a topic in greater depth, we suggest further reading at the end of some chapters and in a general bibliography. We also use quotations from a wide variety of sources to offer different perspectives, to reinforce what we say and to entertain you.

Each chapter in **A Guide to Learning Independently** *has a particular focus*. However, the ideas and techniques mentioned in any one chapter cannot be neatly separated from those in any other chapter, any more than your learning can be segmented. Use this introduction and the 'What to do now' section to familiarise yourself with the whole book. Use the Contents list to become familiar with the theme of each chapter. When working with a chapter, use the Index and cross references to move backwards and forwards through the book, to think about the ideas and techniques in different contexts.

This book is intended primarily as a *guide and reference* for people who have some opportunity for independent learning, no matter how small. It is intended for students who are past the age of compulsory schooling, and for people who want to learn how to use the resources of formal tertiary education for their own purposes in learning. However, the learning techniques presented in the book can be used in structured classes, and sections of the book can be used by people who need help with activities such as creative writing, producing business reports and running discussion groups.

You are likely to find the book valuable if you're a student at university or college, especially in first or second year. You'll find it useful if you're in the final years of high school, whether or not you're going on to tertiary study. If you've left school and are taking technical or training courses, the book can help you with basic learning skills. If you're a student who has little contact with teachers, perhaps because you belong to a large institution or because you're studying part-time or externally, the book offers information otherwise available from frequent face-to-face contact with teachers. If you're a student straight from a highly structured school situation, the book will help you adjust to taking responsibility for your studies. If you're returning to study after an absence from it, you can use our suggestions to help you gain confidence in yourself as a learner.

A Guide to Learning Independently can be used in several different ways, each of which involves actively trying the ideas and techniques in your learning and studying. Don't simply read the book. Acquaint yourself with its contents, and then use it as a guide and reference when the need arises. *Firstly*, you can use the book on your own. Refer to it, for example, when you need help with learning skills, such as using the library or writing an essay. Read chapters such as 'Learning and Remembering' and 'Learning from Evaluation' if you're thinking about the nature of formal tertiary education. *Secondly*, the book can be used when working on your study and learning with other people. You might, for example, use the chapter on 'Developing Your Own Writing Voice', to work on your writing with other students. The process of working with other students can enrich your learning and make it less solitary. You can also use the book when working on your learning skills with a teacher, so you can both relate our suggestions to your particular learning activity. For example, refer to the chapters on 'Defining and Researching a Topic' and 'Writing Assignments' when working on how to prepare and write an essay. *Thirdly*, teachers can use this book too. A teacher within a subject area can refer students to sections of the book which would be most helpful to the particular individual or group. Study skills teachers and counsellors can also use the book in their classes or with individual students.

However, all the ideas, information, techniques and suggestions we offer as co-authors are of little value to you as a student unless you're reading, writing, listening, talking, asking questions, experimenting, stretching your mind — unless you're engaged in learning. Exploring and practising alternative approaches to learning and study provides a basis from which you can choose those approaches which are most effective and satisfying for you. This experience with alternative ways of learning is also essential if you are to change habits which no longer suit you. Such changes take time and practice, and suggestions which are easy for us to make may take courage and persistence for you to apply. But defining your purposes, building on your strengths, and working on your weaknesses as a student are crucial to learning independently. This book is intended to help you discover these challenges and pleasures.

* * *

'Students' minds are like containers to be filled.'
'Education is to sharpen that tool which is the mind.'
'Knowledge is to be built up, block by block.'

These are a few of the metaphors commonly used to describe formal education. But such metaphors describe learning as essentially confined and defined, rather than as a process of growing and changing.

Each of us is born with a great curiosity, and this curiosity is essential for us to survive and learn. We learn as we ask and think about what we need and want to know. We are learning all the time, whether or not we realise it. We learn from what we do, from what happens to us, from our jobs and our pastimes...the list is endless. And we learn more easily when actively involved and when using what we learn in doing or talking, thinking or dreaming.

Learning is often thought of largely as an approved activity which happens in certain places (schools, universities and colleges) at certain ages (usually between five and twenty one) and in certain ways (in classrooms, according to a curriculum taught by teachers). But this formal study is only one part of our learning, and is designed to achieve only particular objectives. At the heart of all of our significant learning, formal and informal, are the questions we ask because of who we are and what we need to know.

Formal educational institutions can help you ask and pursue your own questions. There are teachers in these institutions who care about learning and about you as a learner, who can convey to you the fierce and gentle pleasures of the mind. Having teachers who help you ask your own questions, who share their knowledge and experience and who are also questioning and learning for themselves is an invaluable part of formal education. There are also students to talk and argue with, to theorise and fantasise with.

However, formal education can be one of the most effective methods for squashing curiosity or channelling it in artificial and unnecessary directions. And without curiosity, you're limited to learning what's presented to you rather than discovering how to learn, how to ask your own questions and communicate and exchange ideas. Knowing how to learn makes it possible for you to continue learning after you finish formal education. Otherwise you're restricted to learning a particular body of knowledge, which may soon become outdated.

Using the resources of an educational institution for your own purposes entails thinking about what's expected of you — and why. Who decides what you should learn, and how and when this should be taught? Who decides when and how you should be required to prove what you've learned? These decisions, made partly by teachers, reflect what many others see as the purposes of a university or college in our society. These 'others' include government bodies, academic committees, administrators, professional organisations, employers, and individuals who hold power in our society. If you want to use formal education as part of your purposes for learning rather than simply following other people's goals, try to identify and examine and question the assumptions and purposes of the people who shape tertiary education. Will you accept what these people expect, what they require? If not, think about your options.

Formal educational institutions expect a lot of you. As with most work, sometimes you'll be involved and enthusiastic, and sometimes you'll have other priorities in your life which detract from your study. Learning is a personal process, not simply a commodity or a meal ticket which you'll acquire after a set programme of study, so keep your questions and your purposes in mind. Play with ideas — speculate, hypothesise, fantasise. Do the ideas offered excite you or make sense to you? If so, grab them with both halves of your brain. Read, write, draw, experiment, for the sake of your own learning and pleasure and discovery of a craft. Learn how to communicate your own questions and ideas, and try hard to understand what others are communicating. Don't reject an idea or a topic or a course out of hand because of your biases or lazinesses or fears. Be willing to take a risk, to reach a little further than you're sure you can reach. Don't expect to understand all you read or hear or say.

Real, active learning of your own isn't easy — it's hard work. But the hard work is not that of a dutiful conscience, it arises from the joy of intense involvement. One of the most challenging things you can do is to attempt to be aware of your purposes for learning, to question profoundly what and how you learn, to communicate your ideas clearly and to understand the thoughts of others. This process of learning is one of growing and changing, and that's more exciting than filling bins or sharpening tools or building with blocks.

What to do now

1 Read through the Contents list.

2 Flick through the book and choose a chapter which would be especially useful to you now, or start with Chapter 1 'You' or Chapter 5 'Learning and Remembering'. Read thoroughly the chapter you've chosen.

3 Choose a topic which interests you, locate it by using the Contents list, then look it up in the Index, and read the relevant pages of the book.

4 Turn to Table 8.1, 'The Anatomy of a book', and apply the questions in this table to *A Guide to Learning Independently*.

5 Look back over 'Read This First!'

6 Any questions or ideas? Ask someone else — another student, a teacher, a friend — for their thoughts on your questions and ideas.

1 You

My plea here is simple. Look at yourself long enough to know you are there . . . and then go as you choose.

Bob Samples

This book begins with you. It begins with you because asking questions and thinking about yourself and your lifestyle can give you insights into your individual learning style. With these insights, you can make your learning and study more satisfying and effective.

Your body, your emotions and your beliefs, who you live with and where you study — all these affect your learning. Your physical state and your emotions influence your ability to learn, and too little sleep or exercise may affect your enthusiasm for study. A belief in the value of hard work may make you a conscientious student. An argument with the people in your household can create difficulties when you try to concentrate on study, and moving house or changing jobs can leave little time and energy for formal learning.

As people and as students we're all different. If you're slow and ambling, a study task may take you longer. This may leave you feeling inadequate, or you can enjoy the leisurely savouring of new ideas. At the other extreme, if you've a high energy level and live at a fast pace, you might wish you could occasionally slow down enough to integrate in more depth what you learn, or you might enjoy the speed with which new insights come to you. There's no one way of learning and studying that suits everyone. And because you change daily, weekly and monthly, there's no one way of studying which always suits you. So you need to get to know who you are and examine how you live.

This chapter contains two parts — your self, and your surroundings. Each section of the chapter gives you information, asks questions and makes suggestions. It's a chapter to work with, to take time with. Consider the questions and suggestions carefully. Here are some ideas on how to use them.

- Read each set of questions in turn and write down your answers or ideas on them, perhaps in a special notebook or a journal [see 'Keeping a journal', Ch. 11]. When you've read and thought about the whole chapter, look back over it and revise any notes.

- Read through the whole chapter and think about those questions and suggestions which are relevant to you at present. Later re-read the chapter and focus on other questions. Re-think your responses if you or your lifestyle have changed significantly.

- Discuss the questions with one or two friends or with a group of people.

- If you want to read more on a topic, check the further reading at the end of the chapter or in the general bibliography.

Your self

This section looks at aspects of your self that directly affect your learning and your study. As a first step to thinking about your self, centre your attention on your body. Stop for a few minutes. Centre your attention on your face — your forehead, eyes, nose, mouth, jaw. Are they relaxed? strong? tired? tense? Move your awareness down to your neck, shoulders, spine. Focus on each part of your body — down to your toes. How does your whole body feel now?

What do you like most about your body?
What do you like least?
How does your body feel now?

Now **stop**. Did you actually spend time thinking about and answering these questions, or did you just read them? If you didn't answer them, go back and think about them seriously. Get in touch with your body before you go on to the next set of questions. This chapter centres on you, but can only be effective if you become *actively* involved with the questions and ideas it contains.

Body rhythms

Certainly people show consistent, life-long predilections for morning or night activity. Physiological differences may be found in the circadian rhythms of the so-called lark people, who are most alive by morning, and the owls, who perform at their best late in the day, yet the owls are generally penalised by the usual scheduling of school hours.

Gay Gaer Luce

Your body has many rhythms and cycles. Each day, for example, your temperature and pulse rate fluctuate slightly, and you pass through the same pattern of dreaming several times each night. Monthly cycles apparently occur for males as well as females. Perhaps you go through cycles where your desire for physical activity alternates with your desire for mental activity. One of the difficulties in studying for final exams is that you often need to be mentally active during the first bright spring days when you'd prefer to be outside and physically active after the hibernation of winter. If you're a night person you may be unwilling to leave your bed for an early lecture on a gloomy winter morning, or if you're a day person, you may find it difficult to concentrate during an evening class. A cup of coffee may revive you for that evening class, but regularly using stimulants to help you cope with study is self-defeating in the long run. Discovering your individual body rhythms can help you plan study times when you're more mentally active.

Are you a lark or an owl?
Are you aware of patterns in your body's needs for sleep? for exercise? for food? for sex?
How is your study related to these patterns?

- Determine when during the day you're usually most alert mentally and when you feel physically ready to study.

- Try to schedule your classes and your study during your alert times. If it's necessary to study when your energy level is low, plan to do work which demands less intense concentration.

Sleep

I haven't been to sleep for over a year. That's why I go to bed early. One needs more rest if one doesn't sleep.

Evelyn Waugh

Sleep needs vary for different people. If you're frequently irritable and can't cope as well as usual with minor problems, you're probably getting too little sleep. How well you concentrate on study is influenced by how much sleep you have.

Do you often sleep so much that your mind feels drugged?
What effect does a late or interrupted night's sleep have on your concentration next day?

Can you think clearly after a nap? Does a brief nap or a couple of hours sleep refresh you for long periods of study?
When do your sleep needs vary, for example, when you are emotionally upset or physically active? Do you often have to change your sleep times, for example, because of shift work or a restless baby? How do these changes affect your study?

- Think about your sleep patterns for the past two weeks. Determine your minimum sleep needs and the amount of sleep you think you need for a good night's rest.

- Try to work out how your sleep patterns help or interfere with your learning.

- Try to plan your most demanding study periods for times when you can get enough sleep.

- On a night when you can't fall asleep, try deep breathing exercises and relaxing your body completely [see 'Tension and relaxation']. If this doesn't work, get up and do something rather than lie in bed and worry about not sleeping.

- If you often have difficulty getting enough sleep, allow time to wind down before going to bed, and don't drink a lot of tea and coffee during the evening. Give yourself two or three periods of deep relaxation during the day. Relaxing your body fully from head to toe is different from sleeping, but can be almost as refreshing.

Food and drink

> One cannot think well, love well, sleep well, if one has not dined well.
> Virginia Woolf

A breakfast which is more nourishing than tea and toast, or a lunch which is more than a bag of chips or a doughnut, helps you concentrate during class or private study. A light evening meal instead of a large dinner makes it easier to focus on your study or during an evening class. If you generally feel tired and irritable because of poor eating or heavy drinking, studying is difficult at any time.

Do you prefer to eat one large meal a day or frequent small meals? Do you try to study after a large meal?
When settling to study, does preparing something to eat or drink help or hinder you?
Do you often drink so much alcohol that you cannot think clearly next day?

- Make sure your diet is well balanced. Essential protein is available from complex carbohydrates such as beans or rice as well as from meat and dairy products, but refined carbohydrates such as ice cream, alcohol and soft drinks add little to your diet except calories. If you generally lack energy, check that your diet isn't deficient in minerals and vitamins, particularly iron and the Vitamin B complex. If you don't have much money, eating properly takes more planning and a knowledge of nutrition, but it can be done.

- Avoid studying after a heavy meal.

- If you feel the need for food during a study session have a small amount of protein food, such as a piece of cheese, a glass of milk, or a handful of peanuts. Sugary food gives you a temporary lift then leaves you more tired than before.

- A judiciously chosen treat can help you when you settle to work or reward you when you finish.

Physical exercise

> Exercise is bunk. If you are healthy, you don't need it: if you are sick, you shouldn't take it.
>
> Attributed to Henry Ford

Physical exercise can provide a welcome break from mental activity. It helps your studying because it reduces tension, increases the oxygen supply to your brain, improves your digestion and helps you sleep more soundly. Long periods without exercising your body can make it difficult to exercise your mind effectively. However, immediately after strenuous physical exercise some people find it difficult to settle down to study.

What form of physical exercise do you enjoy — for example, a team sport, cycling, swimming, sailing, yoga, sex, dancing, walking?
If you're a physically active person, do you find it difficult to sit still for long periods to read, write or listen to a lecture?
Does exercise usually refresh or fatigue you for learning?
Do you renew your concentration during a study session by taking a short break to move about?

- Choose exercise that feels good to you and do it regularly. Include activity that exercises your whole body, including your heart and lungs, and activity which stretches your body and helps you loosen up.

- Plan to study and exercise when these two activities help rather than conflict with each other.

- If your work is physically tiring, allow yourself time to relax and eat something nourishing before you try to study.

- At times when you need to be especially mentally alert, such as during exams, regular physical exercise helps increase your alertness and concentration.

Senses

All creative activity, as well as much of your pleasure in life, depends on your sensory awareness. Even your ability to absorb and use second-hand information depends on your ability to relate it to your own first-hand observations. Yet, constantly exposed to second-hand information, you may forget to use your senses and may become, to some degree, cut off from the world immediately around you.

Fred Morgan

Your earliest learning is through your senses, but as you come to rely more on abstract reasoning it's easy to forget how vital your senses are to your learning.

Stop for a moment. Shut your eyes. What can you smell? What can you hear? What tastes do you have in your mouth? What sensations do you feel on your skin? Now open your eyes. What can you see?

- At the end of each day ask yourself what you remember most vividly — which sight, sound, taste or touch comes instantly to your mind? Conjure up these sense impressions as you drift off to sleep or write a description of them in a daily journal.

- When you feel like relaxing, take a few minutes to become deeply aware of the smells, sounds, tastes, touch and sights you are experiencing.

Tension and relaxation

"How did I live to be a hundred years old? Well, when I moves I moves slow. When I sits, I sits loose. And when I worries, I goes to sleep."

Liz Carpenter

If you are relaxed you can learn more effectively. To relax, you may need to put aside problems for a while, exercise more often, or learn how to relax your body consciously from head to toe.

Where in your body do you usually feel anxiety or tension?
Do you feel relaxed now? If so, why? If not, why not?
Can you study when you feel tense? If not, do you know how to relax?
While you're studying or listening to a lecture, do you occasionally check to see if any parts of your body are tense?
After a period of study do you suffer from eye strain, headaches, or tension in your shoulder muscles?

- Learn and practise relaxation techniques which help your whole body relax fully — for example, deep breathing, yoga, gentle exercise, massage.

- If you think that your tension is due to physical causes such as eyestrain, seek appropriate help.

- When reading or writing, stretch and change positions occasionally, rest your eyes by focusing on a distant object, and yawn and take several deep breaths to ease any tension around your mouth and jaw.

Emotional energy

I worry about my sexual prime and where to spend it, my smoking habit and how to end it. I worry about the possible connection between the two. I worry about writer's block, whether it's on the West of the East side of town.

Lee Israel

The ups and downs of your emotions influence your learning. If you're feeling cheerful you probably find it easy to study; if you're feeling depressed you may have difficulty concentrating or absorbing new ideas. Most students have emotional problems at one time or another — including anxiety or guilt about study.

What are the most positive aspects in your life at present? List these.
What are the most positive aspects of your studies?
What are you most worried about? List these worries.
What aspects of your studies worry you the most?

- Write down what's worrying you before you begin studying or if you continue to be distracted as you study. Ask yourself if it is more urgent to go on studying or to tackle your worries. Plan another time to deal with whichever is less urgent.

- Spend five to ten minutes each morning remembering your dreams. This becomes easier with practice, and reflecting on your dreams can help you sort out your emotions.

- Allow yourself a set time during the day to think about your problems and try to put them aside for the rest of the day. Talk to a friend about them or write them out.

- Practice physical relaxation techniques or activities which help you deal with your emotions.

- Reading for pleasure can give you a respite from your worries.

- Spend some time away from the place where you seem to worry most. Going for a walk or visiting friends can make problems seem less important.

- If you have a persistent problem, discuss it with someone — a close friend, a sympathetic 'outsider' or a trained counsellor.

- If your difficulties are connected with your learning or lack of it, do some work. A few hours of concentrated study often works wonders if you're feeling overwhelmed with study demands. If you're stuck on a problem, discuss it with your teacher or with other students — often other people have the same problem. Read the relevant sections in this guide for some useful suggestions.

- If you're anxious about a responsibility such as taking an exam or giving a seminar paper, find out as precisely as possible what you want to know about your subject, and study it as thoroughly as you can. Talk to someone with experience in the techniques of exams or seminars, or read the relevant sections in this book.

Beliefs and values

> Everything we do, every decision we make and course of action we take, is based on our consciously or unconsciously held beliefs, attitudes and values. ... Ideally, our choices will be made on the basis of the values we hold; but frequently, we are not clear about our own values.
>
> Sidney B. Simon, *et al.*

What you believe and value directly affects your learning. It can affect your choice of courses, your work within courses, your open-mindedness and how you relate to other students and to teachers. For example, if you're concerned with conservation you might write your assignments on topics related to this area; if you don't believe in genetic engineering you may find yourself in conflict with teachers in a biology course who see no harm in this area of research.

At times your beliefs and values conflict with your learning. For example, a course on Eastern religious philosophy may affect your belief in a Western ethic which is goal-oriented. You may find yourself disillusioned with the studies required for a long dreamed-of profession, or with the realities of formal education. Perhaps you're confronted with a challenge to a cherished prejudice about the superiority of the male sex or of white-skinned races. A new insight into personal relationships can create dissatisfaction with your own.

How would you complete the sentences:

'I believe that human beings are essentially...'
'I believe that our society should be organised so that...

How does what you believe and value affect what and how you learn?

- Try to work out which beliefs and values are most important to you, and try to identify those which are embedded in your upbringing.

- If a conflict of beliefs and values is seriously affecting you, talk it over with a close friend or a counsellor. If this conflict is related to a course, talk to a teacher in that course if possible.

- Think about the beliefs and values of the other people with whom you have frequent contact — your friends, a partner, your teachers, fellow students. Try to work out why they differ from or are similar to your own.

Your surroundings

The environment in which you work and play and eat and sleep influences your learning. If you're a full-time student and your friends frequently drop by, your approach to studying will differ from that of a parent with young children who is studying part-time and taking evening classes, or an external student who lives and works on a farm. If you have a room of your own, you'll organise study sessions differently from a person who works at the kitchen table or in a library. It's not essential to have ideal surroundings before you can study effectively, but often you can make changes which improve your study situations.

This section looks at two aspects of your surroundings which directly affect your learning — the people you live with and the places where you study — and suggests alternatives which can make study easier.

Who you live with

On Mondays mum has a tutorial, so I have to go around to Grandma's place for tea. That's all right. She lets me watch television.

8 year-old girl

The time and energy you have for study can be dramatically increased if you manage to work out a satisfactory living pattern with the other people in your home. This usually takes time, and even if you have a comfortable arrangement, there'll be difficult periods as you all adapt to the inevitable changes in your lives. But any time and effort in this direction is well spent to increase your enjoyment of formal learning. If the people you live with co-operate in making your study possible, you'll have more energy and enthusiasm for study.

Do you live on your own, or with others — parents, relatives, friends, other students, a partner/spouse, children?
Do your working hours coincide with those of the other people in your house? Are the others also studying or do they have some idea of the demands of being a student? Are they considerate of your study needs? Do they resent the time you spend studying? How do you arrange time with them and time to study?
Do you have responsibilities in your household, such as domestic chores, financial burdens, or caring for young children or a sick relative? Do these responsibilities leave you little time and energy for study? How might they be reallocated?
Are you under pressure from people such as your partner or your parents to succeed in your studies? Why? Are their criteria for success the same as yours?

- If there's a persistent or major problem in your living arrangements which makes it difficult for you to study, talk about it as soon as possible with the person or people you live with. Describe how you feel about the problem and suggest ways it might be handled, particularly what you can do about it. Listen to suggestions from others concerned and see if you can come to a workable compromise. If compromise doesn't seem possible, think seriously about the priority that formal learning has in your life [see 'All work and no play...', Ch. 2]

Where you study

If you're deeply involved with what you're learning, you can concentrate just about anywhere for short periods of time. However in formal learning, you also need to concentrate for sustained periods and to study subjects which aren't of immediate importance to you. It's then that your surroundings become important.

Location

Where do you prefer to study? Does a relatively impersonal environment such as a library help you study?
Are the books and references you need readily available where you study?
Are there other people around where you study? Are they also studying? Do they help or hinder your learning? Why?

- Decide whether you study more effectively at home or elsewhere. If necessary, try to reorganise your time so that you can study in the location where you learn most effectively.

Study spots

> You say I'm well read.
> Thank you but —
> I owe my deep and liberal knowledge
> To the 100 watt bulb
> in the loo
> And not college
>
> Margaret Norton

If you don't have a quiet study place at home where you can leave your work spread out, can you arrange one? How?
What objects on your work space help you study — a box of file cards, a dictionary, photographs, a collection of shells, a bunch of flowers? Why?
Can you study effectively outdoors?

- The association of one place with a particular study activity helps you settle down to study more quickly and also enables you to leave it behind when you finish. You might choose a comfortable chair to read a book, but prefer a library desk when organising essay notes.

- If possible, find or create one or two places where you can regularly study — a desk in your bedroom at home, a corner table in a library or a chair in a quiet room at a friend's house. You may be able to screen off a corner of a room or to move a table into one corner of a backyard workshop.

- Create a work space which includes objects which prompt you to study and is organised according to your needs for space and order. Having your own work space, no matter how small, is much preferable to packing away your papers and books each time after you use them.

Comfort

You concentrate better on studying if you're physically relaxed (but not too relaxed!) — if you're sitting in a comfortable position, with lighting that cuts down eye strain, and without distracting noise.

Are you more comfortable when studying at a table or desk, or when sitting on a couch or bed? Do any of these positions help you study for a sustained period?
If your study places are too warm, too cold or too stuffy, how can you alter this?
What type of noise distracts you? How long can you concentrate fully with 'background' music playing?

- Prevent eye strain by avoiding glare or uneven lighting on your book or work surface. Try to use adequate direct and indirect light or a 14-watt white fluorescent desk light. Light the whole room as evenly as possible, and position yourself so that light falls over the shoulder opposite your writing arm to avoid a shadow on your work space. Prop up your book at a constant angle so your eyes don't have to accommodate to different distances.

- To reduce noise distraction, avoid irregular noise and exciting music, use ear plugs or head phones, or study when your household is at its quietest.

- If you're cold, put on an extra layer of clothes, wrap yourself in a blanket, or turn a heater on at a low setting rather than attempting to study in a stuffy overheated room. If the weather's hot, study at the cooler times of day.

* * *

The questions and suggestions in this chapter have focused on you — because you are central to this book and to what, why and how you learn. Reading and following guidelines which tell you how to make your formal learning more effective is useful only if you adapt these guidelines to your own personality, lifestyle and surroundings.

> If a man does not keep pace with his companions, perhaps it is because he hears a different drummer. Let him step to the music which he hears, however measured or far away.
>
> Henry David Thoreau

Further reading

Currer, Norman. *Foods We Should and Shouldn't Eat*. Rigby, Australia, 1960.

Faraday, Ann. *Dream Power*. Pan Books, London, 1973.

Faraday, Ann. *The Dream Game*. Perennial Library, Harper and Row, New York, 1976.

Hall, Dorothy. *The Natural Health Book*. Nelson, Melbourne, 1976.

Iyengar, B.K.S. *Light on Yoga*. Allen & Unwin, London, 1966.

Lewis, H.R. and Streitfeld, H.S. *Growth Games*. 2nd edn. Souvenir Press, London, 1972.

Luce, Gay Gaer. *Body Time: The Natural Rhythms of the Body*. Paladin, Granada Publishing, St Albans, England, 1973.

Royal Canadian Air Force. *XBX Physical Fitness*. Penguin Books, Middlesex, England, 1960.

2 Planning When and How You Study

This chapter looks at planning when to study and at how to go about studying and concentrating. It begins with examining your life to determine the place study plays in it.

All work and no play...

> It is impossible to enjoy idling thoroughly unless one has plenty of work to do.
>
> Jerome K. Jerome

As a student you're likely to be involved in campus or community activities, socialising, sport, hobbies, personal relationships, domestic chores, childcare or a paid job. These involvements may enhance your learning, for example, if you're a keen athlete taking physical education courses; or they may conflict with your study, for example, if your drinking mates scorn your study. What part does study play in your life?

- List four activities which take a lot of time and energy in your life at present. List four activities which you think should take the most time and energy, and the four on which you would like to spend the most time and energy.

- Then ask yourself if your non-academic activities and interests leave you sufficient time and energy for formal learning, and whether they increase or decrease your satisfaction with that learning.

- If other involvements prevent you from learning as well as you'd like, consider cutting down on these involvements, reducing the number of courses you're taking, or reducing the time and effort you put into a course.

- If there is a significant difference between your current involvements and those you feel you should or would like to have, consider changing your priorities. Think about why you are at university or college, and how important your formal learning is to you.

Learning can be one of the most creative and satisfying pleasures you experience. However, there are inevitably times in your formal learning when you have to make yourself work — when you're not interested in a topic, when you have difficulty with an assignment, or when you have other things on your mind. It is at these times that planning can be useful.

Planning how to spend your time can give you the opportunity to explore the pleasures of using your mind and can help you cope with times when it's difficult to study. If you're happy working to a plan, don't make it too ambitious, and don't let it rule your life so that you rarely do anything spontaneously. Any schedule needs to be flexible.

Whether or not you like to plan your time, examining your objectives and workload for a year is important.

Planning a year's study

> The road to hell is paved with good intentions.
>   Proverb

Your objectives.   Planning a year's study involves formulating your objectives for the courses you'll take, and drawing up a schedule of work to be done. For each course think about:

— where it fits into the overall objectives of your formal education
— how it's connected with your other courses
— your knowledge of the course content
— your interests or questions concerning the subject
— skills you want to acquire, and
— grades you hope to achieve.

Your workload.   Plan your workload for the year, taking into account the time you spend in class, listening to tapes or reading course materials, preparing and producing assignments and reports, and reviewing material after a class or when preparing for exams.

One value of planning is that it minimises the stress that usually accompanies last-minute assignment writing or studying for exams. It's all too easy to delude yourself that there's ample time to complete an assignment or to study. Look realistically at your other study commitments for the same period and think about the activities necessary before each assignment is complete. Ideally, you would also allow 'just in case' time — just in case you have a cold in the week you plan to study, just in case you have an unexpected visit from an old friend when a major essay is due. Give yourself time for the pleasure of exploring areas arising from your study but not directly related to your current goals, needs or pressures.

A method to use. Try the following method of planning your year's study.

- At the start of a year, find out as precisely as possible what work you want to do or are required to do in that period. Do you have exams, major and minor assignments, weekly preparation for tests or classes? Draw up a calendar or buy and use a year planner to show at a glance your study schedule and other commitments.

- Allow time for:
  - choosing and defining a topic
  - searching for and selecting material (including any field work)
  - researching and organising material
  - reading and notetaking
  - writing (or taping or filming), and
  - editing your work.

  Each of these is an activity in its own right and can require a deceptively large amount of time. Writing a report, for example, is not merely a final chore to be hastily completed after your practical and field work is complete. If possible, allow more time than you think necessary for each activity.

- Estimate how much time you have to devote to an individual piece of work. This largely determines the depth and breadth of your approach to the topic, as well as the quality of the end result.

Within the framework of your long-term plan, you can also plan how to spend your week.

Planning your week

'There's lots to do; we have a very busy schedule —
   'At 8 o'clock we get up, and then we spend
   'From 8 to 9 daydreaming.

'From 9.00 to 9.30 we take our early midmorning nap.

'From 9.30 to 10.30 we dawdle and delay.

'From 10.30 to 11.30 we take our late early morning nap.

'From 11.30 to 12.00 we bide our time and then eat lunch.

'From 1.00 to 2.00 we linger and loiter.

'From 2.00 to 2.30 we take our early afternoon nap.

'From 2.30 to 3.30 we put off for tomorrow what we could have done today.

'From 3.30 to 4.00 we take our early late afternoon nap.

'From 4.00 to 5.00 we loaf and lounge until dinner.

'From 6.00 to 7.00 we dilly-dally.

'From 7.00 to 8.00 we take our early evening nap, and then for an hour before we go to bed at 9.00 we waste time.

'As you can see, that leaves almost no time for brooding, lagging, plodding, or procrastinating, and if we stopped to think or laugh, we'd never get nothing done.'

Norton Juster

To draw up a weekly study plan requires some knowledge of your lifestyle and of yourself as a learner, such as whether you often write with ease, or when during the day you're likely to be most alert mentally. Do you work best in bursts of intense activity for several days or weeks, with brief periods of relaxation in between; or do you prefer a regular daily or weekly work session?

If you prefer not to plan your time or find it difficult to keep to a plan, try setting aside and using a regular time each day or week for concentrated study, or making and using a list of 'things to do'. These strategies can ease the worry of apparently having a lot of work and no time in which to do it. Use some of the suggestions in this chapter when your workload overwhelms you.

If you haven't thought much about how you spend your time, **the following exercise** will make you more aware of this. As it concerns a short period, the exercise is only an indicator of your current activities. But it can help you realise what priority study has in your life, how other activities can help or hinder your study, and where your time 'vanishes' to.

1 *Examine how you spend your time.*   For a few days or a week, preferably near the beginning of semester/term/quarter, note how much time is occupied by:

— formal classes

— private study

— relaxing and socialising

— domestic chores and family activities

— travelling, and

— sleeping and eating.

Note particularly any activities which take up a lot of time. Look for hidden time-consumers, such as watching TV. Indicate the times during your private study when you concentrated at your best. Make sure your record is accurate — recording three hours' work on statistics is misleading if you spent part of that three hours on the telephone chatting to a friend, fixing yourself a snack or watering the garden.

At the end of the week, estimate the number of hours you spent in each of the areas listed above, and ask yourself the following questions about your data.

Were there times when I studied more effectively, such as early in the morning or when I had the entire day to study? Why?
Did I work more effectively in some places than others, for example, in the library or at home? Why?
How did the amount of time I spent in classes compare with the time I spent on study out of class?
Did I have a particularly heavy workload this week?
Did I usually work more effectively in short periods and then lose my concentration, or did it take me a while to settle into study so that I needed longer periods for serious work?
Is my study connected with any of my other activities?
Did I prepare myself for long periods of serious study? How? Was this effective? Did I relax afterwards?

Now that you have some data on how you spent a few days or a week, are you happy with how you spent your time? Did you spend enough time studying effectively? Would you like to make any changes? If so...

2 *Map out a week's work.*   Take into account your findings and include the following:

— look at your long-term calendar and see what work is due soon
— chart in your short-term formal study commitments, such as giv-ing a seminar paper
— mark in any informal commitments connected with your study, such as an appointment with your tutor
— indicate your other commitments
— write out a list of what you want to accomplish during the week and when
— plan to study when you're usually able to concentrate most effec-tively
— plan relaxation and social activities so that they and your studies complement each other, and
— set aside time at the end of each day's study to review your work.

At the end of the second week, think back on how your week has resembled your plan. Don't worry if you didn't keep absolutely to your schedule — instead examine *why* you didn't.

Efficiency concerns the best ways of doing an assigned job. Effectiveness, on the other hand, concerns the *best use of time* — which may or may not include doing the particular job in question.

Edwin C. Bliss

*   *   *

Both your long-term and weekly study plans need to combine flexibility and a commitment to realistic goals. You can best use your plans by reviewing them several times during a course. Adjust them according to your current study needs and purposes, and to take account of other changes in your life. At the beginning of a course you explore and familiarise yourself with the areas to be covered, so you probably spend a high proportion of study time in research and in classes. Half-way through a course you're likely to be relating new materials to what you have already learned and to be planning and producing written work as well as attending classes and doing research. Near the end of a course you review what you've learnt, and are probably involved in completing major assignments and preparing for exams.

Planning *when* to study is a beginning. To make full use of the time you've set aside, think also about *how* to study.

Concentrating while you study

"How *can* you go on talking so quietly, head downwards?" Alice asked, as she dragged him out by the feet, and laid him in a heap on the bank.

The Knight looked surprised at the question. "What does it matter where my body happens to be?" he said. "My mind goes on working all the same."

Lewis Carroll

Concentrating is not always something you have to work at — if you really want to know or do something you can concentrate easily, possibly for a long time. When concentrating fully you're so absorbed in what you're doing that you are unaware of time passing or of what is going on around you. Watch a small child building a sand castle, or two friends involved in an intense argument.

However, if you're required to learn about a topic which doesn't particularly interest you or to study for a purpose which doesn't coincide with yours, or if you have to study at times or in ways which are difficult for you — then you have to make an effort to focus and sustain your concentration. Have you ever noticed that during a lecture many of the audience suddenly become restless, or that shortly before the end of a lecture many people change position, look at their watches and prepare to leave? The length of time for which you can concentrate fully depends on factors such as your enthusiasm for what you're doing, your skill at a particular task, your emotional and physical state, and your surroundings at the time.

You don't have to assume the position of Rodin's Thinker or to sit at a desk with pen in hand to concentrate. Why not let your ideas sort themselves out while you surf, watch the sunset, go for a long walk, or drive to college? When you do read and write, concentrating is not simply reading every word on a page or putting lots of words onto paper. Full concentration involves actively questioning your material. Without this questioning you won't understand what you read or be able to organise what you write and share your ideas and knowledge with others.

This section suggests methods of concentrating more effectively in study sessions of at least an hour. These sessions might include reading, notetaking, writing, organising or editing material, or listening to tapes. Concentration during class or while working with other people involves similar principles.

> Experience as a mother has taught me a lot. Gone are the days of spending uninterrupted hours writing an essay or compiling a report. I'm lucky if I get half an hour now. But this maternal conditioning has its advantages. I'm now capable of making the maximum use of the time that is available and then switching off when family demands become pressing. Learning to use the available time to maximum advantage is one of the main secrets to success of the part-time student mother.
>
> Vivienne

Have you consciously thought about your study habits — when, where and how you prefer to study? How do you settle down for a study session? For how long can you concentrate fully? What do you do when you find it difficult to concentrate? There will be times when you can only concentrate for short periods, or when you can't concentrate at all.

However, you can concentrate longer and more effectively if you know how to cope with distractions which can arise at certain points in your study. While you are warming up or preparing for concentrated study, your mind is often partly elsewhere. After you have been concentrating intensely for a short time, you may suddenly become impatient with your task, be unable to capture a particular thought or think through a specific problem clearly, and you may begin to feel stiff from sitting still. After long concentrated work, you feel less mentally alert because you're reaching the end of your concentration span for a particular subject. When you can no longer concentrate at all, outside thoughts or events intrude and you feel generally tired.

1 Warming up

Demanding physical exercise requires a warm-up session; so does strenuous study. You can begin this mental warm-up during your previous activity. When driving to the library, you can plan what you'll study; while doing household chores you can mull over ideas for an essay; while finishing a task, visualise yourself sitting down at your desk with a cup of coffee and beginning to study. When you actually sit down at your study place, deliberately preparing your mind for study can motivate you to study, help you eliminate conflict or anxieties from your mind, focus your mind on the task at hand, and increase your ability to understand what you learn so that you remember it more easily.

If you have difficulty settling down to study, the following suggestions may help.

(a) Consider **how you feel** emotionally and physically. If you feel good, direct this energy to learning. If you're not in the state of mind for studying, decide if you need to study at this particular time. If you don't, plan another time to work. If you do, use techniques that help you set your problems aside [see 'Emotional energy', Ch. 1]. Try a brief energetic walk, a run around the block, a cup of tea, or a short chat with a friend.

(b) Seat yourself **comfortably**, with everything you need at hand (books, blank papers, coffee, lecture notes).

(c) Decide on your **time limits** for this study session. If you don't have outside time constraints, set the minimum time to become involved in your subject. Set a maximum time, so you don't feel overwhelmed by apparently endless work and so you can focus your energy fully. Don't make these times so inflexible that you feel you must stop work precisely at the time planned. Plan to reward yourself after you've completed your study by doing something you particularly enjoy — go to the beach, visit a friend, watch a special TV programme or prepare your favourite snack.

(d) Decide **what to study** while your mind is fresh. Will you start with the subject or activity you find easiest? Will you tackle an assignment that's been worrying you or which you've been intending to do for a long time?

Think about the study activities you have to choose from. You might:

— read for a tutorial paper or an essay
— edit the final draft of an assignment
— write the first draft of an assignment, a short story, a lab report, or a journal entry

— prepare an annotated bibliography or illustrations for an assignment
make a tape recording
— listen to a radio programme or a lecture tape, or
— learn data by heart.

Set yourself a goal to accomplish. If you've a large task, tackle it one section at a time.

(e) Begin your study with **a brief warm-up task** which helps you concentrate. Use this task only if it's necessary — not if it's a form of procrastination.

• Do some routine tasks which are part of the subject, such as filing lecture notes or compiling a list of important vocabulary.

• Revise previous work in the area, for example, summarise notes, write comments on a discussion. This revision brings ideas to the front of your mind, and can give you a sense of achievement if you're overwhelmed by the study before you.

• Foreshadow a topic by asking yourself 'Why am I studying this topic?' 'To whom do I want to communicate my ideas?' For example, are you studying to clarify ideas for your own benefit, or to prepare for a tutorial? Brainstorm your topic by jotting down as many ideas on it as possible — don't worry about the order of these ideas or how far-fetched they seem. Fill your mind with the subject.

• You might preview a book you'll use [see 'Previewing', Ch. 8], or you might read a section of the book and try to identify the central idea [see 'Central ideas', Ch. 8].

If you still have trouble concentrating, ask yourself why and what you can do about it. What must you change to help you concentrate better? Try Chapter 1 for suggestions on coping with problems such as tension or a noisy study place.

2 Sustaining your concentration

"Fan her head!" the Red Queen anxiously interrupted. "She'll be feverish after so much thinking."

Lewis Carroll

Some people study mostly in short, intense bursts with frequent breaks in between; others need to study for long periods to become fully immersed in their task. Your concentration span also varies for different activities and how involved you are in what you're doing.

- When studying intensely, you occasionally become aware that you're distracted by something and feel impatient with your work. Set yourself another five minutes in which to work. If your impatience still persists, give in to it. After the five minutes, take a short break while you **physically loosen up** — stand up and stretch, walk around, consciously relax. Leave your study spot for five minutes or so — get a cup of coffee, glance through a newspaper, organise your desk. Don't take a break for too long or you may require another warm-up.

- When you have been studying for a long time so that your ability to concentrate is diminishing and can't be alleviated by a short break, you need to **mentally recharge**. Remotivate yourself by reviewing the material you've just covered, trying to get an overall picture of it. This often gives you a feeling of achievement as well as reminding you why you're studying a particular topic. Look ahead at what you intend to do next. Preview the rest of the book or chapter. Jot down or tape record ideas for the next section of an assignment. Switch to another subject and work on that until it becomes stale, then return to your first subject or go on to a third.

3 Losing concentration

Try to recognise when you can't concentrate any further. There is little point in believing you're studying when you're simply staring at the words on a page, when you repeatedly can't find the words you want, or when your mind is far away.

- When you feel you're losing concentration, review what you've been studying. If your task is part of a large piece of work, think about where the part fits into the whole and which part you'll tackle next.

- Decide when you'll study again — in an hour's time, the next morning, a day later.

- Then stop studying and relax. Reward yourself — enjoy that special treat you promised yourself earlier.

* * *

It takes time and practice to plan when to study and to learn how to concentrate fully so that you enjoy your formal learning and accomplish what you set out to do. It takes time and practice to become aware of and create your own study patterns and to discover the concentration techniques that you find most helpful. The alternative to spending this time planning when and how to study is to study when others expect you to or to just bumble along as you always have. Being in control of when and how you study is crucial to learning independently.

Further reading

Bliss, E.C. *Getting Things Done — The ABC's of Time Management.* The Macmillan Co., Australia, 1977.

3 Becoming an Independent Student

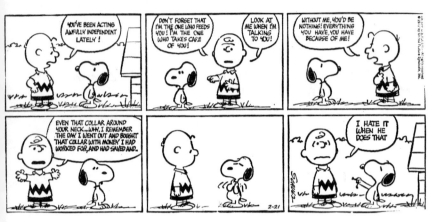

Starting university or college can be bewildering as well as stimulating. Whether your study is full-time or part-time, internal or external, the adjustments you have to make are considerable and you'll be faced with the challenge of learning independently. You're likely to spend the first couple of weeks mostly in organising your timetable and in finding your way round campus and through administrative requirements. Hopefully you can do most of these things during an orientation period before classes start. You'll also begin to recognise faces among staff and students, and may discover some of the social activities that can be part of a tertiary student's life.

This chapter looks at adapting to independent study within formal institutions — thinking about why you're studying, deciding what to study, handling difficult situations, making contact with teachers and other students, and combining study with other work.

Your expectations

> The true University of these days is a collection of books.
> Thomas Carlyle

In Australian society, universities and colleges have a mystique which shapes expectations of them. *One* common image is that these institutions have little to do with the 'real' world, that they are full of professors who expound esoteric theories and young student radicals who do little but take part in demonstrations. A *second* and somewhat contradictory image is that of superior training institutions where doctors, lawyers, architects, engineers, teachers and the like are prepared for their profession. A *third* image is of a community of scholars who dwell in the hallowed halls of higher learning, of professors who pursue ultimate truths and new scientific revelations and impart their insights to highly intelligent students. A *fourth* image which some staff and students come to hold is that

> ... universities have become huge bureaucracies with an academic mind and no heart, careless and ignorant about students and their intellectual needs, organised by managers and managerial professors absorbed in their own pursuits, giving service to the existing social order and dispensing its conventional wisdom, bereft of a philosophy and the social imagination to create a new and compelling conception of their own future.[1]

If you enter university or college with high expectations, this image may be disillusioning. On the other hand, it can help dispel the 'awe-ful' mystique embodied in the second and third images, and can help you realise that sometimes when you're having study problems the causes may not lie solely with you.

Universities and colleges can be intellectually exciting places, but are also bureaucratic institutions like any other large work place. Academics are people with a variety of concerns which can include highly specialised research, a lively curiosity about things of the mind and the world in general, and an involvement with teaching; but like other people, they have their share of human bias and ignorance. Students usually manifest interest in learning, but otherwise are impossible to categorise.

Learn something of the systems and people who shape an institution and your opportunities for learning, and try to take part in the decision-making process. You'll have your own decisions to make as well.

Choices and decisions

"Would you tell me, please, which way I ought to go from here?"
"That depends a good deal on where you want to get to," said the Cat.
"I don't much care where —" said Alice.
"Then it doesn't matter which way you go," said the Cat.

---

[1] Harold Taylor, *Students Without Teachers*, McGraw-Hill, New York, 1969, p. xii.

"— so long as I get *somewhere*," Alice added as an explanation.

"Oh, you're sure to do that," said the Cat, "if you only walk long enough."

Lewis Carroll

Your main experience of formal education may have been in the structured environment of compulsory schooling where from your first day at school the Department of Education and the teachers were responsible for directing what, when, how and where you learnt. You may have attended private schools such as a single-sex denominational school, or a boarding school where your learning and life were very structured; or you may have gone to an alternative school where ostensibly you were free to learn what and when you liked.

In tertiary education, you make many decisions about why, what, when, how and where you learn. Unless you were lucky enough to have teachers and schools who allowed you to develop your abilities for learning independently, this may be your first experience of making such decisions about your formal education.

Why are you studying?

You make your first choice when you decide whether or not to go to university or college. After secondary school, it should be your reasons which determine whether part of your learning takes place within the formal education system. Often there are pressures which seem to give you little choice, but the choice is there if you are aware of it. Why have you chosen to further your education — because your parents want you to, you can't find a job, you want to become an engineer, or you like studying ideas and discovering facts? If you're returning to study after some years away from it, why?

> Most people let themselves be pushed by chance or other people's expectations into environments of which they make the best, rather than into those which meet their inner needs.
>
> Michael Deakin

What will you study?

You also decide which programme to enrol for, which courses to study, and whether to study full-time or part-time, internally and/or externally. In some situations you'll have little choice, such as in a highly structured programme with many required courses, or when confronted with yet another set of rules and regulations. Even so, you should be the one to decide whether to take that particular programme, or whether to comply with a particular rule or regulation.

Choosing courses

Deciding which courses to take depends on why you're studying. It also depends on the course content and workload, and the people who organise and teach the courses. Your choice is likely to be influenced by administrative and academic requirements such as prerequisite subjects or quotas on course intakes.

To help decide on your courses, consult as many sources as possible. Look through the official handbooks and read any student guides to courses and teachers. Remember, however, that most handbooks and guides go to press six to nine months before a course starts, so any information they give may be out of date. For recent information on courses, talk with staff, such as department or programme chairpersons, deans, academic advisers and counsellors.

If you can't find a course on a subject you'd like to study, ask a staff member in a related subject area if there's some other way you can undertake this study [see 'Pursuing your questions', Ch. 4]. For courses which interest you, find out who organises and teaches in them, and look for students who've taken them. Talk to these staff and students to find up-to-date and detailed information on the aims and content of courses, on the likely workload for preparation and assignments, on assessment methods, and on books or materials you're expected to buy. The students will also have opinions about the teachers in the course. Attend any pre-course orientation activities and do any recommended preliminary work. If you can, find out what's expected of you in the first couple of weeks of a course and start on this.

If it's more convenient or enjoyable for you, study part-time or take some or all of your courses externally. You can benefit from being a part-time student taking only one or two courses at a time, especially if you've a lot of other demands on your time, or have been away from study for a while. If you're an external student, your choice of courses may be more restricted than for internal students. Seek information on courses as early as possible, so you can enrol in time for course material to be sent to you.

If you're taking several courses, try to calculate your total workload and plan a weekly class timetable. If you've a choice of times and teachers, decide which classes to attend. The combination of courses you planned may be impossible because of timetable clashes or difficult because of a high, combined workload. These difficulties can occur even for popular or required combinations of courses. So if you still want to take all these courses, check with the organisers if alternative arrangements can be made.

Unless your choice of courses is very clear, if possible delay your final choices until the end of the first or second week of teaching. This gives you a chance to find first-hand information on the courses which attract you, and to meet some of the teaching staff and students. You can't know all there is to know about a course at this stage, but you can check preliminary information against your own experience in the course.

Choosing teachers

Where you've a choice of teachers, sit in on their classes, read any handouts they write, and contact them personally. Look for a course organiser who clearly sets out objectives, organisation, content, workload and assessment for a course and who is open to your comments and questions. Look for teachers who know their subject, stimulate your enthusiasm and are willing to help you improve and extend your skills in studying. A good teacher whose subject areas are only broadly related to your interests can help you follow these interests better than a poor teacher whose interests coincide closely with yours. How well you learn with a particular teacher also depends on how your personalities interact. The lecturer you listen to for several weeks or the teacher with whom you work for a whole course are important to your learning. Be prepared to change courses or teachers if, after a fair trial, you find you're not learning as much as you'd like.

How you spend your time

You largely decide on your study timetable — and you may be surprised at how much work is involved in being a serious tertiary student. The time you're expected to spend in formal classes or studying outside class time varies. For example, fine arts or achitecture students usually spend much more time in classes than arts or social science students, while courses without a large component of practical work usually require more time outside class for research, writing and preparation. Whether or not you attend a class, read a book or hand in an assignment on time depends on your enthusiasm for a subject, your desire to pass a course at a particular standard and your response to teachers and programmes. Some teachers and programmes are more flexible about these matters than others.

Except for formal class time such as lectures, tutorials and laboratory sessions, you usually decide whether to study in the library during the day or at home in the evening, to sit in the cafeteria or the local student pub talking to friends, to work at a job or be with your family. Hopefully you'll have time to explore both social and academic student life, even if you're studying part-time or external-ly. Universities or colleges are more than institutions with collec-tions of courses, and being a part of campus life can be a lot of fun.

Adjusting to independent study

As well as changes you make as you begin to learn independently in formal education, becoming a student entails practical and emotion-al adjustments in your lifestyle. Some aspects of your self and your surroundings which influence study are presented in Chapter 1. If the people you're close to support you as a student, the changes usually won't be too difficult. If not, be prepared to spend time and energy in establishing a new lifestyle as a student as well as on study itself; and you will need to be certain that you do want to be a tertiary student.

Coping with difficult situations

As a student you'll inevitably find yourself in situations which are difficult to cope with. One technique which many students have found useful and which can be used to cope with difficult situations such as exams, is the 'imagine the worst' approach.

Imagine you find yourself in an exam room, and are faced with a question which requires an essay answer. You have the sinking feel-ing that all you know on the topic could be put down in half-a-dozen sentences. What do you do? Panic instantly? Start scribbling furiously in the hope of inspiration? Leave the exam room? Most students worry about not being able to answer exam questions and imagine themselves in this situation. But their imagination stops there. You can help yourself cope with this problem ahead of time by also imagining what you'll do about it.

Now continue imagining that you put down your pen, sit back, stretch a bit, and take several deep breaths. You read the question again, slowly and carefully. You pick up your pen and start to jot down anything which comes to your mind on the topic. You don't try to order this knowledge, but concentrate instead on recalling as much of it as you can. If you start feeling rushed, you deliberately pause for a few moments, and then continue. When you feel you have all your knowledge before you, you check that each item is re-levant to the question. You then organise your information into one or two main points. When this is done, you start writing, concen-trating on saying what you want to, as clearly as you can. You avoid the temptation to pad your answer with irrelevant facts or long-winded language. If at any stage you find yourself feeling rushed, you stop for a minute and concentrate on relaxing. You may just sit and look out of the window as a way of relaxing. When you've finished saying what you want to, you sit back and feel pleased at knowing more about the topic than you thought you did. Then you check your essay over carefully to make sure it answers the question and is clearly expressed. Finish.

Imagining the worst *and* imagining how you will handle it do not guarantee you'll answer the question successfully. Nothing can. However it does make that outcome a lot more likely. See 'Exams' in Chapter 5 'Learning and Remembering' for some help, and Chapter 12 'Writing Assignments' for ideas on essay-type answers.

Part of the 'imagine the worst' approach is to think beforehand about why you are worried about an exam. Is it because you might fail a course, of which the exam is part? Imagine yourself failing the course, and then go on to imagine your alternatives once you've failed. Can you sit for a supplementary exam, or repeat the subject? Think about why you want to pass the course. Can you realise these aims in other ways? It can be invaluable to realise that there are often alternatives to some of the difficulties you face. If you know that you always panic in exam situations, despite knowing your subject well, it may be possible to arrange with your teacher for alternative forms of assessment. You may be able to select a course where exams don't count for all or most of your final assessment.

'Imagining the worst' can be used to help you cope with other difficult situations apart from exams. Are you anxious that you will make a fool of yourself in a discussion group? Imagine this happening — then go on to imagine yourself handling the situation. Think about why you're anxious, and what you can do about the causes of your anxieties. Do you need to prepare more thoroughly for the group so that you feel more confident about contributing to the discussion? Getting to know a couple of other group members outside the discussion time might make you feel that you have sympathetic listeners for anything you say during a discussion. Getting to know other students also enables you to share your feelings and experiences in discussion groups and other learning situations. Such sharing will probably lead you to discover that you're not alone in your anxieties. Other students may have helpful advice on how to cope with a situation which is worrying you. If you are all worried, try 'imagining the worst' together and see what alternatives you come up with.

Now stop, and think of a situation which is worrying you at present.

Imagine the worst that could happen — then imagine yourself coping with it. What are your alternatives after the worst has happened? Which ones seem most viable? Think about why you are worried, and what you can do to deal with the causes of your worry. Share your anxieties with others and see what they have to suggest. And perhaps most important of all — don't accept that you have to be worried. Is it really a matter of life or death?

Contacting people

It is anything but easy to enter a classroom full of people whom you feel must be more intelligent than you, and quite demoralising when your worst fears are realised, you think. Still you must persevere.

Brian's Wife Jenny's Mum

Adjusting to independent study takes time and practice and often courage. Many of the adjustments involve approaching other people — asking questions of a remote professor, seeking help from a teacher you see only once a week, putting forward your own thoughts in a seminar, or making contact with a stranger sitting next to you in a class. To deal with these anxieties, you often need to take the initiative in contacting people.

As a part-time or external student, you may have particular difficulty contacting teachers and other students. Perhaps you enjoy the pleasures of being a solitary scholar and your opportunities to learn independently, and your isolation can partly free you from the pressures of competing with other students. But you may miss sharing the pleasures and problems of study with other students, and if no one in your community sees tertiary study as valuable, you may feel particularly isolated.

Maximising your access to other people's ideas and to learning facilities is one aspect of part-time and external study which takes a lot of time and energy. Personal contacts with a teacher and students can make a big difference to the depth and enjoyment of your formal learning, particularly if you start your studies with high expectations or are worried about your academic abilities.

Approaching teachers

Only an unrealistic teacher would expect you to know everything about a subject you're studying or expect you to write a perfect first essay. You are expected to ask for the help and information you need. Teachers usually appreciate students whose questions and comments show genuine thought and enthusiasm for learning, and like most people, teachers take pleasure in discussing their special interest and explaining what they know to others. Often the students that a teacher comes to know best are those who ask questions, seek advice or are keen to discuss ideas — and it's more satisfying to teach people you know than to impart information to a collection of names and half-remembered faces.

What's the worst that can happen when you approach a teacher for help? Perhaps you persistently have trouble finding them. If so, try to arrange an appointment or leave a message. Perhaps you won't receive a helpful answer to your question. If the teacher is too busy, make an appointment for another time. If he or she isn't skilled at clear explanations, look to another teacher, a student, or a book for your information. Perhaps the teacher you approach is cursory or condescending. If so, maybe he or she is having a trying day, so ask if you can come back another time. Maybe the teacher is inadequate as a teacher. Nevertheless, teachers are paid to help you learn, so if you want to, persist with your request. If you don't want to persist, look elsewhere for help. There are always one or two friendly, helpful teachers or advisers on campus who can help with your contacts with other teachers, with your study, and in some cases with your personal problems.

If you study externally teachers like to receive communication from you other than the assignments you're required to submit. Send a letter telling your teacher a little about yourself. Make a 'phone call to ask about comments on an assignment or to thank your teacher for help. Send an informal tape to talk about ideas not covered in lectures or to discuss your concerns about your work or about course requirements. If you can arrange to visit your teachers on campus, you'll be able to visualise the place and person to whom you're sending your work, rather than simply delivering it up to the postal service and to a marking pen with a person at the other end.

These contacts help your teacher come to know you as an individual, and enable them to make comments on your work which are directed to your individual strengths and difficulties. Your teacher may also be encouraged to make more detailed comments and to return your assignments more promptly — important factors when you have to wait anxiously for an evaluation of your work to arrive in your letter box or mail bag.

Getting to know other students

Having at least one or two fellow students with whom you can toss around ideas and share study problems is an invaluable part of a student's life. Sitting by yourself in the cafeteria, not knowing anyone in the first weeks of class, not being part of student social life or being an isolated student, can make you feel very alone. If you find university or college strange, if you have difficulties with your work, or if you feel shy with other students, you can be certain that other students feel this way too. Help someone else as well as yourself by talking to the person you sit next to in class, or by contacting another student and not always expecting them to contact you first. Take part in some of the social or academic activities on campus. If you have trouble with work or with a teacher, mention it to a couple of students in your class. They may have ideas on what you can do, and if they share your problem you can tackle it together.

What's the worst that could happen when you try to make contact with other students? They don't seem interested? Perhaps they're shy, or preoccupied with other things — try another time or approach someone else. Perhaps they don't seem interested in your particular study problems — find other people you can ask for help. If you continue to have difficulty getting to know a few other students, talk this over with a friend or counsellor. However, most students are willing to talk about courses or teachers, the test next week or the essay you're supposed to finish in two days' time. You won't become close friends with everyone you meet, but you'll find some people with whom you enjoy spending time.

If you're an external student, check with the external studies unit to see if there are other students in your area. Try to make contact with someone who has taken or is taking the same course as you, but even talking to somebody studying different courses can provide you both with invaluable moral support. If you can sit in on the occasional class on campus you'll have a chance to meet other students and share your learning with them. If you're nervous at the thought of attending special on-campus sessions, you'll usually find that some other students feel the same way. Once you actually meet each other, you're likely to have plenty to say.

Contacting the people around you and on campus helps you come to know them as individuals, to learn about the real people behind your images and expectations of what teachers and students are like. It's one of the most important parts of your learning.

Combining study with other work

Your job may be directly related to the subjects you're studying, for example, if you're a veterinary student working part-time in an animal clinic or a parent studying children's literature. Even if your job isn't directly connected with the subjects you study, it may require you to use your mind imaginatively to solve problems and to grapple with new ideas. In this case, your brain won't feel rusty when you tackle formal study. Useful connections between your job and your study can be particularly important if you're an external or part-time student with little opportunity to discuss your learning with teachers or other students. However, close connections between your work and study can sometimes create problems, for example, if you read a book which criticises teaching methods you use, or if courses you take for further job qualifications seem irrelevant.

The amount of energy you put into your job affects your energy for studying. The high level of energy and creativity which you devote to a satisfying job can carry over to your studies. If your studies are less stimulating than your work, you may rapidly lose interest in them. A job which isn't satisfying but is financially necessary may demand a lot of your energy. If you do heavy physical work or spend your day looking after children, sometimes you'll be too tired to study, but at other times you'll welcome the change to mental exercise.

If you work in a high speed job, you can find yourself impatient with the leisurely pace of some courses, especially if you've only limited time off work for classes. If a course doesn't regularly require work to be handed in, the apparent aimlessness of your study may be frustrating. However, study can provide you with a relaxing change from a high pressure job — and the workloads in most courses become demanding soon enough.

The overall time that your job requires, the particular hours that you work and the travelling time from home to work to class all influence your study. They affect your choice of courses, how much time you can spend on private study, and sometimes make external study the only possibility.

Financial decisions may affect your study. If, for example, you have to find a part-time job to finance your education, you'll have less time for study itself. If you've been without an independent income as a secondary school student or housewife, you may have to justify your desire to study to the people whose income will support you. You may feel under pressure to 'succeed' or to choose vocational courses, particularly if your study calls for extra money to pay for books or travel or child care.

* * *

Allow yourself time to discover what university or college is like for you. Expect to feel both confused and excited in the first six to twelve months while you settle in, while you begin to understand what's expected of you and to define some of your own objectives. During this time, as well as trying to pass courses, put some energy into learning how to learn and into making contact with staff and students. Remember that outside school you have learned many things on your own, and that you do know how to learn when you want to.

Think about what you want from university or college, and how you can reach your objectives. After a while it may make sense for you to defer your study for a short period or to leave university or college because of other interests, because your studies aren't sufficiently stimulating, or for pragmatic reasons. (If you are thinking of withdrawing from study, find out what you need to do in case you later want to return.) If you continue to study, your objectives in your formal learning will probably change. Any serious attempt to come to grips with new ideas, especially those which raise questions about yourself, your world and your beliefs about learning always engenders confusion and suggests new directions to consider. Learning that is important to you changes you, often in unexpected ways. Universities or colleges can offer you real learning if you explore what's offered and if you are able to make your own independent decisions about learning.

Further reading

Edwards, Hazel (ed.). *Women Returning to Study*. Primary Education (Publishing), Richmond, Victoria, 1975.

Gilbert, John (ed.). *Staying the Course: How to Survive Higher Education*. Kogan Page, London, 1980.

Victorian Institute of Secondary Education. *Choosing a Post-Secondary Course?* Victorian Institute of Secondary Education, Melbourne, 1980.

Wesson, Gwen (ed.). *Brian's Wife Jenny's Mum*. Dove Communications, East Malvern, Victoria, 1975.

4 Asking Your Own Questions

Knowledge is a process in the minds of living people. It is what we do as we try to find out who and where we are, and what is going on about us.

John Holt

You ask questions all the time, both consciously and unconsciously. When you walk, as you take each step, your foot is seeking out information to relay to your brain. When you pause at an intersection and glance both ways, you're checking the traffic. You learn when you have a question in your mind — whether as a small child continually asking 'Why?', or later as you learned about dinosaurs, gardening, jet aeroplanes or your sexuality. You learn when you're curious, when you want or need to know.

In formal education usually teachers ask the questions and you provide answers. However, to understand what you learn so you can use it, you need to ask questions arising out of your experiences and knowledge.

This chapter looks briefly at a few types of questions and suggests some fundamental questions you can ask when thinking about or researching a subject which interests you. It's designed to stimulate you to ask your own questions and to pursue them in your formal education.

What questions might you ask?

Just before she died she asked 'What is the answer?' No answer came. She laughed aloud and said: 'In that case what is the question?' Then she died.

Last words of Gertrude Stein, quoted by Donald Sutherland

What questions do you have on your mind right now? Questions about your work? Your personal relationships? Your ideas? Your social life? Who you are?

A **simple question** such as 'Should I cook lamb chops or a stew for dinner?' 'Did I leave my glasses behind?' can be answered without much imagination, perhaps with a 'Yes' or a 'No'. Questions such as these close off other possibilities and leave you with the option of only a limited answer. This may be all you need, when checking if you know a fact, such as 'How many grams in an ounce?' 'Where is my clavicle?'

If you're looking for information on a subject such as basic human needs, to ask 'Do humans need food to survive?' is asking a closed question, while the **complex question** 'What types of food do humans need to survive?' opens many possibilities. Complex questions demand time and careful thought when you attempt to answer them. Some complex questions you can never answer. 'Did I make the right choice?' 'What would have happened if I hadn't gone to university?' Perhaps you check your horoscope or consult the *I Ching* in an attempt to find answers to such questions. It's tempting to believe that there are absolute or 'Yes/no' answers to questions which can't be answered so simply. Often an answer which is right today may be wrong tomorrow, or an answer which makes sense for you may be a mistake for someone else. Are there any answers which are always right? Much of what you are told is true later turns out to be not quite the whole truth; and many so called 'objective facts' are actually the results of a consensus of the subjective opinion of the people concerned.

> What men really want is not knowledge but certainty.
> Bertrand Russell

The **language** in which you ask questions shapes your answers. If you ask 'Is intelligence determined by genes or environment?' you've precluded the possibility that both or other factors might be important, as well as making assumptions about what intelligence is. Such 'either'...or...' questions are examples of how language limits your exploration of a topic and encloses what you can learn.

> Every language conceals within its structure a vast array of unconscious assumptions about life and the universe, all that you take for granted and everything that seems to make common sense...
>
> N.J. Berill

When you're curious about a subject, there are some basic questions you can usefully ask. *As you read the questions suggested here, apply them to a topic which interests you.*

Why do I want to know?

> Tiger got to hunt,
> Bird got to fly;
> Man got to sit and wonder, "Why, why, why?"
> Tiger got to sleep,
> Bird got to land;
> Man got to tell himself he understand.
>
> Kurt Vonnegut Jr.

Asking why you want to know about a topic can clarify what you want to find out and how to go about your search. How did you become curious about the topic in the first place? What's *your purpose* for seeking the information? Perhaps you want to share it with others, use it to pass an exam, complete an assignment or progress through a sequence of practical skills. If you need to remember information for a short while, such as for a seminar paper next week, how you go about learning it will differ from your approach if you need the information for long-term use.

What do I want to know?

What do I want to know? What interests me about this topic? What seem to be the most important aspects? These are some of the *the first questions* to ask yourself when you want to find information on a topic. For example, if you're interested in convicts in eighteenth-century Australia, ask yourself 'What do I want to know about this subject?' You might have questions about who the convicts were, why they were transported, how many were women, their living conditions, the number of convicts who were political prisoners, how they were organised and used in the colonies, and their role in the economy of the new colonies.

How do I know that . . . ?

> Artists can colour the sky red because they *know* it's blue. Those of us who aren't artists must colour things the way they really are or people might think we're stupid.
>
> Jules Feiffer

Perhaps you 'know' that hens lay eggs because you were told this as a child. Perhaps you 'know' that the sun will rise tomorrow because in your experience it always has. Perhaps you 'know' that Galileo invented the telescope because you read that he did.

What are the *sources* of your knowledge? The first-hand evidence of your senses is one source which can be deceptive — for example, if you believe that the world is flat because your eyes tell you so. Much of what you know is not from first-hand experience. Sometimes your knowledge comes from personal or cultural *biases*, such as the belief that technological progress is always desirable or that a woman's primary role is to be a wife and mother. You may be unaware of these biases. If you're making a generalisation, question the nature and reliability of your sources of knowledge. Can you prove that hens lay eggs or that the sun will rise tomorrow? If you can't prove it, it may still be true, but you need to be careful before you assert its truth.

On the topic of convicts in eighteenth-century Australia, ask yourself 'What do I already know about this topic, and where does my knowledge come from?' If you 'know' that most convicts were petty thieves or that women convicts were prostitutes, asking yourself how you know these 'facts' should lead you to examine whether or not they really are facts, to ask 'Do I know that these statements are true?'

Why?

> ... and books that told me everything about wasps except why.
> Dylan Thomas

'Why?' is one of the most important questions you can ask, especially if it enables you to *identify assumptions* which may be hidden. As an example of this, debates about education frequently ask 'How can we do this particular thing better?' while the question 'Why are we doing it in the first place?' is not dealt with. It might be more useful to ask 'Why are teachers trained?' instead of 'How can teachers be trained better?' or to ask 'Why am I going to write this report?' before you ask 'How can I best go about writing it?'

If you have a problem to solve, you might ask only how to solve it, for example, which methods you should use to remember material for exams. If you also ask why the methods are effective, you can decide if they suit you and will find it easier to remember how to repeat them and to use them in different exam situations.

When? Where? How? Who? Why? What?

Asking these questions one after another is a *brainstorming* exercise to let your mind generate ideas without having to justify their immediate relevance. It's a useful way to stimulate your initial thinking about a subject and to provide new directions if you're stuck while researching. For example, if given the adage 'Know thyself', you could ask:

— Who said this?
— When?
— Where was it first used?

— What was its original context?
— How has it been interpreted?
— Why has it been important?

What happens if...?

'What happens if...?', or 'What might happen if...?', are the *cause-and-effect* questions that experiments ask, whether the experimenter is a three-year-old child pulling a cat's tail or a professional researcher testing a hypothesis. Experimenting involves manipulating your environment to see what happens, sometimes predicting what is likely to happen, and then describing what happened. For example:

What happens if you drop a piece of paper and a heavy lead weight from the top of a high tower?
What happens if you write an assignment as a dialogue instead of in prose?
What might happen if you always told the truth?

What if...?

Why, sometimes I've believed as many as six impossible things before breakfast.
                                                                    Lewis Carroll

Imagine living in the sixteenth century and asking yourself, 'What if the sun rather than the earth is the centre of our universe?' What answers might you arrive at if you ask 'What if our traditional energy sources are no longer available by the end of this century?' or 'What if Robert Ardrey's theory that humans are predatory killers is true?' These questions require that you transcend your customary frameworks for viewing the world. Using your imagination and *suspending disbelief* enables you to look at the world through new eyes.

You don't need to ask the above questions in a particular sequence, but are likely to move backwards and forwards among them. What you want to know and the questions you ask will be influenced by how much you already know about a subject. For example, when confronted with a new subject you can immerse yourself in it by asking **general questions**, such as 'What is evolution?', 'What is Freud's concept of the unconscious?', 'What is carbon bonding?', 'What is China like?', 'What are marsupials?' By contrast, when familiar with a subject you can ask **specific questions** to lead you further into the material. For instance, you might ask about reproduction in kangaroos because you already know something about marsupial reproduction. Chapter 6 'Defining and Researching a Topic' suggests a systematic way of asking questions about a topic.

Pursuing your questions in formal education

> The t-eacher's work, therefore, begins when that other person asks a question. No question, no teaching. But it is important to understand what a teacher can do and does with his answers, and what he cannot do. He does not give knowledge. Knowledge cannot be *given*. If you ask me a question all I can do in my reply is try to put into words a part of my experience. But you get only the words, not the experience. To *make meaning* out of my words, you must use your own experience.
>
> John Holt

Without curiosity, learning is dull and mechanical if it occurs at all. Wanting to know, enjoying stretching your mind, feeling wonder or delight at a new experience or idea — all these need a mind which is receptive and questioning.

Unfortunately, the crucial part your curiosity and questions play in learning is often forgotten or disregarded. Formal learning is frequently based on a model which assumes that there's a body of knowledge to master, and a particular way to master it; and the proof of your mastery lies in correctly answering set questions. This model of learning is most evident in the exam process but can also underlie work such as essays, tutorial papers and laboratory reports. If you're given a topic for a tutorial paper, do you approach it by asking your own questions, or as you think your teachers expect? If you read a lot for an assignment, but feel uncertain about what to write on the topic, perhaps you're trying to guess what you're expected to write, rather than reading and writing about what seems most relevant and interesting to you. In a discussion group, are you hesitant to take an active part because you fear you might say the 'wrong' thing, or give the wrong answer?

> We kill, not only their curiosity, but their feeling that it is a good and admirable thing to be curious, so that by the age of ten most of them will not ask questions, and will show a good deal of scorn for the few who do...
>
> John Holt

No teacher can tell you what you want to learn, but he or she can help you discover this. Teachers with an active curiosity who are interested in you as a learner can help you articulate your questions and can stimulate your curiosity in new ways. They can also help you rediscover the confidence and skills needed to pursue your own questions in formal education. Obviously some teachers and assignments allow you more scope than others for asking the questions which interest you. If your learning is to be satisfying and mean something to you, you need to ask your own questions, even with teachers who prefer you to answer theirs.

Independent study

The basic questions of why, what, how and when you learn apply to any independent learning, and can be applied to an individual assignment or to your formal tertiary education as a whole [see Ch. 5]. Studying independently requires thinking about and formulating your objectives. It involves studying a subject of your own choosing, on your own initiative, and making your own decisions about how and when you study it and with whom. Independent study differs from 'individualised' learning and self instruction methods, in which you study alone but are supervised and controlled.

Studying independently entails asking yourself the following questions:

- What do I want to study, and in what depth and breadth?

- Why do I want to study this particular topic? You might explore an interest more fully, acquire specific skills, or examine previous work in a new context.

- How will I study the topic? Perhaps you want to conduct library research, interviews, or laboratory experiments, or to undertake field work, or to read extensively [see Chs. 5, 6 and 7].

- How do I want my work to be evaluated? You need to decide what work to produce specifically for recorded assessment, and who'll evaluate your work and by what criteria [see Ch. 15].

- How much time will I spend on this study?

- With whom will I discuss my work?

If you usually rely on your textbooks and lecture notes for the right answers without questioning their information or assumptions, you may find it frightening to consider asking your own questions. Perhaps you've become so accustomed to teachers asking you questions that you've largely forgotten how to ask your own, or have lost the confidence to ask them. Even if a teacher encourages you to approach a topic in your own way, you might be so unaccustomed to this that you prefer to retreat into the safety of looking to the 'experts' for the answers. In this case you're probably assuming that your task at university or college is to meet the requirements of courses and teachers, rather than seeing them as resources enabling you to move towards your objectives and to think about your questions. So perhaps the first question you should ask yourself is 'Why am I at university or college?' 'What are my objectives?' 'What are my questions?'

A few universities and colleges allow you to complete part or all of your study programme independently. Sometimes you can obtain credit for exploring in depth a topic not available as a formal course. If independent study appeals to you, explore the possibilities for this method of learning within your institution. If you develop a serious academic interest which you want to explore further, you may decide to go on to study as an honours or postgraduate student.

Within a course, the extent to which you're allowed to work on your interests varies. In some courses you can spend most of the time exploring your interests without close supervision. Other courses allow you little scope for independent study; the work you do is assigned by teachers and you are told what to read, what experiments to conduct, and how to present your written work. When you do have the opportunity for independent study within a course, this often takes the form of an individual or group project for which you choose the topic and the methods of research.

* * *

Often your learning becomes largely a matter of asking more exact or more intricate questions, rather than finding answers. Despite a formal education system which talks of having 'done maths' or 'done history', it's impossible to learn all there is to know about any subject. When pursuing your own questions, you may realise that the more you know, the more there is to learn, which leads you on to further questions.

What questions would you like to pursue in your formal learning?

Further reading

Boud, David (ed.). *Developing Student Autonomy in Learning*, Kogan Page, London, 1981.

Dressel, P.L. and Thompson, M.M. *Independent Study*. Jossey Bass, San Francisco, 1973.

Postman, Neil and Weingartner, Charles. *Teaching as a Subversive Activity*. Penguin Books, Middlesex, England, 1971.

Marshall, Lorraine and Bain, Andrew. *Taking an Independent Study Contract*. Murdoch University, Western Australia, 1979.

Percy, Keith and Ramsden, Paul. *Independent Study: Two Examples from English Higher Education*. The Society for Research into Higher Education, University of Surrey, Guildford, England, 1980.

5 Learning and Remembering

Oft in the stilly night,
When the mind is fumbling fuzzily,
I brood about how little I know.
And know that little so muzzily.

Ogden Nash

Why do you remember the things you do?
Why do you forget?

If you want to know how to ride a bicycle, you practise with great concentration, and persist with your riding despite the occasional spill. Once you can ride with skill, even if you sell your bicycle you always remember how to ride one.

A small child who wants to learn how to build a tower of blocks concentrates intensely while trying various ways to make the blocks stay put one on top of the other. After repeated attempts, she comes to understand the most effective way to build a tower of blocks. This skill is later remembered to build other towers — of books, of dolls, of cushions.

If you concentrate on learning what you want to know, you're more likely to understand and be able to use it. Remembering what you learn well enough to use it depends on why and how you learn. If you learn to ride a bicycle because you want to, and if you learn at your own pace, you easily recall the skill. You're less likely to remember it if you learn because someone else decides you should and teaches you in the way they think best. Whether or not you want to learn depends on you — what you already know, how you learn, your current interests and how you feel at the time.

This chapter begins by looking at how you filter what you learn and remember, and at why you might want to remember. It discusses how you learn in order to remember — by learning what, when and how suits you, and by using methods which help you learn material. Deliberately learning in these ways makes it more likely that you'll be able to use what you learn later and recall it in situations such as exams.

Filters on what you learn and remember

"I could tell you my adventures — beginning from this morning," said Alice a little timidly; "but it's no use going back to yesterday, because I was a different person then."

Lewis Carroll

Your mind and body unconsciously select and interpret what you learn and remember from your daily life, and what you remember changes with time. Five people witnessing a car accident have five different versions even if asked soon afterwards to describe what happened, and a year later each person will have yet another version of the episode. They may even 'recall' things which didn't actually happen, such as events which could have been expected to occur but didn't or details of a 'long argument' between the drivers which was in fact only a couple of remarks. What each of the five recollects is their personal experience of the accident, modified by their experiences in the meantime.

What do you remember about today?
What immediately comes to mind?
Try recalling in order everything that's happened since you woke up.

What do you remember from yesterday?
What do you remember from last week? Why?
What memories do you have of your last birthday?
Do you remember your first day at school?
What's your earliest memory?

Spend about half an hour answering these questions. If you finish in less time, go back and see how much more detail you can recall. Can you work out why you recalled what you did?

Share the questions with someone else. How do your memories differ from theirs? How are they the same? Why?

The past which we remember is partial and distorted; it has been edited by the censors to exclude events which are disturbingly painful or disturbingly pleasurable.... The history we recall tends to be propaganda which preserves the status quo of personal identity.

Sam Keen

Now stop for a moment, and let yourself become aware of everything your senses are telling you. Smells? Sights? Sounds? Tastes? Touch? Of what are you most aware? After your first sense impressions, what else do you begin to notice? What thoughts are running through your mind?

Trying to be fully aware of even one fleeting moment makes you realise how much you forget — perhaps for a short time, or perhaps for all of your life. Some things you need to 'forget', in the sense of taking them for granted. Imagine you wanted to be fully aware and decided to consciously breathe every breath. You'd soon give up because you wouldn't have time for anything else. Other things you 'forget' by pushing them below the surface of your mind — items that have little interest for you, that have unpleasant associations, or that don't fit with your view of the world.

Sometimes you forget things you'd like to remember. Have you ever read a childhood autobiography and marvelled at the amount of detail the writer recollects? Few people remember such detail without making a conscious effort to do so. Keeping a diary or taking photographs can make you more aware of your surroundings and help you remember them. Photos or diaries also help you realise how much you forget. Have you ever read back over a diary entry from several weeks or years ago and been amazed at how your memory of that time has changed and how much you've forgotten?

Try it now. See if you can find a letter, a poem, or a diary you wrote, or a photograph you took. Look at it and conjure up your memories of that time.

Remembering isn't just something you set your mind to do — **your senses** are involved too. Do you have a good memory for faces? For 'phone numbers? Or for jokes? Some people remember mostly what they see, and can see a word once and remember how to spell it; others remember what they hear, and can repeat verbatim snatches of dialogue from a movie.

Your experiences lead you to knowledge and beliefs about yourself and your world which influence what you're aware of at any moment. If you've been a keen surfer or sailor for several years, you're more likely to know and remember how the wind and waves have changed from one season to another than will someone who plays cards for their recreation. If you've worked as a carpenter, you can pick up and remember new information about the craft because of your previous knowledge.

Your active interest in a subject increases what you remember about it. A football fan can tell you in detail about the previous wins of her club, but if she's not interested in horse racing she will have no idea who won the Melbourne Cup. If you're concerned about the role of women in Australian society, you'll remember facts from a history of Australia, which others without your concern wouldn't notice. Such an interest can be kindled by another person's enthusiasm. Skilled teachers who care about their subjects can hold your attention so that you remember far more than you expected to. You may remember a conversation with someone you met at a party because you were entertained by them.

How you feel emotionally and physically also influences what you learn and how vividly you remember it. If you're alert, perhaps because you're feeling exuberant or slightly uncomfortable, your chances of remembering that particular time more fully increase. Your surroundings influence how you feel and are part of what you remember. Have you ever picked up a book you've read and been reminded of when and where you read it? And items you can recall in one situation you can't remember at all in another.

Your senses, experiences, interests and your current state of being act as filters on your life, both past and present. They affect what you're most aware of and what you find easy to concentrate on and to learn, and so influence what you remember from the information you're offered.

Why remember?

> ...no one who is not conscious of having a sound memory should set up to be a liar.
>
> Michel de Montaigne

Remembering enables you **to learn more** about yourself and your world. Newborn human babies seem to operate mostly by reflexes rather than by consciously knowing and remembering. But toddlers in their second year are able to call on what they've learned, and can form a concept such as 'dog-ness' by remembering the characteristics of dogs which aren't present and comparing them with a dog which is. As an adult, the more you can remember, the less you have to relearn. The more you can remember concepts, the more you can solve problems and cope with new situations and ideas. If you can recall the fundamentals of Darwin's theory of evolution, you can move on to further related knowledge instead of relearning the theory repeatedly.

When you find **pleasure** in what you learn, you probably want to remember it. Perhaps you do this unconsciously because your senses and curiosity are more active, or perhaps you deliberately heighten your sense awareness. You may relive the experiences in your mind, in a diary or through photographs. You may learn by heart the words of a song which please you. Maybe you want to remember an intriguing idea, so you can contemplate it further.

If you need **to use what you learn**, you're more likely to remember it. To cross the road and live, you learn and use an array of skills which become habits, or unconsciously recollected knowledge. If you need to prune fruit trees, you have a reason for using and remembering what you learn about pruning. If you want to use an idea in a discussion paper, you try to understand the idea and its links to your topic so that you remember it fully enough to explain it to others.

Some things you're required to remember **for reasons not directly your own**. You might enjoy learning the manual skills of flying a 'plane but not want to study the navigation theory required for a pilot's licence. In your formal education you're expected to remember material so that your progress towards course objectives can be evaluated and recorded according to tangible criteria. For example, you may be required:

— in an exam, to show that you remember and understand the rudiments of a particular subject
— in an essay, to recall information well enough to argue a case
— in a report, to remember and describe a sequence of steps in an experiment
— in a tutorial, to review and present a summary of your reading on a topic
— to remember material in the short-term, such as dates or data for a seminar paper, and
— to remember material for long periods so you can take a final exam, a subsequent course or a future job.

These requirements are based on the assumptions that in formal education there's certain knowledge worth having, certain learning skills and abilities worth acquiring, and a specific sequence and time limit in which this learning should be acquired. These assumptions shape why and what and how you learn and remember. Those assumptions you disagree with can still influence your learning and remembering if you decide to accept them as a means to your own ends. For example, even if some course material doesn't interest you, you may study it for an exam, because you accept the exam as necessary to acquire a qualification you want.

> "But what did the Dormouse say?" one of the jury asked.
> "That I can't remember," said the Hatter.
> "You *must* remember," remarked the King, "or I'll have you executed."
>
> Lewis Carroll

How you learn to remember

There are times when your assumptions and objectives about learning and remembering differ from those of your teachers. At such times, what you learn will be difficult to recall. However, you're likely to remember what you learn if your curiosity about a subject remains alive. To sustain your curiosity, there are certain prerequisites for learning.

1 What is important to you.   You need to learn according to who you are — your interests, your experiences, your questions [see 'Beliefs and values' Ch. 1, and Ch. 4].

2 *When you are ready.*   You need to learn at a place and time and in a way that makes sense to you, at 'the moment of readiness'. You're not always ready to learn in a school classroom between the hours of 9 am and 3.30 pm or during specified hours each week in a lecture theatre. If you're not ready, it's more difficult to concentrate on and to understand what you're supposed to learn, and you're more likely to forget what you do learn unless you use memory techniques such as those mentioned later in this chapter.

3 *A way that suits you.*   If you've some insight into how you learn informally, your formal learning can be enhanced. If you're learning to drive a car, do you prefer to get in the car and start driving, to read a book on how a combustion engine works, or to talk to a friend who's just learned to drive? If you want to find out about kangaroos, do you go to look at them in the zoo or try to study them in their natural habitats? Do you ask other people about them? Do you read books on the subject? Do you take a course in marsupial physiology? Learning in a way that suits you enhances your ability to remember.

4 *Building on what you already know.*   You need to learn by building on your skills and experience, on the patterns and beliefs which shape your world and your language. Even if you know only a little about a new area, you have a context in which to understand your new learning and so will remember it more clearly. Have you ever attempted to read a book you don't understand and then some time later read it more easily and remembered it? By the second reading you've acquired new knowledge to which you can relate the book's contents.

If you're required to reproduce ideas or information that you can't relate to something familiar, you have to resort to rote learning and mnemonics, acrostics and rhymes such as '30 days hath September'. One of the most powerful tools to help you remember unfamiliar material is linking it to familiar information and concepts. For example:

- If you're required to review a book on a new topic, your recall of the book will be more thorough if you already know the principles which underlie a good book review.

- You're more likely to remember the intricacies of Darwin's theory of evolution if when you first learn it you test it against species differences with which you're familiar.

- Analogies, similes and metaphors based on comparisons with familiar ideas and information are effective ways of learning and remembering new material. For example, the metaphor 'the body politic' helps you think about a political system in new ways by comparing it to your own body, and what you learn from such a metaphor is likely to stay in your mind.

> I can give you nothing that has not already its being within yourself. I can throw open to you no picture-gallery but your own soul... I help you to make your own world visible. That is all.
>
> Hermann Hesse

When you come to learn about a new topic in a class, study session or assignment, spend some time recalling what you already know about it. Think about what you want to learn and, if you have a choice, how you want to learn. This preparation provides reference points or a framework for your learning and enhances your ability to remember.

Selecting what to learn. However, even if you're able to learn what, when and how you want to, you can't possibly remember everything. Every minute you 'learn' a great deal of information, but most of it you remember only if prompted. To retain some things, you need to 'forget' others, focusing your conscious awareness to select what you take in and learn. To remember what a teacher is saying, focus on just that and ignore other things of which you're indirectly aware, such as what the teacher is wearing.

If as a student you have to digest large amounts of information, the time you could spend learning to remember it all is better spent selecting what you need to remember and discovering how to record and retrieve it [see 'Filing information', Ch. 6]. Some information and ideas you can use without needing to remember them. Relying on someone to tell you where your socks are or on calculators to perform your arithmetic may be described as laziness — but you can't remember everything at a given time, and it's essential to consciously select what you want to remember. If you're allowed to take a calculator or your course text into an exam, what you need to learn and remember is how to use either aid and selected key information.

Learning thoroughly

Once you've selected what you want or have to learn, you need to learn that material thoroughly. Even material you thought would be dull or difficult can be unexpectedly interesting if you set out to learn it thoroughly, if you make a game or challenge of learning it well.

A variety of ways for the same material

Take in the same information in as many ways as possible. If a friend explains to you the difference between a ketch and a schooner, you're more likely to remember these if you also see a diagram of each and then sail on them. If you read about a topic as well as discuss it and listen to a lecture on it, your recall of what you've learned will be greater. This approach is particularly important if you're trying to remember complex material, for example, the elements of existentialist philosophy or the intricacies and implications of Einstein's theory of relativity. Such material can only be understood and remembered after repeated encounters.

Before, during and after classes and study

> "— but there's one great advantage in it, that one's memory works both ways."
>
> "I'm sure *mine* only works one way', Alice remarked. 'I can't remember things before they happen."
>
> "It's a poor sort of memory that only works backwards", the Queen remarked.
>
> Lewis Carroll

Thorough learning from a class or study session partly depends on what you do before, during and afterwards. Many of the chapters in this book use this principle as their framework, and you'll remember more of what you learn if you use the approaches they describe. 'Concentrating while you study' in Chapter 2, for example, describes warming up, concentrating fully, and concluding a study session. The chapter on lectures discusses how to make the most of a lecture by preparing, questioning as you listen, and reviewing and using the material soon afterwards.

Study session techniques

There are techniques which you can use in a study session to enhance your ability to remember what you learn.

- Vary the length of your study sessions according to the material. Your mind can only take in so many statistics at once and you won't remember effectively if you try to learn masses of figures all at once. In contrast, you need time to understand a philosophical argument well enough to remember it.

- When learning details from two similar subjects, study a contrasting subject in between so you don't confuse information. This applies, for example, if you're trying to remember dates from two similar history courses, or studying verb tenses in Spanish and Italian. Avoiding interference between subjects is especially important in the early stages of learning and for long-term recall.

- When trying to remember concepts, studying related subjects provides a framework, because the differences and similarities between them enhances your understanding of each. For example, this approach can help when studying concepts of human nature in Rousseau's philosophy and in humanistic psychology.

Memory keys

One way of consciously remembering is to précis the essential parts of what you've selected to learn, and then to find memory keys for each of these parts. These keys can then be used to open your memory of each part and its associated details. You unconsciously use such keys when an unexpected memory is evoked because you hear a particular piece of music, walk past a certain street, or drink a once-favourite drink. In your formal learning you can use memory keys consciously, for example, to recall the discussion in a seminar. Summarise the structure and main points of the discussion, represent these by key words or phrases, and use these keys to review and recall the discussion.

What would you choose as memory keys to help you remember each paragraph in this section 'Learning Thoroughly'?

Patterns and principles

If you learn by comprehending the patterns and principles, structures and relationships which link individual ideas and information, it's easier to remember these items than trying to do so one by one. Learning in patterns also makes it easier to recall information you thought you wouldn't need, since you can search for it by reconstructing the patterns in which you learned it.

Using what you learn

If you think back over an event from your day, what you remember depends on what has happened to you in the meantime, even if that time has been very brief. When you use your knowledge of an event in a new context, you don't reproduce it exactly unless it has absolutely no meaning for you. You extend your memory of the event to take in the context in which you remember it — if you describe the event in a journal, your surroundings, as you write, influence and become part of your memory.

Unless you continue your learning by recalling it, you forget even things you wanted to learn. Going over your day helps fix it in your memory, and recording the day in a journal makes it available for you to relive, to 'use' again. Discussing the ideas from a lecture with other people who've shared it has a similar effect, with the added dimension of the others' perceptions now becoming part of yours.

Use what you learn as *soon*, as *often* and as *widely* as possible if you want to remember it. You recall the alphabet easily because you've used it over and over again in different situations. When you first learn to ride a bike, if you practise every day and in many different conditions you're likely to remember the skill more quickly than if you practise once a week and have to spend some of that weekly time in re-learning. Unless you've an exceptional memory for figures, you're unlikely to remember statistics, such as the population of Australia, unless you use them frequently. If you want to remember an important idea, write it down and try it out on various people. You'll come to a new understanding of it each time and remember the original idea more fully. To remember material for long-term use (for instance, for exams), use it by revising it periodically and relating it to new knowledge you've acquired.

> ...Funes not only remembered every leaf on every tree of every wood, but even every one of the times he had perceived or imagined it. He determined to reduce all of his past experience to some seventy thousand recollections, which he would later define numerically. Two considerations dissuaded him: the thought that the task was interminable and the thought that it was useless.
>
> Jorge Luis Borges

Exams

One situation for which you're likely to need to remember material is exams. Your memory in exams depends as much on being prepared for the exam situation as it does on learning material well. Even if you know material, you may be unable to recall it effectively if you go to pieces in an exam room. 'Coping with difficult situations' in Chapter 3 suggests how to handle the exam situation. Table 5.1 on page 54 looks at techniques to help you remember what you've learned when you read the questions on a limited-time, no-books exam.

Look back at the section on 'Why Remember?' What do you remember from this section?
Why do you recall what you do?
How could you remember this section more effectively?

Without remembering, each day, each event, each moment would be a totally new experience. How fully you remember depends largely on how thoroughly you learned in the first place, and what you recall is unique to you as is why, what and how you learn. As you learn in your formal education, think about how you can learn in order to remember more effectively.

Table 5.1   Exam techniques

1 If you're uptight before an exam, try to relax (see 'Tension and Relaxation', Ch. 1).

2 When you are given the exam paper and before you start writing, take the following steps.

- Carefully read the instructions which should tell you how you're expected to answer the paper, how many questions you should answer and the value of each.

- Read through all of the questions.

- If you have a choice, decide which questions you'll answer or at least which questions you'll start with.

- Decide how much time you'll need to spend on each question because of its value, and according to how thoroughly you can answer it.

- Decide on the order in which you'll answer the questions. Answer first the questions you know most about and which are easiest. If you run out of time, you do so on a subject which will earn you fewer marks.

3 When you're allowed to start writing, jot down any thoughts or ideas you have about each of the questions you'll answer. These jottings can be useful memory triggers when you actually come to answer the question.

4 For essay-type questions, analyse the wording of the question [see 'Defining a Topic', Ch. 6] and plan your essay [see 'Writing to a Plan', Ch. 12]. Include your plan in your exam booklet.

5 Write as quickly and as clearly as you can.

6 For multiple-choice questions, don't waste time over questions you can't answer. Be careful about guessing answers if points are deducted for incorrect responses.

7 When answering mathematical problems, include all of your calculations. Even if your answer is incorrect, the examiner can see where you went wrong and you may gain some points for your method.

8 If you have a memory lapse in the middle of a question, leave a few pages, go to another question, and later return to the first question.

9 Answer as many questions as you can. If you only answer the questions you know well, you're unlikely to make up enough marks to pass.

10 If you run out of time, jot down the main points you were going to make.

11 Try to leave time at the end of the exam to read back over your answers. Correcting poor expression or spelling or checking your calculations can make an important difference.

Further reading

Highbee, K.L. *Your Memory. How it Works and How to Improve it.* Prentice Hall, Eaglewood Cliffs, New Jersey, 1977.

Hunter, Ian M.L. *Memory.* 2nd edn. Penguin Books, Middlesex, England, 1964.

6 Defining and Researching a Topic

As a student in a tertiary institution, most of the work you're expected to do is in the form of assignments in which you communicate your ideas and knowledge to others. These assignments are usually written or oral (essays, discussion papers, reviews, projects and reports), or occasionally audiovisual. In addition to assignments, you're expected to gather information for lectures, discussions, practical sessions or field trips.

Before you begin research you should clearly define your purpose and topic, as these definitions largely determine the material you select for research. However, as you work with this material, the information you gather reshapes your original definition and may even lead you to change to another topic. Defining and researching your topic are interdependent processes, rather than two separate activities.

This chapter looks at defining the purpose of an assignment, and at choosing, defining and researching a topic. The approach outlined is applied in this chapter to assignments, but it also applies to researching a broad course area or when preparing thoroughly for a key lecture or seminar. The chapter is intended mostly for students who have difficulty selecting and defining a topic and finding their way through reference lists, rather than for those undertaking advanced research.

The purposes of an assignment

"Why, if a fish came to *me* and told me he was going on a journey, I should say 'With what porpoise?'"
"Don't you mean 'purpose'?" said Alice.

Lewis Carroll

The first step in defining and researching a topic is clarifying the purpose of an assignment.

Teachers who design and teach courses usually do so with particular **purposes** in mind and each assignment set should follow from these purposes. These purposes may or may not be explicitly stated — it's not uncommon for teachers to be unaware of their purposes and underlying assumptions. Some of these purposes may be to acquaint you with an issue central to a subject area, to stimulate you to question your attitudes, to give you practice in the skills of a discipline, to diagnose your ability to write clearly and logically, or to give your teacher some tangible work by which to evaluate your progress.

You also bring **your own purposes** to a course or an assignment. You may enrol for a course to follow up an interest, to work with a particular teacher, or to complete a prerequisite. You might undertake an assignment to obtain background knowledge for your main area of study, or so you can practise communicating your ideas and receiving feedback on them.

Many students worry about what their teachers expect of them. How do you find out what your teacher expects for an assignment? You should be told the aims of an assignment and how you're expected to present it. Beyond those requirements you can't be expected to second-guess your teacher's mind. If you attempt this, your assignments are likely to be cautious and dull. It's *your* interests which give your assignments originality, so spend your time researching and presenting these interests as effectively as possible. Most teachers prefer a well-researched and well-argued original approach rather than a rehash of familiar textbooks or their own lectures.

At times your purposes for an assignment conflict with what's expected of you. You may be expected to give a seminar paper on a topic which doesn't interest you, or to present a written report when you feel a videotape would be more effective. When such conflicts arise, ask your teacher if you can choose an alternative. Many teachers welcome such initiative and allow you to pursue your own topic and form of presentation. If an alternative isn't possible, your discussions with your teacher should at least give you a clear idea of his or her purposes for the assignment. It's then up to you to decide whether you agree with these purposes. If you can't use the assignment to pursue your own purposes and questions, you may need to find an alternative [see 'Independent study', Ch. 4].

Choosing a topic

Some topics are *general*, such as 'The ecology of eucalypt forests', 'Romantic literature', 'Journalism', 'The French Revolution', or

'Scientific Method'. Others are more *specific*, for example, 'Discuss the Hindu ideas of forgiveness and tolerance', 'Define Marx's concept of the proletariat', 'Examine the likely effects on the local flora and fauna of the freeway proposed for your capital city' or 'How should Piaget's theory of stages in children's development be applied in teaching mathematics in Australian primary schools?'

Deciding on a topic can seem deceptively simple — a matter of choosing from a list of suggested or set topics, or selecting a topic from anywhere within the subject matter of a course. However, your decision also involves defining possible topics. Start making your choice by thinking about the possibilities of each one. Explore a couple of options and choose between them as you define them in some detail, or decide on one topic at the start and change your mind if your initial exploration suggests that it has limited possibilities. Often a topic which at first doesn't seem very interesting may become attractive as you explore it.

- Your choice of topic is affected by what you already know. If you're given a list of topics and are uncertain which to choose because some of them are unfamiliar, find out more about these options from someone who knows about them and from a reference such as a specialist encyclopaedia or a course text. If you've limited time to gather information, choose a familiar topic. If you've ample time, decide whether to explore a previous interest further or to learn about a slightly familiar topic.

- Your enthusiasm for a topic also affects your choice. For example, if you are interested in women's history you might choose a topic such as the suffragette movement. If you're an athlete, you might write on the physiology of marathon runners.

- Your choice of topic is often influenced by the information sources available. Being aware of sources other than libraries, lectures and your teachers can increase your choice of topics [see Ch. 7].

Unless your choice of topic is quite clear from the start or unless you have little time in which to choose, keep several options in mind. Allow yourself time to define their possibilities further, and to find out if the resources you need are available.

Defining a topic

The following six points should lead you to a written definition of your topic.

Questions to ask

1 'What do I already know about the topic?'

Ask yourself this question and jot down any ideas you have. Use any available lists of study questions to start your mind ticking over. Brainstorm your topic by asking 'Why?' 'Who?' 'What?' 'When?' 'How?' 'Where?' about it, or ask 'How do I know that...?' to check the validity of your existing knowledge. See 'What questions might you ask?' in Chapter 4 for more questions to start you thinking about a topic.

2 'What might I focus on within the topic?'

Ask yourself 'What interests me about the topic?' 'What aspect of it do I want to explore?' 'What seems most important about the topic?'

For example, for the general topic 'Scientific Method', you might be familiar with the work of various writers on the questions 'What is science?' and 'Is there a scientific method?' and want to look further at the ideas of Paul Feyerabend, John Kemeny and Karl Popper.

3 'How much breadth or depth can my assignment have?'

Ask yourself 'Given any requirements of the assignment (such as length or format) how many questions can I answer?' 'How much key information can I present?' 'How many main ideas can I convey?' 'Should I concentrate on presenting a broad overview of the topic, or on exploring one or two facets of it in depth?'

For example, in the topic 'Scientific Method' you may focus on the question 'Is there a scientific method?', contrasting the opinion of Paul Feyerabend (who argues that there is no single scientific method) with the views of John Kemeny (who posits that there's one basic method common to all scientific activity). You make this decision because the length and time set for the assignment don't permit you to look at many writers in detail, and because you want to contrast two theories on the question.

4 'What is the topic about?'

With specific topics, analyse the wording of the topic so that you understand more clearly what you're expected to discuss and the possibilities that the topic offers. There are several questions you can usefully ask.

- What are the assumptions behind the topic? For example, the topic 'How should Piaget's theory of stages in children's development be applied to teaching mathematics in Australian primary schools?' assumes that Piaget's theory should be applied to maths teaching in Australian primary schools.

- What key words shape my approach to the topic? The topic may include words such as 'define', 'discuss' or 'evaluate' which direct how you should approach it [see Table 6.1 on page 61].

- Does the topic contain words or ideas I don't understand? For example, the possible uses of the word 'concept' in the topic 'Define Marx's concept of the proletariat' may not be clear. Consult a dictionary or, if a topic isn't clearly worded, ask your teacher to explain it more fully.

- How many parts are there to the topic? For example, in the Piaget topic you would need to describe Piaget's theory of developmental stages before discussing its possible applications to maths teaching in Australian primary schools.

With general topics or topics of your own choice, devise a specific title which clearly and accurately defines the topic. As you're still in the process of defining your topic, you're unlikely to be ready to choose a final title. However as you develop your definition, revise the wording if necessary.

5 'What subject headings are central to the topic?'

Compile a list of these headings as preparation for finding information. For example, before interviewing someone or using indexes, make a list of alternative or related terms for your subject headings. The reference cards in a library catalogue can help with this. To find information on immigrants look under 'Emigrants', 'Immigration' or under the nationality of a migrant group. To find references to the changing composition of the Australian workforce, look up 'Unemployment', 'Trade Unions', 'Women, working', as well as the obvious heading 'Workforce, Australian'.

6 'How will I approach the topic?'

> The trouble is that essays always have to sound like God talking for eternity, and that isn't the way it ever is. People should see that it's never anything other than just one person talking from one place in time and space and circumstance.
>
> Robert M. Pirsig

'How subjective will my approach be?' 'To what extent will I include my personal opinions?'

Table 6.1 Directive words

"When *I* use a word", Humpty Dumpty said, in a rather scornful tone, "it means just what I choose it to mean — neither more nor less".

Lewis Carroll

Analyse	Show the essence of something, by breaking it down into its component parts and examining each part in detail
Argue	Present the case for and/or against a particular proposition
Compare	Look for similarities and differences between propositions
Criticise	Give your judgement about the merit of theories or opinions about the truth of facts, and back your judgement by a discussion of the evidence
Define	Set down the precise meaning of a word or phrase. Show that the distinctions implied in the definition are necessary.
Describe	Give a detailed or graphic account
Discuss	Investigate or examine by argument, sift and debate, giving reasons for and against
Enumerate	List or specify and describe
Evaluate	Make an appraisal of the worth of something, in the light of its apparent truth or utility; include your personal opinion
Examine	Present in depth and investigate the implications
Explain	Make plain, interpret, and account for in detail
Illustrate	Explain and make clear by the use of concrete examples, or by the use of a figure or diagram
Interpret	Bring out the meaning of, and make clear and explicit; usually also giving your own judgement
Justify	Show adequate grounds for decisions or conclusions
Outline	Give the main features or general principles of a subject, omitting minor details, and emphasising structure and relationship
Prove	Demonstrate truth or falsity by presenting evidence
Relate	Narrate/show how things are connected to each other, and to what extent they are alike or affect each other
Review	Make a survey of, examining the subject critically
State	Specify fully and clearly
Summarise	Give a concise account of the chief points or substance of a matter, omitting details and examples
Trace	Identify and describe the development or history of a topic from some point or origin

— adapted from Harry Maddox *How to Study*, 2nd edn., Pan Books, London, 1967, pp. 119–120.

Your approach to a topic is always **subjective** to some degree. Even a set, specific topic can be tackled in a variety of ways, and your particular approach is reflected in what you include and omit from the possible material. Even if you're presenting a report in which you try to be as objective as possible, the words you use carry with them personal associations for you and your audience. So the question to ask is not 'Shall I take an objective or subjective approach?' but rather 'How objective will I attempt to be?' Whatever your approach, state it explicitly and let your audience know your beliefs or biases on the subject. See the Appendix 'Discrimination' for examples of bias.

In an assignment such as a laboratory report you're required to report only what you see as facts. In other assignments such as a philosophy essay you may be expected to include your own ideas with supporting arguments. Many assignments are open to a combination of these approaches. Your scope for presenting personal opinions or theories often depends on the conventions of a particular discipline and the personal preferences of your teacher. If you feel unsure about including your opinions, even when asked to, remember that practice in communicating your ideas and arguing them is a vital part of learning — and given practice and some encouraging response it does become easier. Usually it also makes your assignments more interesting to read.

> . . . my purpose is to employ facts as tentative probes, as means of insight, of pattern recognition, rather than to use them in the traditional and sterile sense of classified data, categories, containers.
>
> Marshall McLuhan

The **direction** of your approach depends on your purpose and interest. 'Will I simply describe aspects of my topic, or will I also attempt to analyse this description?' 'Will I compare two different aspects of a topic, or set out to clearly define all its components?' 'Will I argue a case for or against a particular controversy relating to the topic, or review the range of opinions on it?' [see Table 6:1]

(a) You're asked to write an essay on 'The Philosophy of Descartes'.

- You might concentrate primarily on explaining the impact made by Descartes' ideas, give social and historical detail to explain why his ideas had such impact. You include some description of the life and personality of Descartes, but select such description for its relevance to the ideas under discussion.

- Perhaps you decide to take one of Descartes' ideas, such as 'I think, therefore I am', and to focus mostly on examining the implications of that idea. You look at how Descartes' proposition puts him in a particular school of thought, and you avoid biographical details.

- You could critically evaluate the implications of Descartes' ideas. You decide either to make your own analysis of the ideas without the aid of secondary sources, or to review other people's analyses.

(b) You've chosen to write about the topic 'Women in the paid workforce'.

- You intend to give a broad overview of most facets of the topic and to interrelate these on a descriptive framework, because you have considerable previous knowledge of the topic.

- You want to present a general introduction to the subject and then focus on specific case studies so that you can suggest areas for further research.

(c) You're given the topic 'World Population' and you decide to focus on the changes in birth and death rates in Third World countries.

- You could concentrate on describing these demographic changes with selected graphs and statistics so that a detailed written analysis is unnecessary.

- You might analyse demographic statistics for one country in the light of various theories on population trends.

Group Assignments. If you're working on a group assignment, see Chapter 10 for suggestions on discussing ideas and information with others. In addition to the points mentioned in the previous section, defining a group topic involves agreeing on a central theme or question which the whole group will explore; deciding which specific aspects of the topic each person will research; and clarifying how each person's work contributes to the main theme or question.

Your initial definition

Before you begin full-scale research for an assignment, write down your initial definition of your topic, indicating the focus and depth or breadth of your approach, and outlining possible main points. Your definition may be reasonably clear at this stage if the assignment is short and straightforward. But it's more likely that you'll have a couple of possible approaches and a number of likely points from which you'll choose as you acquire detailed information about the topic. If you have trouble defining a topic, write down any ideas you have and discuss them with other people. Trying to express your thoughts accurately in writing or to others often helps you clarify them.

Deciding which material to use in research

Once you've defined your purpose and topic as far as possible, think about where and how you'll find material on it [see Ch. 7]. You'll be given information in lectures and other classes, supplied with reference lists for courses, discussion groups, lectures and assignments, and perhaps directed to sources such as the mass media and individual people. At times you may have to search out and know how to use less obvious sources so that you don't overlook significant material.

This plethora of material can be overwhelming, particularly as the information on any one subject is increasing rapidly all the time. You may feel bewildered because you want to or are apparently expected to absorb so much. When researching a topic it's easy to become sidetracked by fascinating but irrelevant information, held up by little or no information, or bewitched by mystifying technical language. You can avoid these pitfalls by keeping your purpose and your definition of the topic in mind. Obviously you can't use or absorb everything, so as well as being aware of potential material, you'll have to decide which material is most useful to you.

This section gives some hints on selecting and evaluating material for your purpose, and for its relevance and complexity. It also looks at the practical aspects of selecting material — buying, copying and borrowing.

Selecting relevant material

You may be given a list of references to choose from. If not, check the available information sources and make up a list of material relevant to your topic. Consult your teacher and any course guides, handouts or reference lists for suggestions. Ask for guidance on which material is essential, and which material to read first. Look for both primary and secondary sources on your topic [see 'Identifying primary and secondary sources', Ch. 7]. The length of your list should depend on the time available for your research.

When defining your topic you should have drawn up a list of the specific subject headings you intend to research. Keep this list firmly in mind. Browsing through material which is vaguely connected with your topic can be highly enjoyable, but it's time-consuming and shouldn't be confused with seriously selecting material for full-scale research. When browsing, however, you may come-across material which isn't precisely on your topic but deals with the general principles underlying it. An article on scientific methods, for example, can spark off ideas about an individual question on physics. Other material may provide valuable background, for example, a conversation with a person who lived through the Depression may help you understand a specific aspect of this era more fully. Occasionally an idea can be illuminated by juxtaposing it with material from an unexpected source, for instance astronomy with *Alice in Wonderland*, semantics with Sufi philosophy, poetry with Peanuts.

Look for material on your topic which isn't obvious or recommended. A book you own, for example, may contain suggestions for further reading, or an organisation you contact for information may refer you to another source.

Evaluating your selection

Education... has produced a vast population able to read but unable to distinguish what is worth reading...

G.M. Trevelyan

Once you've selected relevant material, choose from your selection by evaluating the material on the basis of the purpose for which you need it and its complexity for you.

According to your purpose

For what purpose will you use the material you're evaluating? Is it preliminary reading for a lecture or for a discussion paper, follow-up reading to a field trip or study material for an exam? Chapter 8 looks at purposes you might have for reading a book, and Table 8.1 on previewing suggests questions which help clarify how useful a book is for your purpose.

Some material, such as a course text, you'll use for more than one purpose. Sometimes different materials you use may complement each other, such as two books each with information on a different aspect of your topic, or a lecture and a course text which present the same information from different angles. Some materials you'll choose between because they are repetitive, such as two radio programmes which cover essentially the same ground.

Complexity of material for you

You can only understand a textbook when you are at the point where you almost don't need to read it, where it helps you comprehend (if it is any good) some higher-order connections among things which you separately have already worked your way through or around.

David Hawkins

Previewing material can help you discover the complexity of material for you and hence the background knowledge you require to use it.

- The subject may or may not be interesting or familiar to you and may or may not accord with your beliefs and biases. If an area is new to you, you won't understand all the material in it, but its very newness can be exciting. Don't automatically reject apparently difficult material — even as a beginning it may provide you with one or two important ideas, and later you may find it easier to understand and very stimulating.

- The writing style, format and organisation of material can make it easy or difficult for you to follow.

- Perhaps you're more comfortable using some media than others. For example, perhaps you usually take in more from journal articles than from lectures because you can re-read difficult sections in an article. Any medium becomes familiar if you use it often enough, but if there's no time for this before selecting material, opt for media which usually yield you the most information (and learn how to use the others later).

If material you're required to use seems too advanced or too simple for you, discuss this with your teacher and with other students. There may be other material you can use or you might need to choose another topic.

Buy, copy or borrow material?

Your choice of material depends on its availability. Sometimes you'll encounter problems with material you want to use because you can't buy or borrow it from a library. Often you can avoid these problems by doing your research well in advance, arranging to borrow material from friends, and asking your teacher if an alternative reference is possible. Otherwise you may need to reconsider your choice of a topic in the light of available resources.

Some material you're likely to want to refer to again, such as a course text or a reference book you need for a final exam or for a seminar paper. If you do need to consult material more than once, you may want to obtain your own copy — to buy a book, to tape a lecture or an interview, or to photocopy an article (subject to copyright laws). If you can't have your own copy, try to borrow the material, or if your information comes from a person or a place, arrange to visit them again. Take full notes from borrowed material if you need to use it heavily.

When deciding which books to buy, be wary of relying on course booklists given in handbooks. Such lists are usually drawn up six months or so before a course starts and may change substantially, or a different edition or translation of a book may be recommended. Before you buy books or start your reading, check with a teacher from the course to find out if there have been changes.

Whether you buy, copy or borrow material depends on:

— the amount of money you have
— if the materials are easily available from the library, from another student, or from a teacher
— how heavily you'll use the material in a course
— whether you have easy access to a library
— how heavily yu rely on course materials and references for stimulation, for instance, if you've little opportunity to discuss your work with other students
— whether you prefer to underline books or articles you read, and
— whether or not the material will be useful in other courses or in a future job.

Using research material

Preparing to use material

Consider the **skills needed** to select information from the material you'll use. For example, you gain more from a book if you're aware of what's involved in the activity of reading and how you might improve your skill in this activity. You learn more from a lecture or radio programme if you've thought about how these media convey information and the skills required for effective listening. See 'Examining a source' in Chapter 7, and the introductions to Chapter 8 on reading and Chapter 9 on lectures.

Previewing material, that is, surveying material as a whole before you work with it, acquaints you with its general organisation, content and presentation. This previewing enables you to consider how you could best use the material for your purpose, for example, how detailed your reading of a book should be or whether to take notes on a television programme [see 'Previewing', Ch. 8].

You have to record, store and retrieve useful information, so give some thought to how you'll do this. **A filing system** evolves as you use it, but have a basis for your filing before you start researching. If you've defined your purpose and topic, these can form the basis of your system.

In the preliminary stages of your research, give some thought to **how you might communicate ideas and information**. A written essay or report isn't automatically the most appropriate means for expressing ideas. If, for example, you're researching children's poetry, a taped essay which includes poetry readings may be most effective. If your topic is animal behaviour, you may decide to use photographs or videotape to convey your findings. Asking yourself, 'To whom do I want to communicate the information I find?' can help you decide how to convey your information.

> "Don't grunt," said Alice, "that's not at all a proper way of expressing yourself."
>
> Lewis Carroll

As you work with material

Questioning and evaluating

> Where there is much desire to learn, there of necessity will be much arguing, much writing, many opinions; for opinion in good men is but knowledge in the making.
>
> John Milton

You should have already previewed your material for its overall relevance to your purpose and topic. As you work with a book, listen to a lecture or watch a film, question and evaluate the information offered. This involves examining the purpose, content, structure and presentation of the material for its general quality and for its specific relevance to your topic and purpose. See Chapters 8 and 9 for details on evaluating information from reading and lectures. Be prepared to discover that some of the material you've selected may not be as useful for your purpose as you hoped, and don't expect that set or suggested references will automatically suit your definition of a topic. If you feel material is of limited use to you, abandon it as a source or try to incorporate a criticism of it into your assignment.

As part of evaluating information in your research, hopefully you'll learn to *interpret primary sources confidently*. In some assignments you're expected to use both your interpretation of primary source material and opinion from secondary sources [see 'Identifying primary and secondary sources', Ch. 7]. For example, when you conduct an experiment, you may be expected to interpret the data yourself and to refer to other people's interpretation of data from the same experiment. In an essay you may be expected to criticise a well-known author's works and to use other critics' evaluations of these. If you feel uncertain about presenting mostly your own ideas, and think that you should play it safe and rely mostly on secondary sources, practise the following:

— get to know your primary source material thoroughly, and see what ideas and interests this sparks off in you

— refer to secondary sources to help clarify points you don't understand in the primary source material
— read selectively among secondary sources and critically examine
other people's interpretations of the ideas or data you're studying, and
— use secondary sources for occasional new insights and for any
unexpected connections they may make.

Above all, trust your own intelligence and common sense in questioning and evaluating ideas.

> In a private debate the scholar Salih Awami said to Sufi Rahimi:
> 'What you have just said lacks references and proofs through quota-
> tions from ancient authority'.
> 'Not at all,' said Rahimi, 'for I have them all here, chapter and
> verse.'
> The scholar went away, saying, 'That was what I wanted to know.'
> The next day he made his famous speech on Rahimi which began:
> 'The lecture which you are about to hear from Sheikh Rahimi lacks con-
> viction. Why, he is so unsure of himself that he actually adducted writ-
> ten proofs and authorities to what he says.'
>
> Idries Shah

Selecting, recording and filing information

As you evaluate material, select information and record it in an
easily accessible form, for example, underline an article, tape parts
of an interview, or take photographs. You'll probably record most of
your information in note form even if preparing an oral or audiovisual assignment. See Chapters 8 and 9 for more on selecting information and taking notes from reading and lectures.

Some information you don't need to record and keep because it's
relatively accessible or because it's unlikely that you'll need it in future. However, some information which you may want again is
available to you only once (such as material in an interview or radio
programme) or is difficult to find again (such as information from a
person who's awkward to contact or a book which isn't readily
available). In these instances as you select the information you
want, think how you can best record and store it.

The basic reasons for systematically filing information are so that
you can easily find it again, add to or subtract from it, and re-
arrange it when useful. Use stationery such as looseleaf paper and a
ring binder, a box of file cards, a concertina file or several filing
trays to make it easier to arrange and re-arrange material as necessary.

Methods for filing information depend on the specific purposes for
which you need it. Often it's convenient to organise and file material according to its content or its source, as in the following examples.

- To follow the development of themes within a course, keep your lecture notes in sequence in a looseleaf folder. You can then interleave notes from tutorials, fieldwork and reading wherever their content is related to a theme.

- When preparing to write an essay in which you're expected to base your ideas on a careful examination of primary source material, keep your notes taken from the reading of primary sources separate from those from secondary sources.

Organise and file your material in chronological order (such as dates on lecture notes) or alphabetical order (such as authors of books read) and/or numerical order (with each item or each page of notes numbered). Record the source of your information in detail in case you want to find it again or cite the reference.

Read material and edit notes before you file them, ask yourself if you're likely to use the material again. Keeping all 'to-be-read-or-edited-material' together without attempting to file it before reading it indicates whether you're being realistic about the amount of information you take in and use. An efficient filing system is of little use if all it yields is an impressive collection of file card boxes whose contents you've mostly forgotten, or a stack of folders full of photocopied articles you intend to read one day.

> Knowledge is of two kinds. We know a subject ourselves, or we know where we can find information upon it.
>
> Samuel Johnson

Organising and integrating ideas and information

As you research and think about your topic you need to organise your ideas and the information you find and to integrate these. The following method is one way of doing this.

- Write each of the possible central points on to separate sheets of paper or cards.

- Enter relevant information and ideas (and references to any graphic or audiovisual material) under the appropriate heading.

- Add a new heading if you decide on another major point, or delete a point which comes to appear insignificant. If you've much more information for one heading than for others, consider if you should base your whole assignment only on the idea in that heading. If necessary, reorganise and delete material.

- Check the number of major points you want to make against the possible assignment length and the time available. It's usually better to err on the side of making a few points clearly, with plenty of evidence and examples and explanation, rather than trying to cover all possible major points superficially.

Organising your information and ideas in this way helps you see the central points more clearly. You begin to understand how they could effectively be related to one another, and the order in which you could develop them so they reflect your approach to the topic. Your researching, thinking and organising should extend and clarify your definition of the topic. As you continue your research, you're likely to revise the content of your definition and to structure that content. Ask yourself 'What statement can I make which captures the focus of the whole assignment?' 'How can I convey my central theme/thesis/argument to my audience?'

Expressing your ideas

Talking to others about the information you find and your ideas helps you begin to sort out your thoughts and become accustomed to putting them into words. As you carry out your research, it's often valuable to write individual paragraphs or sentences (or to make part of a tape) so that you capture an idea you may use later. Put these ideas down when you think of them in case they vanish, and if you have a half-formed idea in your head, try expressing it without editing and see how it takes shape [see 'Free writing', Ch. 11]. Often you'll discover that trying to express your thoughts accurately leads you to other ideas you can use.

Towards the end of your research

When your research is almost complete and you're ready to begin your assignment, allow yourself time for **sorting out your ideas**, for your thoughts to sift and settle. Do this rather than read another book or conduct another interview, especially if you're finding it difficult to work out what you want to say in your assignment. Look at your notes as a whole to refresh your mind about your ideas on the topic and to review the information you've selected from your material.

Talk again about your information and ideas with others, perhaps in a discussion or writing group, so that you begin to express your thoughts. New ideas and relationships will emerge within the material, and difficulties in deciding and articulating what you want to say often resolve themselves. Ask yourself again what strikes you as most important and interesting about the topic to provide you with a focus for the assignment.

Your revised definition

The initial definition of the topic with which you began your research should have reflected your purpose for the assignment, indi-

cated the focus and depth or breadth of your assignment, and outlined your likely approach to the topic and your possible main
points.

After your research, your revised definition should still reflect your
purpose and approach. Your focus should have developed into your
theme/thesis/argument and the main points should now be definite.
The structure of your assignment — how you'll organise your main
points — may be quite clear now or may still be tentative. In either
case, leave some flexibility in your definition so that if necessary you
can revise it further when expressing your thoughts and information
in writing your assignment [see Ch. 12].

* * *

An assignment is designed for a specific, limited purpose, rather
than to find out all you're ever likely to know on a topic. Defining
and researching a topic should enable you to select from your current knowledge of that topic, even if your knowledge continues to
grow and expand in areas far beyond the focus of your assignment.

7 Using Libraries and Other Information Sources

We live in the midst of information networks. You are a point in many networks, sometimes giving information and sometimes seeking it. No one can learn all there is to know about a subject, so you can be both a learner and a teacher in subjects which interest you. Even as an interested beginner, you probably know enough about an area to teach someone else a little about it. If you can't answer someone's queries on a subject, you can probably direct them to another part of a network where they're likely to find what they want to know. Which network you plug into when seeking information depends on what you want to know, why you want to know it, and whether you know how to use available information sources.

This chapter centres on the processes involved in making effective use of libraries and other information sources, while emphasising the need to be aware of a wide range of possible sources. The chapter looks at choosing sources relevant to your topic and at examining the sources you decide to use. We begin by looking at libraries, as they are heavily relied on as a source of information in tertiary institutions.

Libraries

Choosing libraries

If you have access to more than one library, explore each one to find out what it offers you. Look at it as a place to work. Consider its facilities, material in your areas of interest, and staff expertise and helpfulness. A large library may have most of the material you need, but you may prefer a small library where the staff are familiar with your interests and where you feel more at home. Or the small library nearby may be frustrating because it never seems to have the books you want, and you may prefer a large library with a postal loans service.

Libraries have many different functions, and include:

— large state libraries, with special sections such as archives
— university libraries, often with individual subject libraries attached
— government departmental libraries
— specialist collections, such as a historical society library, a photographic collection, a substantial private collection
— public libraries serving a local community, and
— school libraries.

Your State Library can help direct you to the libraries most useful to you. Don't forget your personal library, and those of your friends. Remember that through inter-library loans and computer-based information services you have access to material in libraries other than the one or two which you can visit most easily, or from which you usually receive books.

To use libraries fully, you need to know what materials they offer, learn how to gain practical access to the materials they contain, and learn how to find items in them.

Making full use of libraries

1 *Knowing what materials libraries contain*

Explore the libraries to which you have access to find out what materials they contain. The following list may include materials you hadn't considered or which are unfamiliar to you.

(a) *Books and other printed material.* These are a familiar source of information to most of us. Chapter 8 suggests ways of reading printed material fully. Apart from books, some libraries contain:

— periodicals, journals, newspapers, bulletins and other serials, with current issues usually on display and back issues shelved or available on microfilm
— government publications, such as reports, yearbooks, and manuals, and
— pamphlets on a wide range of subjects.

One important group of books in any library is **the reference collection**. You probably are aware of standard references such as *The Encyclopaedia Britannica* and *The Oxford Dictionary*, but reference collections can also contain works such as:

— specialist encyclopaedias or dictionaries, such as *The Encyclopaedia of Philosophy, Dictionary of Film Makers*
— atlases, gazetteers, guidebooks, such as the *Archaeological Atlas of the World, Bartholomew Gazetteer of Britain*
— yearbooks and almanacs which give relatively up-to-date statistical information and which are often government publications such as *The West Australian Yearbook*
— handbooks which contain useful and detailed information for people in specific fields such as teaching, writing, surveying, skindiving
— resource directories which are catalogues of useful material, people and places, from a grand scale such as *The Last Whole Earth Catalog* and *The New Woman's Survival Catalog*, to a local scale such as a directory for a particular city or small interest group.

To find works on a subject, it can be extremely useful to consult some bibliographies, indexes and abstracts in the reference collection as well as using the subject catalogue.

● Bibliographies list books by a particular subject, author, printer or country, for example, *The Current Bibliographies on African Affairs, The Internatinal Bibliography of Economics, A Bibliography of Sex Rites and Customs, The Australian National Bibliography*.

● Indexes are usually:

— indexes to multi-volume reference works such as an encyclopaedia
— indexes issued by publishers of a periodical, for example, the *Scientific American Cumulative Index*
— indexes to a number of general periodicals issued by an independent publisher, for example, *APAIS* (The Australian Public Affairs Information Service), issued by the National Library, Canberra, and
— indexes to periodicals in special fields, for example, *Index Medicus* in the medical field.

● Abstracts include a précis of books and articles in a field, as well as indexing them, for example, *Psychological Abstracts*. Some libraries have computer-based information services which offer information available in abstracts and indexes, and store, classify and facilitate retrieval of this information. These services are used primarily for advanced research rather than for providing general reference material.

To make efficient use of bibliographies, indexes and abstracts you need to develop a list of subject terms central to a topic [see 'Defining a topic', Ch. 6].

> Twenty-two acknowledged concubines, and a library of sixty-two thousand volumes, attested the variety of his inclination . . .
>
> Edward Gibbon

(*b*) *Non-print material.*   This may include:

— graphic material, such as maps, prints, illustrations, paintings and models
— audiovisual material, such as slides and photographs, audiocassettes, videotapes, films, and overhead transparencies
— microfilm, for example, of back issues of newspapers
— microfiche, such as the Human Relations Area File, and
— collections of ephemeral material, such as newsletters, posters, advertisements, and lapel buttons.

It takes time and practice to become familiar with the contents and organisation of a library, and to learn how to use library facilities. This familiarisation is a means to learning more about subjects which interest you, and the exercise at the end of this chapter can help you with this. To update and extend and diversify your knowledge of the information that any library has to offer, explore its resources when new subjects stimulate your curiosity.

2 Gaining access to information

To be able to use materials a library offers means learning to use catalogues and equipment such as photocopiers, tape recorders, and videocassette players. Ask one of the library staff to show you how to use this equipment as most students who aren't initially confident with equipment rapidly become so, once familiar with it.

3 Learning how to find items

(a) Ask the *library staff* — they are usually helpful with anything from the most basic to the most esoteric of queries.

(b) Become familiar with the *layout* of a library — where the different types of materials are located, and where facilities such as photocopiers and audiovisual equipment can be found. Most libraries have maps and publications describing their layout and operation, but it's easy to fall into the habit of only using one section of a library and being unaware of what other areas have to offer. Learn about the *operation* of a library, for example, how the borrowing system operates or how to ask for an inter-library loan.

(c) Find out what extra information *the information or reference desk* holds to enable you to locate material. There may be a print-out of material currently on reserve, a list of journal issues, information about material in special subject libraries elsewhere on campus.

(d) Find out which *system the library uses* for cataloguing, classifying, indexing and shelving the material it contains. For example:

— some libraries have catalogues for author/title and for subjects, while other libraries put all cards in one alphabetical file

— some libraries use classification system other than the familiar Dewey system

— methods of shelving materials such as large books, pamphlets and audiovisual material vary from one library to another

— the alphabetical order of catalogue cards may vary, for example, in how entries for authors with hyphenated names are filed, and

— some libraries use microfiche catalogues instead of card catalogues.

(e) Learn to use the information on the *catalogue cards*. Taking time to do this (ask the library staff to help you) can save you many hours later on and gives you access to much greater breadth and depth of information. There are two general types of catalogue card.

● Reference cards direct you to alternative headings for a topic (such as 'Motor cars...*see* Automobiles'), or to related headings (such as 'Naturalists...*see also* Ecologists'), or to more specific headings (such as 'Biology...*see also* Marine Biology').

● The author/title/subject card, gives you information on an item, its location in the library, and related subject headings. These cards include:

— the call number for an item, which gives you its exact shelf location and also appears on the item itself

— a location symbol, which indicates the sequence of materials in which the item is shelved, for example, books, journals, pamphlets, oversize books. (Your next step is to find out where this sequence is shelved.)

— the classification number, which arranges material by subject
— the author's symbol, which is used to sub-arrange books on the same subject, and
— publication details for an item, which includes the publisher, place, date of publication and edition. (Note that the date of first publication may differ from the publication date of the particular edition or reprint which the library holds).

To look up an item in the author or title catalogue, you need the correct spelling of the author's name and the correct wording of the title. If you can't find a book in the catalogue, check that you have been given an accurate reference.

(f) *If the item isn't on the shelf in its exact location:*

— check if it's on the shelf but slightly out of order
— check the catalogue to make sure that you copied the call number accurately
— if you did, find out if the item is on loan
— if it is, you can ask for it to be recalled, and
— if it isn't on loan, check if it's being held elsewhere in the library such as in a reserve collection.

If none of these steps help you find the item, it's probably in use in the library by another reader or waiting to be re-shelved. Try the shelves later on.

(g) *If you aren't able to visit the library easily*, perhaps because you're a part-time or external student, be particularly well-informed about the facilities you need to use most often, such as photo-copying services and special loan arrangements. When you send in a request for help, or if you do manage to visit the library, be very clear about the sort of information you're seeking. Explore other library facilities near you, which books you'll use most heavily, and be prepared to buy them [see 'Buy, copy, or borrow material', Ch. 6]. The cost of mailing books or making special trips to a library can soon add up to the price of several books, and libraries don't regard provision of textbooks as one of their functions.

'It may be all very well in cities, where they have unlimited funds, to let nasty children ruin books and just deliberately tear them up, and fresh young men take more books out than they are entitled to by the regulations, but I'm never going to permit it in this library!'

'What if some children are destructive? They learn to read. Books are cheaper than minds.'

Sinclair Lewis

Choosing relevant sources

Not even the largest 'multiversity' can offer all the resources needed by students today. One possibility, in our mobile society, is freedom for the student to go wherever he is likely to find what he needs.

University Without Walls

An initial step in choosing information sources for a topic is to become aware of a range of possible sources. As a student in an educational institution, you have some obvious sources such as:

— classes, including lectures, lab sessions and discussion groups
— people, including teachers and other students, and
— printed and audiovisual material, such as course guides, laboratory manuals, handouts, recommended books and library materials.

You limit your potential sources if you look only to educational institutions and libraries for your information and ignore the groups and individual people in your community. So before automatically consulting your lecture notes or going to a library for information, ask yourself 'How would I find what I want to know if I wasn't a student with access to these sources?' You can learn much in your formal education from people who aren't considered experts or teachers. If you're studying local history, for example, you can gain a wealth of information from people who've lived in your community for a long time. If you're studying insect behaviour, the person next door who has kept bees for many years can be extremely helpful. But it's easy to overlook sources of information outside libraries unless specifically directed to them. And as a learner in the late twentieth century, the mass media form a large part of your information networks and a large part of the reality in which you live.

Being able to use a range of information sources requires:

— defining your purpose and topic as clearly as you can
— locating a range of potential information sources
— choosing sources which suit your subject, and
— examining sources to find out how to use them most effectively.

Defining your purpose and topic is discussed in Chapter 6. This section and the next look at the other processes involved in using a range of information sources, and as examples of these processes refers to three broadly different sources of information — organisations, people and the mass media. We now look at identifying primary and secondary sources in relation to your topic, and at mastering the skills necessary for using a source, in this case for gathering primary information.

Identifying primary and secondary sources

The information sources available to you vary according to your subject. Sometimes you can go directly to your subject for first-hand information. For example, if your subject is the ideas of Mao Tse-Tung you may be able to obtain and read his writings, or if you're studying goldfish behaviour you might have facilities so you can conduct experiments on this. At other times, you'll have to rely on other people's reports about your subject. For example, you may read a journal article about Mao Tse-Tung if you can't obtain his books, or you might ask an aquarium owner about the behaviour of goldfish. Often you'll use both first-hand (or primary) and second-hand (or secondary) information.

If you're studying a local community group and you gather your information on them by attending several meetings, your source is also your subject and is described as *a primary source*. If you read a newspaper article on the group to obtain your information, the article is *a secondary source*, that is, the information doesn't come directly from your subject.

Similarly, if your subject is a scientific research organisation, a filmed interview with the head of the organisation is a primary source whereas someone else's written report about the interview is a secondary source. If you are studying an historical event, the testimony of participants and witnesses are primary sources, while a source of secondary information would be a book written by an historian using these testimonies.

You can limit your choice of material and your choice of topics by classifying an information source as either primary or secondary when it can be both. Teachers and libraries, for example, dispense secondary information about a range of subjects, but they themselves can also be subjects for a study and thus a primary source. You may study a commercial organisation such as a mining company and use it as a primary source, but overlook the secondary knowledge the company holds on subjects related to its operations.

Communities offer a wide variety of organisations which can be used as primary and secondary sources, depending on your topic. The following are just a few of the possibilities:

— public agencies and institutions, such as museums, government departments, art galleries, courts, scientific research organisations
— commercial businesses, such as mining companies, factories, insurance companies, shopping centres, and
— community groups, such as church organisations, business associations, environmental groups, women's health care houses, ethnic broadcasting groups.

Some organisations offer library and public information facilities. You also have access to services and organisations designed to provide information, such as Legal Aid, Citizens' Advice Bureaux, and local government information offices. Often a person or group can refer you to further sources.

Do some preliminary research and decide on some questions you want to ask before contacting people and organisations for information [see 'Defining a topic', Ch. 6]. Make inquiries to find out who's most likely to be helpful for your purpose and don't hesitate to make an initial polite request for information. You may be surprised at the help people are willing to give, and this process of finding material is a valuable learning exercise in itself.

Tools for using a source

Other chapters in this book look at tools for using sources such as books and lectures. Here we look briefly at the tools needed to gather primary information.

When you're curious about a subject you can learn much by **observation**. Listen and look closely, and use your senses of taste, smell and touch if appropriate. If you can observe a subject more and more intently over a period of days or weeks, you'll come to see it with new eyes. You can observe the natural physical environment — phenomena such as a sunset, a bird, trees, rain and mountains. You can observe your manufactured and technological environment, with its aeroplanes and advertisements, its transistors and telephones. You can observe the people in your world such as parents, friends, work colleagues or strangers.

Observing people and seeking information from them are activities you engage in for many of your waking hours, and you consciously or unconsciously learn much of what you need to know from your interactions with others. Deliberately seeking information from and about people requires carefully directed observation if you're to obtain useful information on a specific topic. You need practice in the skills of observation, even if you're 'only watching' people to describe them, or 'just talking' to a person to find out very specific information.

However, observation alone can't tell you all you want to know. No matter how acute your observations, don't mistake them for a sophisticated analysis. Skilled researchers are very cautious about drawing conclusions from their research.

> Natural science does not simply describe and explain nature; it is part of the interplay between nature and ourselves; it describes nature as exposed to our methods of questioning.
>
> Werner Heisenberg

As well as careful observation you also need considerable familiarity with the appropriate **research techniques** if your observation is to be extended and directed towards specific ends. Research techniques are more of a hindrance than a help if used without sensitivity to the complexity of people and of environments, or if used in the belief that they provide 'objective' answers. But if used cautiously they can be appropriate tools in your search for information.

Anyone interested in human beings and why we act as we do won't want to limit their inquiry to reading books or listening to lectures. The raw material of all our understanding of human behaviour is observations of people — ourselves and others. These observations include study of how people act in certain situations and what they report about how they feel and why they do things. From these observations we infer their motives, their values, their attitudes, and their opinions. Social science has developed a whole array of tools to assist in these analyses. These tools include questionnaires, interviews, field studies, participant observation, laboratory studies, and unobtrusive measures.

Each of these techniques is an entire skill area in itself and consists of a whole series of sub-techniques. For example, an interview may be open-ended or closed, structured or unstructured, in-depth or limited. The proper construction of a reliable and valid questionnaire is a skill requiring months or years of training and experience. Unobtrusive measures for observing people can range from activities such as measuring carpet wear patterns in an art gallery to find out which paintings are most popular, to gathering statistics from pharmaceutical companies about sales of oral contraceptives to Catholic and non-Catholic communities.

Each technique has its own characteristic strengths and weaknesses. The nature of the question being asked, the population being studied, the resources available, and the preferences of the questioner, all influence the choice of appropriate techniques. This area of 'research methodology' is one of the most complex and difficult in the social sciences and scholars spend entire lifetimes studying small aspects of it. One should no more expect a beginning student in the social sciences to be able to construct these research instruments properly than one would expect a biology student to be able to design and build an electron microscope. The difficulties are of the same order of magnitude.

The interpretation of the results of these information gathering techniques is equally complex and requires an equally sophisticated level of skill if it is to be properly done. The path which leads from initial formulation of a question in the mind through gathering data from observations of people to drawing valid conclusions from those observations, is a long and thorny path which is pitted with traps for the unwary. Expert guidance is essential.[1]

Humans don't follow neat patterns of behaviour, don't act in totally predictable ways, and are distinctly prone to present a researcher with a mass of complex material to analyse. As you acquire information, your clear definition of what you wanted to know will hopefully remain the same in substance but will inevitably change in shape as you come to grips with the uniqueness of

---

[1] John Raser, 1980, written for this book.

another human being. To acquire skill in using research techniques, practise them and learn from your successes and failures how each technique can best be applied. Even when you've considerable skill with such tools you'll continue to learn more about their use because of the unpredictable nature of your 'subjects'. It's a challenge which is worth as much creativity and effort as you can muster if you're interested in who we are and what we do.

Examining a source

> The media shape both content and consumer and so are practically undetected. We recall the story of the Russian worker whose wheelbarrow was searched every day as he left the factory grounds. He was, of course, stealing wheelbarrows. When your medium is your message and they're only investigating content, you can get away with a lot of things — like wheelbarrows, for instance. It's not the picture but the frame. Not the contents but the box. The blank page is not neutral; nor is the classroom.
>
> John M. Culkin, S.J.

As well as choosing relevant sources, examine each information source you use so that you can plan how to use its contents effectively and how to understand and evaluate it more fully. If, for example, you're going to interview a person, think about the process of interviewing and about the skills you'll need to obtain information on your topic. *Other chapters in the book look at the processes involved in using the sources of books and lectures. Here we look at the mass media as an example of analysing a source and at planning how to use that source systematically.*

The discoveries to be made from observing and using the information in the mass media are plentiful — if you accept them as a significant information source in your formal education. How can you observe and analyse the nature of the mass media?

The medium used

The mass media are part of your daily life. When you read a daily paper or watch the TV news, you see your community, your society and your world as they're reflected, selected and shaped by the media. What you see, read and hear is happening now, and you expect the media to provide you with more up-to-date information than that in books. But this simultaneity makes it difficult to stand back from the information the media convey. For example, it's difficult to evaluate and use a documentary shown on TV last night in the same way as you would a book. And because the media deal almost entirely with topical issues and events, they frequently select information which will make 'a good story' rather than presenting a balanced view of a subject. Use the media — but keep their limitations in mind.

1 Comparing mass media with traditional sources

Another way to learn about the nature of mass media is to compare them with information sources traditionally used in formal education. Listening to a ten-minute current affairs commentary or a full-length play on the radio requires a different approach from listening to a fifty-minute lecture. To criticise the content of a radio programme as though it were a lecture delivered by a person in front of you is to ignore the way the medium itself shapes the content and your perceptions in each instance. The same is true if you evaluate feature articles in a daily newspaper as though they were written with exactly the same aims as a book which took a year to write and which you can take a year to read.

> The newspaper format...offers short, discrete articles that give important facts first and then taper off to incidental details, which may be, and often are, eliminated by the make-up man. The fact that reporters cannot control the length of their articles means that, in writing them, emphasis can't be placed on structure, at least in the traditional linear sense, with climax or conclusion at the end.
>
> Edmund Carpenter

Like books and traditional lectures, radio programmes and newspapers present you with information in a one-way process. Their messages come to you with little possibility of engaging in immediate dialogue with them. If you recognise this, you can see that you need to question and evaluate and use the information they convey if you're to understand and remember it. This entails discussing it, writing about it, or applying it to a problem you need to solve. In this way you think actively about the information, and make it your own. As with listening to a lecture, it's easy to delude yourself that you've learned something from listening to and looking at a TV programme, when all you've done is passively receive words and images.

You may also realise that, unlike books and lectures, the media mix direct information with advertisements and trivia which convey information indirectly. When using the media as sources, look out for both types of information.

Indirect information includes:

— examples of attitudes to sex in our society as seen in a family comedy series or in recent films.
— political attitudes and issues as presented in the 'letters to the editor' columns and the cartoons in daily newspapers, or

— a mystification of science and technology revealed in the way advertisements use the word 'scientific' and in the lack of informative, accessible technical reporting.

Much directly informative material is broadcast on the Australian Broadcasting Commission's TV and radio, including:

— regular programmes in areas such as science, women's issues, current affairs, wildlife and music
— individual series or programmes on the ideas of people such as Jung and Darwin and Einstein and on issues such as nuclear power and racial discrimination, and
— performances of Shakespeare's plays and dramatisations of novels by modern Australian authors.

2 Theories about the media

The work of theorists such as Marshall McLuhan is an invaluable stimulus to observing and analysing the mass media. McLuhan explores the concept that 'the medium is the message'. This implies that the way you learn is what you learn, that the framework of your learning forms the content of that learning. For example, in a geology textbook a description of a large earthquake tells a very different story about the event from a TV newscast which includes film and sound footage. McLuhan argues that the nature of the media with which people communicate have always shaped societies more than the content of the communication. Part of his thesis concerns how the mass media are used, by whom and for what purposes.

> Effective study of the media deals not only with the content of the media but with the media themselves and the total cultural environment within which the media function.
>
> Marshall McLuhan

3 Practical experience

'Hands on' experience is one way to learn about the nature of the mass media — making films or videotapes, writing or taking photographs for a student newspaper, preparing a broadcast for community radio, working in public access television. Learning about the media by only observing them is somewhat akin to expecting to learn how to conduct experimental scientific research by only observing experiments conducted by others.

How to use a source systematically

Plan how to use the mass media systematically according to their particular demands. The media present you with masses of information, much of which you won't want to use in your formal learning. But be aware of the valuable information that is offered, and make the most of it when you do use it. If you see a TV programme only once, how can you best take in and select the information it offers? If you buy a newspaper every day, how can you decide which items to re-read and keep?

Prepare, evaluate and review material as suggested in Chapter 8 on reading and Chapter 9 on lectures. Think about the nature of the media and how they influence your information. For example, if you've been listening to a radio programme, ask yourself how the same material would have been presented in a lecture or on TV.

Electronic media

TV, radio and film are essentially transient. You usually see a TV programme or a film only once, you listen once to a radio programme. These media are strongly visual and aural, unlike the usual academic information sources of books and lectures. There are several ways to take advantage of the information they offer.

- Use *guides* to films and to TV and radio programmes. Don't overlook the less obvious alternatives in these areas such as community radio or a cinema screening 16 mm films. Go through the guides and pick out programmes which you know or expect will be useful. Note the times for these in a 'Things to do' list, a diary, or a weekly study plan.

- Make arrangements for *recording* a radio programme (subject to copyright laws) if you can't listen when it's broadcast or if you think you may want to replay it. Keep a couple of blank tapes on hand, and buy or borrow a tape recorder with a time switch. Some libraries videotape programmes for you if you don't have access to facilities for this.

- Think about *the topic* of a programme or film ahead of time, talk about it with others, and perhaps arrange to watch or listen to it together and discuss it afterwards.

- If you'll hear or see a programme only once, *concentrate* fully so that you can absorb and select information quickly and competently. Take notes if these would be useful, for example, to remember certain facts or figures or to record impressions [see 'Understanding a Lecture', Ch. 9].

- If you haven't made *notes* during a radio or TV programme or film, but would find these useful, do so immediately after while the material is still fresh in your mind.

- *Review* any notes you've made or listen to a tape recording or videotape you've made as soon as possible after a programme, preferably the next day.

'She reads at such a pace,' she complained, 'and when I asked her *where* she had learnt to read so quickly, she replied, "On the screens at Cinemas."'

Ronald Firbank

Print media

When you read newspapers, magazines and periodicals, you probably browse and skim, glancing through some items, reading a few others in detail, and passing over most. You can re-read newspapers and magazines, but except for a few items of special interest you're unlikely to do so. After all, there's next day's paper and the next issue of a favourite magazine to be read, and today's news article loses much of its impact by tomorrow or next week or next month. What can you do to discover and select the information available in the print media?

- Buy a daily and weekly newspaper (or read them in a library) to see if they contain any useful information.

- Survey several issues of the magazines, periodicals and newsletters in your areas of interest, and decide which ones you really find useful. Subscribe to them for yourself or on a shared basis, or find out if your library will subscribe to them. Look through their contents regularly for useful material.

- Practise the skills of surveying material, selecting what to read and deciding how closely to read it when looking through newspapers, magazines and periodicals [see 'Approaches to Reading', Ch. 8]. Clip out useful items and note on each the page number, date and title of the paper or periodical.

- File clippings so they can easily be found again [see 'Selecting, recording and filing information', Ch. 6].

People don't actually read newspapers — they get into them every morning like a hot bath.

Marshall McLuhan

* * *

Using the media as learning sources requires that you think about the general nature of mass media and about their roles as information providers in both formal and informal learning. if your teachers only occasionally direct you to the mass media as significant sources of information, being aware of what you can learn from the media is essentially something you choose to do for your own reasons. The choice is an important one if your education is to include an understanding of the nature of learning in the late twentieth century.

One way to use this chapter

The aim of this exercise is for you to become more aware of a wider range of information available to you in a particular area. To do this, set aside a couple of days at the beginning of your academic year to do the exercise, or return to it at intervals over a longer period of time. Continue it for as long as you like or regard it as succesfully 'completed' when your knowledge of your topic has been increased.

1 Choose a topic which strongly interests you but which you haven't systematically researched.

2 Define the topic as clearly as possible by asking yourself what you want to know and by listing topic headings [see Ch. 6].

3 Write down as many possible information sources from your community as you can think of. Don't bother at this stage to evaluate how helpful they might be — simply list any people or organisations that might be useful.

4 Use a library catalogue to list material on your subject, and use the library's reference collection to discover further references to your topics.

5 Choose four or five information sources from your community list which you think will be the most helpful for your purposes. Choose another four or five sources from your list of library references.

6 Follow up each of these information sources to find out more about your subject.

Further reading

Babbie, Earl R. *The Practice of Social Research*. Wadsworth Publishing Company, Belmont, California, 1973.

Guenther, Elsa. *How to Study Through Your Library*. 3rd edn. Australian Library Promotion Council, Melbourne, 1978.

McLuhan, Marshall. *Understanding Media: The Extensions of Man* McGraw-Hill Book Co., New York, 1964.

Macbeth, Jim, and Hitchens, Dave. *A Report on Community Information Needs: Research into Information Needs in Perth*. Murdoch University, Western Australia, 1977.

Reus-Smit, Karel *et al*. *Introduction to Social Theory*. Cheshire Publishing, Melbourne, 1974.

Schoenheimer, *H.P. Men and Messages*. Cheshire, Melbourne, 1973.

As you silently read this paragraph, your eyes are moving from left to right in a series of quick jumps along the line of print. Each time your eyes stop and focus on individual words or a cluster of words, the number of words you take in depends on your eye span and your word recognition skills.

You instantly perceive and recognise familiar words by their shape without needing to think consciously about their spelling, pronunciation or origin. However, sometimes you need a context to give a familiar word meaning. For example, how do you read 'read' in 'I have read six books' or in 'I'm about to read the paper'? At other times you need knowledge or experience to identify the intended meaning of a word. For example, do you interpret 'The East is red' to mean that the sun is rising or that China is a communist country?

When you come to a word you've never seen before, such as 'transmogrify' or 'simulacrum', your eyes focus on it for longer. You could re-read the sentence or paragraph to understand the meaning of the word from its context, or you might refer to a dictionary. Perhaps you recognise parts of the word, ('trans-' in 'transmogrify') or you attempt to divide the word into syllables (trans-mog-ri-fy, sim-u-la-crum) and pronounce it to see if you've ever heard the word spoken. Sometimes the word reminds you of another familiar word ('simulacrum' may remind you of 'similar', 'simulate', 'simultaneous' or 'fulcrum'). You might skip the word and move on.

There is much more to understanding what you read than the physical movement of your eyes and your ability to recognise words. When reading the paragraphs above, you gained an overall impression of what was written without needing to identify every word or literally reconstruct the printed message. You filtered the message through who you are as a reader — your experiences and beliefs, your current state of being, your reading purpose, your knowledge and interest in the subject, your reading skills, and your feelings about reading.

I would sooner read a time-table or a catalogue than nothing at all.
Somerset Maugham

Stop for a few minutes to think about and answer the following questions about **you as a reader.**

Do you like to read? Why?
If you don't enjoy reading, why?
What do you read? Historical novels? Science fiction? Biographies? Cookbooks? Newspapers?
When do you read? Before you go to sleep? Whenever you have a spare moment?

While cleaning your teeth?
Where do you most enjoy reading? In the bath? On the bus or train?
Do you have several books on the go at the same time?
Do you talk to others about what you've read?

As a reader, you differ from other people in what you read, when and where you read, and how much you enjoy reading. You have your own reading 'personality' which began developing when you first made contact with words and books as a small child. This reading 'personality' influences how you, as a student, feel about and approach reading. If you like to read novels, you can sit absorbed in them for hours. If you prefer magazines, you may be accustomed to reading in short bursts. If you usually read the paper, you probably read some articles closely and glance through others.

When confronted with reading material for a course, only some of your reading habits are appropriate. You shouldn't read medical text as you would science fiction, and novels in a literature course require a different approach from magazines. However if you enjoy reading and read a lot, you can build on this enjoyment and the appropriate reading skills when you come to tackle academic reading.

If you consciously think about how you put yourself into what you read, you are reading actively. To read actively you deliberately try to be aware of your strengths and weaknesses as a reader, your experience, beliefs and biases, and how you are feeling. If you read actively, you're more likely to be able to discern the author's intended message and to evaluate how this message has been affected by the author's purpose, biases, experience, and beliefs. You will also be more aware of the author's writing style and method of presentation.

> ...she continued with the process of taking a fragment here and a sentence there, and built them into her mind, which was now the most extraordinary structure of disconnected bits of poetry, prose, fact and fantasy...She had in fact not read...any...author, if reading means to take from an author what he intends to convey.
>
> Doris Lessing

This chapter is about reading actively. It focuses on you the reader and on how you can become actively involved with what you read so that you come to know and understand it in detail. The chapter is designed to help you formulate your purposes for reading and suggests a range of techniques appropriate for different purposes and materials. You're likely to use the chapter most fully in conjunction with material you're reading thoroughly, such as a course text, or when discussing material with others. But it's a long chapter, so first look through the headings. Then either start at the beginning and work through it slowly, or dip into sections which are most immediately useful to you.

If a book is one of a dozen suggested references, use the previewing section to help you decide whether to read it. If you want to improve your notetaking, read rapidly through the chapter to that section. The techniques described here apply to reading a whole book, a part of a book, a journal article, a research paper or a government report, and some of the chapter is useful for reading fiction.

Preparing to read

Your purpose

Your purpose influences any groundwork you do before you read, your reading rate, whether you underline or take notes. Before you read, ask yourself 'How thoroughly do I want to understand this material?' 'Why?' 'How much do I want to remember?'

Imagine that you're reading to prepare for a lecture on an unfamiliar topic. A day or so before the lecture you look through a couple of references and try to identify some of the main points or issues of the topic, using guides such as the introduction, index or chapter titles to help you. Or imagine that you have to write a detailed critique of an article. You read it slowly, underlining important points or taking notes, and re-read if necessary.

Sometimes you read the same material for several purposes. For example, you may be required to read the same text for background information for a course as well as to understand several chapters to answer an assignment question. You'll approach the book differently to meet each of these requirements.

Examining your material

When browsing in a bookshop or library, why does one book appeal to you more than another? Perhaps a book's appearance or title attracts you or the author is someone whose writing you usually enjoy. Perhaps it seems relevant to one of your interests or useful for a particular purpose. The layout, writing style or author's approach to the subject may lead you to buy or borrow the book. Each book has its own identity, and you respond differently to each one you pick up.

Previewing

To get the feel of a book you might glance through it, read the dust jacket, look at the pictures or diagrams, think about what the title means and perhaps check through the table of contents and read

Table 8.1 The anatomy of a book

Title/subtitle

What is the author trying to convey in the title (and subtitle)?

Cover/dustjacket

What information does the cover of the book give about the contents, the author, and the book within its field?

How reliable do you think the people are who wrote or are quoted in any information on the cover?

Author/editor/translator

Is there any information inside the book about the author's, editor's or translator's background, other publications, or experience relevant to the subject?

Do you know anything else about the author or any other of his/her writings?

Publication details

When was the book written?

What is the publication date of your copy of the book?

Has the book been revised?

Which edition is the book? Has the book been reprinted?

If the book is a translation, what is the date of this?

Who is the publisher?

In which countries has the book been published?

Table of contents

Is the table of contents sufficiently detailed to be helpful?

Which sections appear to be interesting, familiar or difficult to you?

How do the contents relate to your purpose and to other material you're studying?

Preface/foreword/introduction

If the book includes a preface, foreword or introduction, have they been written by the author or editor, or by someone else?

---

the introduction. *Systematically* previewing material is one of the first steps you take to become thoroughly familiar with it because it gives you some understanding of why the material was written, what information the author has selected, and how that information is organised and presented. Previewing can indicate which parts of the material could be most useful for your purpose and ho thoroughly you want to read different sections.

This section looks at previewing a book, but many of the steps described also apply to parts of books or to articles. There are various steps you can take when previewing a book, but the order of these depends on your preference. You might start by reading the first chapter to become immediately involved with the content and the author's style,

What information do these sections give you about why the book was written, its place in its field, how to read it?

Text of the book

What do the introduction and conclusion tell you about the book?
Are there guides to your reading of the book, such as summaries of chapters, sub-headings?

Graphics/layout

Is any graphic material, such as diagrams, photographs, graphs, tables, charts, maps easy to follow?
How are headings and sub-headings used?
How is emphasis within the text indicated? For example, are italics used?

Glossary

If the book has a glossary, are many words unfamiliar to you?

Bibliography and references

How comprehensive are any footnotes, endnotes or a bibliography?
Does the author use recently published items in references and a bibliography?
Is the bibliography divided into subject areas?
Is it a summary of all sources consulted or only the major ones?
Do the references include other than written materials?

Index

What does an examination of the index add to your understanding of the contents of the book, such as which subject areas are given prominence?
Does the index deal primarily with ideas and concepts, or places and people?
Has the index sufficient detail to enable you to easily locate your areas of interest?

or you may prefer to check through the information that surrounds the text, such as the publication details and the index. As you preview, list the ideas, questions or facts which strike you to give you reference points for understanding and evaluating the book. Then as you read you can look for material relevant to your initial points and add to your list.

Apply the questions in Table 8:1 for a fuller sense of what a book is like. For example, a quick thumb through the index can tell you the major areas covered by the book; and a glance at the publication details gives information about the book in its field, such as how recent it is, whether it's sold enough copies to be reprinted, and whether it's been published in more than one country.

Complexity of material for you

> ...one of the stupidest things the S-chools do is insist that children 'comprehend' everything they read, and read only what they comprehend. People who read well do not learn to read this way. They learn by plunging into books that are 'too hard' for them, enjoying what they can understand, wondering and guessing about what they do not, and not worrying when they cannot find an answer. Few children in school are allowed to act or feel that way.
>
> John Holt

How complex material is for you depends on your knowledge of and interest in the subject, and your related beliefs and biases. Even if you are familiar with a subject, material can be complex because of its style and format, because it's poorly written and presented, or because it expresses original ideas in unfamiliar language. 'Evaluating your selection' in Chapter 5 looks at determining the complexity of material when deciding whether to use it in research. Here we suggest how you can read material which seems too difficult or simple, and the first step in doing this is to try to articulate why this is so.

- If the material seems too simple, check that you really do understand it thoroughly — even basic material sometimes has one or two points to offer, and can provide useful revision.

- If the subject doesn't interest you, read a little of it and use the techniques described later in this chapter to make your reading more effective. On closer acquaintance the material may become more interesting and you can try to relate the subject to one which interests you.

- If you're aware that the material conflicts with your beliefs and biases, discuss these conflicts with a sympathetic person who doesn't share your beliefs. It can help you see your beliefs and biases in a new light if you play devil's advocate to them.

- If you have a mental block about the subject or if the material is in an area unfamiliar to you, read the easiest sections before you attempt more advanced ones. If you can't get past the basics, ask for help.

- If the material is apparently complex, read it slowly and look for one or two important ideas. You may later find it both easier to understand and very stimulating.

The subject area

She took the book to her refuge, the tree, and read it through; and wondered why it was that she could read the most obscure and complicated poetry with ease, while she could not read the simplest sort of book on what she called "facts" without the greatest effort of concentration.

Doris Lessing

How you read is also influenced by the subject area of the material. For example, in maths, understanding what you read can depend on mastering one step at a time. In geography, you frequently refer to maps and other visual material as you read. In literature, reading a literary work to savour the language differs from reading literary criticism to select the central points. How much you're expected to read varies from one subject to another, and this in turn also influences how you read. For example, in subjects such as the social sciences and law you are required to read more than in others, such as engineering or the physical sciences.

As a newcomer to a subject area you may find the special language of that subject difficult to understand, and even familiar words may have specialised meanings. For example, the word 'programme' has different meanings in psychology, computing and education, and the meaning of 'character' is different in literature and mathematics.

If you have difficulties mastering a new language, talk about these difficulties to a teacher or in a discussion group. Listen carefully to relevant lectures, ask for a glossary of terms, or consult a specialised dictionary on the subject. Compile your own list of terms and try reading some basic books on the subject. Don't flounder along in confusion. Make a real attempt to understand the new language, then if you still have difficulties or think too much is expected of you, let your teachers know. The language may be second nature to them, and they can easily forget that it may be incomprehensible jargon to you.

'Twas brillig, and the slithy toves
Did gyre and gimble in the wabe:
All mimsy were the borogroves,
And the momeraths outgrabe.

Lewis Carroll

As you read

How you read material depends largely on why and what you're reading. You probably read a detective story straight through to find out 'What happens next?' With many books you identify with a character or an idea, and affirm or reject what you read on the basis of your experience. Maybe you read with pencil in hand, jotting notes or underlining anything which strikes you as useful, puzzling or appealing. Perhaps you ask yourself questions about what you're reading. Are you conscious of varying your reading rate according to your material? Do you talk about what you're reading to your friends and urge them to read it too?

How you read is also influenced by whether or not you're **sharing your reading**. Reading with others gives you the opportunity to share immediate reactions to material. Some material such as poetry, plays or novels, lends itself readily to being spoken and heard with another person or a group. You may also like to share the problems and pleasures you have with material with your teachers and other students. Because everyone's perceptions of what they read differ, opinions vary, so hearing different viewpoints can help you understand material more fully. To set up a group to read each others' writing, see 'Sharing your writing' in Chapter 11.

Approaches to Reading

> Some books are to be tasted, others to be swallowed, and some few to be chewed and digested; that is, some books are to be read only in parts; others to be read but not curiously; and some few to be read wholly, and with diligence and attention.
>
> Francis Bacon

Different reading techniques are sometimes given names, such as 'skimming' or 'scanning', and actual reading rates of words per minute are suggested for each. Such terms can be confusing, and while generalised reading rate figures may apply, in practice how you read varies. It depends on your purpose, the material, your concentration when you read, and your mechanical skills, such as visual span and word recognition skills. This section describes five different reading approaches which arise from your reading purpose and the material, but it doesn't assign reading rates to each approach. It looks first at the breadth and depth of understanding you're seeking from your material and then at reading rates.

Reading for depth and breadth

Imagine you're planning a visit to a city that you've never visited before. Why are you going there? Five possible purposes are:

— to stroll around the central shopping area for pleasure
— to experience the city atmosphere
— to visit a famous art gallery or a zoo
— to familiarise yourself with the key features of the city, or
— to explore thoroughly as much of the city as possible.

Your purpose in visiting the city influences how you go about preparing for your visit, what you do when you arrive, and how long you stay.

Imagine that you're planning to read a book you haven't read before. Are you going to read this book:

— for entertainment?
— to gain an overall impression of the book?
— to locate a specific idea or section?
— to familiarise yourself with the central concept or theme? Or
— to understand the whole book in detail?

These five purposes and how they influence your approach to reading are explained below.

1 Entertainment. What do you read for relaxation? A favourite magazine? A detective story? A collection of poems? An abstract philosophical work?

Entertainment reading, that is, reading without any specific intention of evaluating or remembering what you read, can be other than reading for relaxation on free evenings or holidays. When studying, it can be a pleasurable way of getting yourself into the right frame of mind for in-depth study in an area, and can provide you with general background on the subject.

When you read for entertainment, you probably read fairly quickly or browse through the material. You might pause to ponder over a particular passage, image, or item of information, but you make no conscious effort to remember what you read. Use entertainment reading as part of formal study when you intend:

— to read the quotes in a chapter of this book as stimulation for reading the chapter in detail
— to enjoy an historical novel before beginning an intensive study of the era in which the novel is set, or
— to read quickly through a biography of a scientist who has worked in your research area.

2 An overview. Reading for an overview of material entails reading quite rapidly, reading the introductory and concluding paragraphs, noting the main themes or facts and forming an overall impression of what you read. You're not concerned with specific details or a complete understanding of the material. Read for an overview when, for example, you want:

— to find out how this book might be useful to you
— to decide whether to read a book in detail, or
— to add to your store of information on a familiar subject.

3 Specific information. To locate (or re-locate) a specific item or section in material, read through most of the material quite rapidly, using such features as the table of contents, the index, chapter headings and sub-headings to guide you to the item or section you want.

Then read the section thoroughly, possibly taking notes or underlining. Use this technique if, for example, your purpose is:

— to look for a specific section in this book
— to locate biographical details on a literary figure, or
— to find evidence for or against a case you will debate.

4 *Central ideas.*   To familiarise yourself with central ideas or facts in material, first take an overview of it. Then read so that the structure of the material and its central ideas become clear, clear enough for you to write them down or explain them to someone else.

Read for central ideas or facts when, for example, you want:

— to familiarise yourself with the main approaches to study presented in this book
— to read an article as background for a research paper, or
— to understand the central conclusions in an experimental report.

5 *A Detailed critical understanding.* When reading to understand an entire book or article as thoroughly as possible, first read for an overview, then for the central concepts or facts. Lastly, read through the material in detail, ferreting out the structure and the underlying assumptions, and evaluating the arguments. Reading in detail doesn't mean laboriously reading every page word by word. It does involve making sure that you read actively, understanding each section as you go, so that you can reproduce clearly what you've read with the material set aside. Take notes or underline to help reinforce your understanding. This chapter explains fully what's involved in reading for a detailed critical understanding.

Read for a detailed critical understanding if, for example, your purpose is:

— to identify the assumptions underlying this book and to evaluate its usefulness to you as a student
— to follow a complex argument
— to understand each stage of an experiment in order to repeat it yourself, or
— to understand material thoroughly so you can build on it in further learning

Reading rates

> Speed, which becomes a virtue when it is found in a horse, by itself has no advantages.
>
> Idries Shah

When feeling overwhelmed by long reading lists or by the time it take to get through a book, you might wish you could increase your reading rate or speed. Although learning to read more rapidly can save you study time, fast reading rates are useful only if you understand and recall what you read as fully as you need to. They do not in themselves ensure better comprehension.

The skill of reading effectively involves **varying your reading rate** according to your purpose and to the difficulty of material for you [see Table 8.2].

Table 8.2   Varying your reading rates

The following example suggests how you might read a chapter in this book.

Chapter 9 'Lectures'

Your purpose	The material	Your rate
To warm up	Boxed quotes	Fast
To read for an overview of the chapter	Whole chapter, especially the introduction and conclusion	Quite fast
To identify main ideas so you can explain them to another student	Whole chapter	Slowly
To locate specific information to help you take more useful lecture notes	Section on 'Taking Notes'	Fast, until you locate the section you want and then slowly within the section itself
To gain a detailed critical understanding of the nature and purposes of the lectures	The introduction to the chapter	Slowly and thoroughly, underlining or taking notes

You can **improve your reading** rate while still understanding what you read.

● Check how fast you can read while still understanding what you read. Time the number of words you read per minute for:

— a light novel you're reading for background
— a journal article you're reading to familiarise yourself with the central ideas, and
— a chapter in a course text that you have to understand in detail.

In each case, when you finish reading set aside the material and try to recall it in as much detail as you need to. If you've trouble with this, your reading rate probably needs to be slower. If so . . .

Table 8.3   Asking questions as you read

As you read a section of a book or article, look for information to help you answer the following questions.

The author's purpose

- Why has the author written the material? Are these purposes explicitly stated? Are there other implicit purposes?
- For whom is the material intended?

Content

- On which aspects of the topic has the author chosen to concentrate and which to omit?
- Is the material presented in breadth or depth?
- What is the main argument or theme in the material?
- What explanation or evidence is used to support these main points?
- How does the author develop the argument or theme from one main point to another?
- What are the author's underlying assumptions? Are these explicitly stated?
- Has a contemporary issue or a particular philosophy influenced the author's purpose?
- Is the author defending a particular point of view?
- Is there any evidence of deliberate bias, such as choice of sources or interpretation of material? See Appendix A for examples of discrimination in language and attitudes.

- Push yourself to read as fast as you can for 10–15 minutes each day for a week, then check your rate and comprehension. Remember your reading rate regresses if you don't read often and keep practising reading faster.

- Make a habit of reading material as complex as your study material. If you're accustomed to material which is more demanding than light fiction or the sports pages, it's easier to read most study material.

- Increase your vocabulary by consulting a dictionary or technical glossary as you read. This slows you down at first, but soon improves your reading when you have to stop less often to identify or stumble over unfamiliar words. List unfamiliar words when preparing to read material, and try to become familiar with the language and concepts of a subject as well as knowing specific terms.

The aim of improving your reading rates is to save you time, but you only save this time if you understand and remember what

- Do the facts seem correct?
- Is any irrelevant material included?
- Does any graphic material illustrate or restate the written content?
- Which of your questions about the subject does the author answer?
- How are the contents related to what you know about the topic?
- Do any items puzzle or intrigue you?

Structure

- What framework is used to organise the material? Is the framework clearly explained?
- How is the content organised and developed within the framework?
- How does the author introduce the subject?
- Does the author recapitulate what has been said at appropriate points?
- How does the conclusion relate to the introduction and to the rest of the material?

Style and format

- In what style has the material been written? For example, is it formal or informal, simple or complex, didactic or persuasive, narrative or analytical?
- How does the style and format influence your reaction to the material?

you read as thoroughly as you need. Without understanding, you have to go over the material repeatedly until you do understand it, and your initial time saving is lost.

Questioning and evaluating

You have already evaluated the material before reading to find out if it's useful for your purpose, how complex it is for you and to check if its subject matter is relevant and interesting [see 'Evaluating your selection', Ch. 6].

For a detailed evaluation *as* you read, take the material section by section. A section may be a group of chapters, a chapter, a paragraph or even a sentence, depending on your purpose and on how complex or familiar the material is. Before you begin a large section, preview it. As you read, ask yourself the questions in Table 8.3. These questions should help you identify the author's purpose and assumptions, understand the content, and evaluate the structure, style and format of the material. At the end of the section, recapitulate what you've read. Check if you understand the contents of the section as thoroughly as you need to, and try to understand the relationship of the section to the whole.

> To communicate . . . experience through print means that it must first be broken down into parts and then mediated, eyedropper fashion, one thing at a time, in an abstract, linear, fragmented, sequential way. This is the essential structure of print.
>
> John M. Culkin, S.J.

If you have difficulty answering the questions in the table, try working on the material with other people. Discuss any differing opinions on aspects such as the central ideas in individual sections and in the material as a whole. Ask 'What did the *author* intend to be the central ideas?' When you finish reading each section, put the material aside and evaluate its usefulness for your purpose. Decide which information you want to underline or include in your notes.

Notetaking and/or underlining

> Books that you may carry to the fire, and hold readily in your hand, are the most useful after all.
>
> Samuel Johnson

You might underline your own books because you want to make your responses to what you read part of the book itself. You might take notes because you don't want to mark your books, because referring to the book later is difficult, or because a précis of the information is more useful for your purpose.

On rare occasions you come across a piece of writing which encapsulates ideas that are especially significant for you, so that you want to photocopy or buy the material. However, usually it's better to close the book or article and try to express what you read in your own words, as this helps you remember it. Avoid photocopying material which you'll never read, as when under pressure and short of time, you may tend to photocopy everything rather than read any one item carefully.

Why take notes or underline?

You may do this:

— to help you see a structure in what you read
— because what you read strikes you as useful, puzzling or interesting
— to remember what you read
— to be able to refer to it later, for instance, for an assignment or for an exam in a few months time, and
— to help you concentrate on and understand what you read.

What to note or underline

This includes:

— key elements, such as central ideas, major characters or crucial information
— the author's purposes and assumptions (explicit and implicit)
— single phrases or sentences which encapsulate key elements or the author's purposes and assumptions
— details or facts which appeal to you, such as a useful statistic or a vivid image, and
— items to follow up, such as a question, an idea that offers further possibilities, a puzzling comment, an unfamiliar word, an explanation you don't understand, an opinion you question.

How can you take notes or underline?

● The *amount* of underlining you should do or notes you should take depends on what you read, why you read and whether you have easy access to the material again.

If you have limited time and access to material, it's easy to opt for the apparent safety of taking notes of everything you read 'just in case' you need the information later. However, if you define your topic before reading, you should take fewer notes and underline less. Having a clear idea of what you're looking for should prevent you finishing up with masses of notes and no idea of how to organise or use them.

Check that you understand what you've underline or written down. Underlining a lot or taking detailed notes can be necessary, but it may indicate your inability to discriminate what is important from what is not, and can give you a false sense of achievement because you have a large quantity of work to show, regardless of its quality.

If you record lengthy quotes or paraphrases to use in assignments because the material 'says it much better than I can', select quotes and paraphrases to use within the framework of *your* ideas and approach to a topic. Although your teachers usually expect you to discuss other people's ideas and work, relying mostly on authorities shows a lack of confidence in your opinions and a belief that there is a Right answer for a topic.

You probably don't need to underline or take notes if you're readily mostly for entertainment, if you're familiar with the subject or if you've an excellent visual or conceptual memory. But if you need the material later, take down at least a bare outline of its contents and notes on where to find it again. Two weeks and six books later you will find it surprisingly difficult to recall what you've read unless you have some record of it.

> "The horror of that moment," the King went on, "I shall never, *never* forget!"
>
> "You will, though," the Queen said, "if you don't make a memorandum of it."
>
> Lewis Carroll

- Develop your own *method* of indicating in your notes or underlining central ideas, information or characters, the author's assumptions or attitudes, the details which appeal to you, and items to follow up. To integrate your own ideas with those from your reading try the system suggested in 'Organising and integrating' in Ch. 6.

  When beginning to take notes, write down full details of author, title and publication. Then on each page of notes, write the title or author and list the book's or article's page numbers in the margin of your notes. This habit is essential for quoting, referencing assignments and checking the exact wording or content of a paraphrase. Use quotation marks to clearly indicate the beginning and end of material you've copied exactly. Clearly identify the beginning and end of material you have paraphrased [see 'Paraphrasing and plagiarism', Ch. 14].

After you read

When you've finished reading, do you close your book or article with a sigh of satisfaction or relief and not think about it again unless you have to use it? To remember and use what you've read, **review the material as a whole**, and use it as soon, as often and as widely as possible.

- Look at the material in relation to your reading purpose. Does the material lead you to revise your definition of a topic? Is the book central or peripheral to your understanding of a topic? Does the material provide the necessary level of information for your research? What parts of the material particularly apply to your theme for a topic?

- Find out whether your initial impressions and any questions raised during your preview have been confirmed or answered. To help revise what you learnt from the text, look again at those parts of the material you examined during your preview. Check through the index, for instance, to help recall what you read and to give you a fuller understanding of the scope of a book.

- Ask yourself the same questions about the purpose, content, structure, style and format as you asked about each section while reading. Review your notes or underlining to ensure that you remember what you've read and to see how the various sections fit together as a whole. List questions which the material has raised and which you want to follow up. Edit your notes, or summarise them further if necessary, and file them [see 'Selecting, recording and filing information', Ch. 6].

Table 8.4 Writing a book review

"...What is the use of a book," thought Alice, "without pictures or conversations?"

Lewis Carroll

The overall purpose of a book review is to interest and inform potential readers and to give them your considered opinion of a book. It should evaluate a book from your perspective rather than simply paraphrasing or describing the book's content.

Depending on your specific purpose in writing it, your review should contain some or all of the following points:

full details of title, author and publication
a brief resume of the book, or what the subject of the book is and how this content is organised
comments on the author's style, or how the book is written
information about the author's purpose in writing the book, or why the book was written
comments on the book in relation to other material in the field including when the book was originally written (and revised), the author's qualifications and experience, whether the book introduces any new concepts or data, and whether the author is reviewing material
comments on how the book relates to your knowledge, your experience, your beliefs
comments, where possible, on what other reviewers said about the book (check indexes such as *The Australian Book Review Index*)
information on the standard of the details such as an index, a bibliography or graphic material
comments on the overall quality of the presentation, such as layout, quality of paper and binding, and
an evaluation of the overall strengths and the weaknesses of the book.

Support any statements you make, including your opinions, with reasons and examples. A few well-chosen quotations can convey the flavour of the author's style as well as illustrating a point. (Give the page reference for a quote immediately afterwards).

Your own honest and well thought-out opinion of a book is of more value to your learning and to your readers than your version of someone else's opinion. A book review can be technically excellent but dull to read unless you convey to your reader the impact the book has on you.

- Think about the material and how it relates to you — your knowledge, your experience, your beliefs.

Whether or not you think about what you've read when you finish reading depends largely on the impact it had on you and whether you're required to use it. You might remember ideas or information, or recall a particular character. You may read further works by the same author or on the same subject, and in time re-read the original book. If a book pleased you or irritated you, stimulated or satisfied your curiosity, you're likely to think about it and discuss it with other people. Articulating your ideas and responses to material helps clarify them, and you may also want to articulate your ideas about a book in a written review [see Table 8.4].

Reviewing this chapter

1 Look through this chapter, taking each heading in turn and recalling what you can about it. Which section can you recall in most detail? Why?

2 Choose one section which is useful to re-read. As you re-read it, think about how you are reading and why.

3 Could you explain the structure and contents of the whole chapter to someone else?

Further reading

Anderson, J., et al. *Efficient Reading: A Practical Guide*. McGraw-Hill, Sydney, 1969.

Buzan, Tony. *Speed Reading*. Sphere Books, London, 1971.

Drewry, John E. *Writing Book Reviews*. Greeenwood Press, Westport, Connecticut, 1974.

Robinson, F.P. *Effective Study*. Harper and Row, New York, 1970.

9 Listening to Lectures

Depending on who you are — your experience, your interests and how you're feeling — you react to and select from what you hear. Each person responds differently to the pitch and intensity of sounds. One person's music is someone else's noise. If you live in the country the noise of traffic can be deafening when you visit the city; for an enthusiastic motorbike rider the roar of a 750 cc engine is music to the ears; and the 'snap, crackle and pop' of a favourite breakfast cereal can be irritatingly loud to someone with a hangover.

Do you consider yourself a good listener?
Do you listen closely to your friends when they talk about their troubles?
Have you ever felt your eyes glaze over as you listened to a teacher's monologue?
Have you ever found your mind far away from the lecture theatre towards the end of a lecture?

There's a difference between hearing sounds passively and actively listening. Concentrating on what you hear is one of the basic skills required for listening to lectures. But even when you're keenly interested in a subject, it can be difficult to concentrate for a long time while sitting passively without the opportunity to respond.

This chapter is about understanding lectures well enough for them to be genuinely useful for your purposes in learning, rather than classes which you go to out of habit. The chapter looks at how you can actively prepare for a lecture and how you can concentrate on what's being said and on taking notes. It suggests that after a lecture you need to review and use the material which has been presented to you.

Lectures are essentially a one-way communication process. The lecturer lectures and you listen, whether the lecture is delivered to ten students in a high school classroom or to several hundred people in a large lecture hall, whether the lecture lasts for five minutes or for an hour and a half. A lecturer may follow the customary format of university and college lectures and talk for almost the entire time with little or no student participation, or he or she may set aside part of the lecture for students to respond to and discuss what's said.

Why lectures?

Lectures are the most common form of tertiary teaching, so it's worth thinking about their purposes. These can include:

— imparting information to large numbers of people
— providing a common ground for formal discussion in a subject
— serving as a starting point for private study
— drawing together the main ideas in a new research area
— providing a preliminary map of difficult reading material
— reviewing literature which is difficult to find, and
— adapting a subject for a particular audience in a way that a standard course text can't.

However, educators debate the effectiveness of lectures in achieving many teaching aims. For example, it's often stated that lectures don't encourage students to think for themselves and that students should discuss ideas thoroughly rather than simply listening to them in lectures. It's also argued that lectures are widely used, not because they're effective, but because they are the cheapest way of teaching large numbers of students. You probably have your own opinions on how valuable lectures are in achieving your purposes for learning.

> I cannot see that lectures can do so much good as reading the books from which the lectures are taken.
>
> Samuel Johnson

Some lecturers think seriously about what lectures can teach and about what they want students to learn from a particular lecture. They adapt their lecturing methods to their purposes, and are willing to depart from the traditional lecture format.

● If the lecturer intends to take a class in stages through difficult subject matter which involves a sequence of reasoning or events, he could use a series of five-minute lectures each followed by a few minutes for students to discuss or work on a related question.

- If the lecturer wants to exchange questions and comments with students in a small class, she doesn't plan a set lecture or time for student participation beforehand. Instead she relies on knowing the subject well and on being able both to present it logically and to restructure it in response to discussion.

'Should a lecturer cover the ground laid down in his syllabus, even when some students don't understand, or go at a slower pace and get behind?' . . . If lecturers considered their courses in terms of the learning being achieved by students rather than as a succession of performances by lecturers, this question would seldom be asked.

Donald A. Bligh

A lecturer's effectiveness partly depends on his or her personality, particularly if — as is often the case — they are not trained in the skills of communicating to an audience. And because lecturing styles and abilities differ, you inevitably learn more from some lecturers than others. A skilled lecturer varies his or her method of presentation, pace of delivery, voice, and position in relation to the audience. He or she may be a story teller, an actor or a humorist. Some lecturers read their lectures, while others use brief notes or speak extemporaneously. A lecturer who's sensitive to an audience and responsive to their shifts in mood and attention is always more enjoyable. You may or may not share a lecturer's enthusiasm for a topic, but a talented lecturer is a pleasure to listen to and can hold your attention almost regardless of the subject.

However, most lectures require effort on your part. If you consistently prepare for lectures, actively concentrate on what's said, and think back over it afterwards, you'll get more out of lectures, even poor ones.

Preparing for a lecture

Usually you'll hear a lecture only once, so preparing beforehand will help you understand it more fully.

- Think about how useful a lecture could be in achieving **your purposes** in learning. For instance, if you're attending a lecture as well as discussing a topic or reading a book on it, why? You might do so to find information which is difficult and time-consuming to locate elsewhere, or to listen to a talented lecturer present a familiar topic in a new way. Your main incentive could be to absorb information for exams and assignments. You may go to lectures simply out of habit or because they are compulsory.

- Prepare for a lecture by thinking about where **the topic** fits within the broader framework of a course — review previous lectures and the course outline. Do some of the suggested reading on the topic and look for other relevant material. You may find material (such as a summary of main points of the topic, a map, a time line or a list of biographical dates) you can take to the lecture to help you follow it. List any questions or ideas that come to mind as you prepare. You can use these as reference points when listening to the lecture, so that you're less likely to be over-whelmed by a mass of unfamiliar information and you should be able to listen and take notes more intelligently.

- Consider your alternatives for **recording the lecture**. You'll probably take notes on a lecture, so think about how you can best do this. You may want to arrange to compare your notes with someone else's after the lecture [see 'Taking Notes']. Check if the lecture will be taped. If not, you may want to tape it your-self if, for example, the topic is unfamiliar or if you want to listen without taking notes. However don't tape lectures indiscriminate-ly — think first about your reasons for wanting a tape rather than notes (and always ask for the lecturer's permission before using a tape recorder).

- Immediately before a lecture, think about **how you feel**. If you're feeling physically or emotionally low, do what you can to make yourself feel better. See 'Emotional Energy', Ch. 1 for sug-gestions on how to put your worries aside. If you need to miss the lecture, have someone else tape it or take notes for you.

To help you follow a lecture, arrive before it starts to collect any handouts and so that you don't miss the introduction. In an intro-duction the lecturer often outlines the lecture, relates the topic to reference material or to the rest of the course, states a problem the lecture will address, or tells a joke or a story to lead into the topic.

Understanding as you listen

"I think I should understand that better," Alice said very politely, "if I had it written down: but I can't quite follow it as you say it."

"That's nothing to what I could say if I chose," the Duchess replied, in a pleased tone.

Lewis Carroll

Thoughts can move faster than speech, so your attention can easily wander during lectures unless you actively concentrate on what's being said [see 'Concentrating', Ch. 2]. To sustain your concentra-tion so that you understand more fully what you hear, try to ques-tion what's being said, anticipate what will be said and frequently review what has been said. Take notes, and try to deal with situa-tions which make concentration difficult.

Questioning and evaluating

Ask yourself questions about the purpose, content, structure, style and format of the lecture. Most of the questions suggested in Table 8.3, 'Asking questions as you read', also apply to lectures. You may have other questions specifically related to lectures such as 'What's the lecturer conveying by his or her position, distance from the audience and voice tones?' The questions you ask as you listen can form the basis for any notes you take.

Taking notes

> "Write that down," the King said to the jury; and the jury wrote down all three dates on their slates, and then added them up, and reduced the answer to shillings and pence.
>
> Lewis Carroll

It's impossible to reproduce the content of a lecture exactly and very rarely do you want as much detail as this. Instead your notes should be your consciously selected version of the material offered. The previous chapter on reading suggests *why* you might take notes and *what* your notes could include [see 'Notetaking and underlining', Ch. 8], and the same points apply to lectures. But *how* you take notes when listening to a once-only live lecture differs from taking notes from printed material you can re-read.

Find a **balance** for each lecture between taking useful notes and listening carefully — taking notes constantly or taking none at all are both of dubious value. In lectures which are meant to stimulate your imagination, spend most of your time sitting back and listening. In lectures which are densely packed with information and ideas you'll take more notes, but select from and condense what's said so that you can listen closely enough to understand. For instance, if you're given a lot of data or examples, you can often summarise what they mean rather than frantically trying to copy them. Sometimes lecturers use phrases such as 'the following three factors are...' or 'It's important to note that...' to help you identify the structure of the lecture and indicate which points to note [see Table 12.2 'Transitional words and phrases']

If you prepare for a lecture and go over your notes very soon afterwards, you can usually strike a happy balance between taking satisfactory notes and listening fully to what's said. Try the following **methods** to experiment with how detailed your notes need to be and how much time you need to spend listening.

- Take as many notes as you think you'll need. Go over these immediately after the lecture, asking yourself if you understand all you've written, and try to reproduce the way in which the lecture developed. If you can't, you've possibly spent too much time writing during the lecture — or the lecture itself was very confusing.

- If you have access to a tape of a lecture or if you can make your own tape, don't take notes but sit and listen intently. Immediately after the lecture and before you listen to the tape, see if you can write down a satisfactory summary of what you've just heard. Then listen to the tape and compare your notes with what you hear.

- If you're listening to a taped lecture, listen to the whole tape once without taking notes. Write notes on the lecture before you listen for the second time. A taped lecture gives you the advantage of being able to stop and replay it at any point — something you can't do with a lecturer.

The above are suggestions and you should develop your own method for distinguishing the structure of what's said — the main points, sub-points and supporting details. Lecture notes in which you can see the structure are easier to remember. Leave space for your own comments, questions or references to follow up, and items to think about further. Include the lecture title and date, and the lecturer's name on each page.

Overcoming concentration difficulties

> Now I lay me back to sleep,
> The speaker's dull, the subject's deep.
> If he should stop before I wake,
> Give me a nudge for goodness' sake.
> Anon.

Try to overcome difficulties which prevent you concentrating on and understanding a lecture. Your concentration is usually better at the beginning of a lecture — if you're able to put aside the thoughts or distractions which were occupying you before the lecture began. You also concentrate better when you know that the lecture is nearly over — unless you're impatient to leave. During a lecture your concentration span is probably about twenty to twenty-five minutes. In a long lecture, revive your concentration by changing your sitting position, by quickly reviewing your notes, or by asking the lecturer a question.

- Try to minimise distractions in your physical surroundings — a hard chair, a wobbly desk, a cold room or loud hammering nearby are not conducive to full concentration.

- If you find it difficult to listen to a lecture tape because you can't see the lecturer's expressions or gestures, listen intently and replay parts of the tape if necessary. If you still have trouble, ask the lecturer for a written copy or an outline of the lecture.

- If a lecture seems to offer little that's new to you, ask yourself 'Am I really listening to what's being said?' If you are, try to anticipate what will follow, relate what's being said to what you already know about the topic, and review any notes you've made as you listen. Make a game of trying to find new information.

- If a lecture contains too much unfamiliar material, make a list of questions on points you don't understand, and ask the lecturer to clarify a couple of these points.

- If the content of the lecture seems irrelevant or uninteresting to you, jot down at least an outline in case the topic becomes relevant or interesting at a later date. Leave the lecture quietly and do some other work rather than sitting through it and complaining afterwards.

- A lecturer may make it difficult for you to follow a lecture because he or she doesn't organise material clearly, doesn't provide a written or oral lecture outline, or doesn't adequately prepare overhead transparencies and other aids. When you can't follow a lecture easily, leave plenty of space for your notes so that you have a chance to go back and add and edit as you write.

- If a lecturer's style is difficult or dull for you, think about why this is so. You can probably do little to change the idiosyncrasies of lecturers' styles, but let a lecturer know if you can't hear or follow what's said. Don't dismiss lecturers you find difficult to follow as useless after only a couple of lectures. They may know their subject well, and as you become more familiar with their individual styles, it's often easier to concentrate on and understand what they're saying.

After a lecture

> Before I came here I was confused about this subject. Having listened to your lecture I am still confused. But on a higher level.
>
> Enrico Fermi

As you hear most lectures only once, **reviewing your notes** as soon as possible — preferably immediately after a lecture or the same day — helps you remember what you've heard.

- Do you understand everything you've written?

- Can you identify the structure of the lecture — main points, sub-points and how the lecture developed from one point to another? It may help to underline the main points as you review your notes.

- Do you need to edit your notes so they reflect the lecture more accurately and read more easily?

- Do you need to expand your notes so you can still understand them in a month or two's time? Do you have a relevant article or other material to file with your notes?

- Would it be useful to express part of your notes in another form, for example, as a flow chart, or diagram or in a pattern?[1]

If you have **persistent problems** in identifying the structure of lectures and understanding your notes:

— listen to a tape of the lecture if you need to
— make sure that you are preparing thoroughly for lectures
— compare your notes with someone else's, and discuss the differences to help clarify ways to improve your notetaking
— read some more on the topic so the lecture isn't your only source of information, and
— ask a lecturer for help with the problem [see 'Contacting People', Ch. 3].

Your problems with lectures may be due to the lecturer. If you have difficulty understanding an important lecture, go and see the lecturer soon afterwards to talk about the topic. Sometimes a person who's awkward in front of an audience is helpful when discussing information on a one-to-one basis. (Think about how you feel when delivering a seminar paper and when discussing the same topic with one other person.) Lecturing is a talent which few people possess naturally, so constructive comments can help lecturers improve their skill. Such comments can be made tactfully by asking questions on points you don't understand and suggesting alternative lecture formats [see 'Why lectures?']. Part of being an active listener is to suggest to lecturers how their lectures could be more effective.

Since most lectures are a one-way communication, **using and discussing the lecture material** is essential if you're to understand it fully.

- Do you have items you want to follow up, for example, an idea which interested you, a reference you noted, a point you didn't fully understand, a quote you want to check out?

---

[1] Tony Buzan, *Use Your Head*, BBC Publications, London, 1974.

- Did the lecturer suggest any follow-up to the lecture such as a reference to read, a problem to solve, an exercise to do, or a couple of questions to think about?

- File your notes for easy future reference [see 'Selecting, Recording and Filing Information', Ch. 6].

Some lectures contain ideas or information that are especially significant for you. These lectures are easy to remember and use. Otherwise, you're most likely to use what you've heard and written down if you need the material for an assignment or an exam or when talking to friends, in a tutorial or seminar, or with a teacher. In a discussion over coffee after a lecture, for example, you can compare notes, clarify points you didn't understand, exchange ideas which excited you, and decide on questions or suggestions with which to approach the lecturer if necessary.

* * *

If you find some lectures boring and pointless, is it because you're sitting back and expecting to be entertained? If you are, think about your purpose for attending a lecture and prepare to take an active part as a hard-working listener. Inevitably some lectures seem a waste of time, and very few people deliver an ideal lecture. To make the most of the range of knowledge and lecturing styles you're offered, take the time to learn how to get the most out of lectures and, if necessary, pluck up the courage to try to change them.

Further reading

Bligh, Donald A. *What's the Use of Lectures?* Penguin Education, Penguin Books, Middlesex, England, 1972.
Brown, George. *Lecturing and Explaining.* Methuen, London, 1978.
Buzan, Tony. *Use Your Head.* BBC Publications, London, 1974.

10 Participating in Tutorials and Seminars

Do you think of yourself as a 'talker' or a 'listener'?
Which people or situations encourage you to talk?
Who do you talk to in your daily life about the weather? About personal matters? about current issues?
Do you find that many of your conversations are about other people? yourself? Ideas? Events? Sex? Religion? Politics?
To whom do you particularly enjoy listening?
Do you think that you learn more from talking to people, from reading, or from watching TV?

Your discussion with other people may be an intense debate, a rambling conversation, a casual chat, an exchange of brilliant repartee or a ritual of polite remarks about the weather. These discussions may be very brief, go on for several hours, or continue intermittently for weeks or even months. Perhaps you use the discussion to sort out ideas, share experiences, play with words, or learn something new.

As a tertiary student, you'll probably learn a great deal from discussions over endless cups of coffee in the cafeteria. However, formal small-group discussion in universities and colleges is mostly conducted in tutorials and seminars. Such groups meet specifically for discussion as part of a course, and usually consist of a teacher as leader and a particular group of students.

These formal group discussions vary widely in structure and content. For example, they may be:

— a mini-lecture where the teacher imparts information

— a group in which the leader remains relatively unobtrusive and the rest of the group decides what to discuss
— a leaderless group which collectively decides on an agenda
— a group where each member takes a turn as chairperson
— a discussion structured around a paper given by a group member or based on set reading
— a meeting which sets out to debate an issue formally, to solve a specific problem or to work on a particular piece of research
— a group which uses role-playing exercises to learn more about the dynamics of human behaviour
— a group which emphasises the less subjective, rational aspects of learning, or
— a group which often shares experiences and feelings as well as discussing intellectual issues.

Such variety is the spice of discussion groups. Within a group, people of different ages, experiences, backgrounds and beliefs have much to offer each other when exchanging ideas, and a varied format and content for group meetings is stimulating. *If you're in a group which lacks variety, this chapter suggests some alternatives.*

I dogmatise and am contradicted, and in this conflict of opinions and sentiments I find delight.

Samuel Johnson

Why formal discussion groups?

Formal discussion groups can offer an opportunity:

— to integrate what you learn from your reading, writing and lectures
— to clarify your ideas and feelings on a subject
— to sort out misunderstandings and problems in your work
— to practise communicating ideas to others
— to have relatively close contact with a staff member, and
— to learn about the uses and dynamics of formal discussion groups.

Sharing your learning in discussion groups can be a co-operative exploration of ideas which offsets the competitive pressures on you as a student. Discussion groups also provide an alternative to the solitary activities of private study and listening to presentations such as lectures. If an educational institution doesn't include formal discussion groups, you might ask that these be established as part of a course you're taking, or create informal ones with other students so you can actively use the information you receive from lectures and reading.

The principles and techniques outlined in this chapter can be used in informal discussions with other students as well as in tutorials and seminars. The chapter deals with some aspects of how discussion groups work, and suggests how you can learn from and enjoy groups more by preparing for them, participating actively, and reviewing and using what's discussed.

Preparing for a discussion

If *few* people prepare for a discussion group, it's probably better to cancel the group or change the topic — and agree to prepare fully next time. If *everyone* in a group prepares, the discussion at least has the basis for success. If *you* prepare, you'll have a clearer idea of what you want to discuss and you'll remember the discussion more clearly.

Be sure you know as precisely as possible **the topic** planned for discussion, what preparation is required, and why. Ask the group leader as soon as possible for suggestions or information if you find the preparation required too much or is too difficult, if you have trouble obtaining necessary materials or facilities, or if you've other demands at the time which make it difficult for you to prepare fully.

- Do any required preparation such as reading or exercises to complete.

- Revise your relevant lecture notes.

- Check reference books and audio-visual material on and around the topic and follow up with more specific reading if necessary.

- Read over any notes you made during or after the last group meeting.

- Formulate in writing at least one brief item to contribute to the discussion — a thought, a question, a piece of information, or a comment on your reading or lectures on the topic.

Prepare thoroughly if you're to give **a discussion paper**.

- Research, plan and prepare what to say [see Ch. 6]. In a short paper, limit yourself to only one or two main points. Prepare a clear introduction for the topic, and a summing-up which could usefully take the form of a statement or a question for the group to debate.

- If you're not duplicating your paper, your listeners will have the material presented to them only once, so prepare visual materials or handouts to help them follow you. If you plan to use data, maps or other information which may be difficult to absorb quickly, prepare photocopies or a blackboard display so the group has the information before them.

- Speaking from notes is less stilted than reading a paper, but you may feel more confident if your paper is written out fully and you can read it. Whichever you choose, rehearse aloud so that you know how long it takes to present your paper. Most listeners become restless after 15–20 minutes, so time your presentation with this in mind. Rehearsing can also help you feel more comfortable about giving your paper, and you can practise varying your presentation to hold the group's attention.

Immediately before the group meets, be aware of **how you feel** and try to put distractions behind you [see 'Emotional energy', Ch. 1]. You might read thoroughly a section from a relevant book to focus your mind on the discussion topic.

Taking your part during discussions

Most groups spend time talking about academic or practical matters such as the next topic for discussion, the set reading, or who'll deliver a seminar paper, but they usually neglect to explicitly consider the personal interactions within a group — **the 'hidden agenda'**. Even group interactions of which every member is aware, such as frequent silences or an over-talkative person, aren't usually discussed by the whole group. The following are a few examples of this.

- The particular combination of people in a group plays a large part in shaping the discussions. For example, groups made up of school leavers who are full-time students approach a subject differently from groups made up of part-time students from a variety of backgrounds. People who are in a minority in a group, such as women in a predominantly male group, often feel less free to speak.

- If people always sit in the same place or two or three people always sit together, this can set up habits of who talks to whom and where discussions centre.

- A person who decides the direction of a discussion may not be a teacher or a person who talks a lot, but someone who asks pertinent questions or who brings an aimless discussion back on track.

- How people contribute to a group is influenced by whether each person's participation is assessed by a teacher, by the whole group, or whether or not it's assessed at all.

- When people contribute to a group discussion, they may be

trying not to appear naive/over-clever/aggressive while at the same time seeming to be witty/intelligent/confident/sexually attractive.

If you have little experience of taking responsibility for formal discussions and are anxious not to appear foolish in front of the other students and a teacher, you're unlikely to initiate discussions on how a group is working. If a teacher is unskilled in dealing with group dynamics, he or she is unlikely to initiate discussion with students about what's happening in a group. But the personal interactions within a group can't be separated from its intellectual discussions, and a group needs to spend time talking about both if it is to realise its full potential. If you feel that a 'hidden agenda' item is being ignored at the cost of group effectiveness and your own learning, try to work up the courage to bring the problem into the open, using some of the suggestions which follow. A basis for discussing both academic work and the interactions within the group can usually be established in the first two or three meetings.

The first few meetings

Instead of plunging straight into talking about a course topic or assignments and assessment, people in a group can devote some time to **becoming acquainted**, perhaps over a cup of coffee or a glass of wine. Names and faces become more familiar if each person, including the teacher, introduces themselves briefly and talks about their interests and hopes for the course. If the group divides into pairs for a brief period to discuss a specific question about a topic or the course, people have another opportunity to get to know each other.

Discussions are influenced by **the physical setting** in which you meet, so consider how you can adapt a meeting place to the group's needs. A cold box-like room occupied by standard institutional chairs and tables and a blackboard is more conducive to monastic silence than heated discussions. What can you do with an inappropriate room? It's often possible to rearrange seating or desks so that everyone is more comfortable and can see everyone else. A leader need not be isolated in front of the group, a large open space in the middle of a group can be closed up, and if the room is carpeted, people may be more relaxed sitting on the floor. Sometimes another place can be found for a group, or you can meet outdoors or in a private home. Meeting outside the formal setting — to have coffee or go to a movie, for example — has an impact on the group's formal discussions.

One of the first topics for discussion should be **the group's role in a course**. Group meetings could serve as a forum for discussing lecture topics or the special interests of members. Some people in the group may see its main role as enabling students to exchange ideas, while other people see the meetings as an occasion for the teacher to tell them more about a subject. Group members need to decide (or be told) if participation in the group will be assessed formally or informally, and if so, how.

Contributing to discussion

'The time has come,' the Walrus said,
'To talk of many things:
Of shoes — and ships — and sealing wax —
Of cabbages — and kings —
Of why the sea is boiling hot —
And whether pigs have wings.'
Lewis Carroll

Each member of a group influences how that group operates, even if by remaining silent. The success of a discussion group depends largely on whether everyone takes responsibility for how the group operates and whether everyone feels free to contribute fully.

The size of a group

A group should be small enough to enable everyone to say something within the time available. Seven to ten people is often recognised as a useful number for a group, but this varies with the purpose of the discussion. Most people feel hesitant about speaking up in front of a large group, yet there should be sufficient people to provide a variety of ideas. If a group is too small, combine it with another group if possible. If the group is too large, it might break into smaller groups for a part of each session or permanently.

Attending regularly

If the same group of people come to the meetings regularly, they become more comfortable with each other and more confident about suggesting ideas, asking questions, admitting ignorance, and responding honestly to what's said by someone else. The give and take that develops lessens the pressure to say something on most topics and to impress others, and because continuing discussions are built up when everyone knows what's been talked about previously, people find it easier to make their own contributions.

Talking and listening skills

'...I find discussion as a whole...difficult, because I've never had to discuss anything before and haven't put my feelings into words...It takes me an awful long time to think about what I want to say and, sometimes, by the time I've thought about it, it's gone.'

A student

Participating fully in a group discussion requires practice in the skills of talking clearly and concisely, asking useful questions and listening carefully. These skills take time to acquire, particularly with a group of people who are initially strangers, and you need to find your own balance between talking and listening for each combination of people.

Participating in a group is not the same as talking a great deal. Some of your *alternatives* are:

— listening closely for most of the time, occasionally contributing a well thought-out remark or question
— attempting to paraphrase what someone else said, to make sure you understood them
— asking questions which begin 'Do you mean that...?', 'What do you think about...?' or simply 'Why?'
— commenting in response to someone who has spoken, as long as you really are responding and not just waiting until they've finished so you can have your say, and
— expressing support for an idea that someone else has put forward.

If you've prepared for the discussion you'll have your own thoughts and questions to contribute. If a discussion group is to help you sort out your ideas and become aware of your biases and beliefs, articulate these and bring them out from inside your head so other people can respond to them. Don't hold back because you feel you have to utter perfectly complete thoughts or always be serious.

Language most showeth a man; speak that I may see thee.

Ben Jonson

If you lack confidence in a discussion group, remember that it takes time to gain experience in the skills of formal discussion and to settle into a new group of people. Even if you like the group members at first meeting, you may still be cautious about venturing opinions until you know them a little better. If you continue to feel uncertain of yourself in a group or if you're not confident about a topic, you can gain confidence by preparing for the discussion, getting to know some other members of the group outside the formal discussion time, and talking to the group leader or a helpful staff member about how you feel. Others who at first seem to know more than you often don't; and even if they do, you still have your contribution to make.

If you talk too much and are aware of this, you'll probably also be aware that other people stop listening or find it difficult to follow what you say. For several meetings try to ask other people questions whenever you feel tempted to talk — you'll probably be surprised at how much they have to contribute.

How much time do you usually spend in talking and how much in listening to what others say?
How much response do you usually give to other people's ideas?
Your answers to these questions will probably vary for each group to which you belong. Can you work out why you put more effort into some groups than into others?

Taking responsibility

Each person in a group influences the nature of the discussion, and the absence of even one person can change the atmosphere of a group. Everyone needs to prepare for and participate in discussions rather than seeing the group solely as the leader's responsibility. If only one or two people contribute, even a skilful leader can do little to make the group satisfactory.

- If you're giving a *discussion paper*, let the group know if you're happy to deal with questions or comments during your presentation, or if you'd rather these were kept until you finish. If you're responsible for the discussion afterwards, try to encourage other members of the group to take part. As well as helping them and improving the discussion, directing this effort to others usually reduces your anxiety about being the centre of attention.

  "Begin at the beginning," the King said, very gravely, "and go on till you come to the end: then stop."

  Lewis Carroll

- The amount of time each person talks in a group varies depending on their enthusiasm for a topic, amount of preparation, and well-being at the time. A common difficulty in a group is having one or two people who are persistent *talkers or non-talkers*.

  Some people prefer to contribute to a discussion only occasionally, but the person who rarely says anything needs encouragement. Most people indicate by facial expressions or body movements when they're ready to speak, and if other people are sensitive to these signs they can give a shy person an opportunity to speak. Someone who's quiet may gain confidence if the group divides into smaller units for part of the discussion. You could suggest that each person prepares a specific contribution for each session or takes a turn to comment briefly on a topic which comes up, as this gives reticent members of the group practice in speaking while limiting more garrulous individuals.

However, the whole group needs to discourage a person who talks too much, and usually this can be done politely but firmly by remarks such as 'That's interesting — I'm curious to hear what other people have to say now'. If what the talker says is irrelevant, the whole group will be grateful to someone who restates the original topic. But if the ooffender fails to take the hint, someone in the group needs to deal with the problem after the meeting.

The teacher's authority in a group

> The authority of those who teach is very often a hindrance to those who wish to learn.
>
> Cicero

The official group leader may not always be a teacher, but he or she may be a student who is giving a paper or is responsible for chairing the discussion. Most groups also have unofficial leaders, even if 'leaderless'. The authority of a teacher-leader usually overrides that of a student, even when the teacher tries to prevent this.

A teacher may have authority in a group because she or he is:

— a group leader appointed by the educational institution

— an assessor of the group members' work

— a specialist in a particular field of knowledge

— a skilled group leader

— a person older than most students in the group, or

— a dominant personality.

Leadership styles

Some teachers consciously try to step back from a position of authority in a group, to encourage students to articulate their own ideas and learn from each other. Such teachers face the challenge of trying to be *a resource person* in a subject rather than an expert or an appointed leader. They try to use their personal skills with people or groups to foster the development of individuals and the whole group, instead of attempting to direct this process. If you're accustomed to having your learning firmly directed, you may find this approach disconcerting.

There are teachers who consciously prefer to be *the definite leader* in a group. This choice is consistent with a model which defines formal education as students receiving information from experts. Teachers who base their teaching on this model are likely to expect to be the focus of the group's comments and questions and use group meetings to give mini-lectures. This approach can work when both teacher and students feel under pressure to cover a prescribed amount of material, but it discourages discussion between students and ignores much of the potential of small-group work.

Some teachers remain as *automatic leaders* because they haven't given much thought to the bases of authority in a group — and even teachers who want to encourage student participation occasionally fall into accepting this authority. An inexperienced teacher may be glad of the security that the role of leader offers, and some older teachers expect younger students to defer to them. Some teachers, because of their personality and experience, are accustomed to leading most groups in which they find themselves.

> He was leader by default — by de fault of de rest of de group.
>
> Anon

Coping with a teacher's authority

If you're a student in a group where the teacher takes the authority you may find it helpful to cope with this authority if you can work out *why* the teacher is the group leader. For example:

- Some teachers don't recognise that their familiarity with the concepts and language of a subject gives them a position of authority in discussing it with students. It's often difficult for these teachers to understand how complex a subject can be for beginners.

- Other teachers have their own plan for a tutorial or seminar because they're anxious to cover a syllabus or eager to convey what they see as the important or exciting issues in a topic. Such teachers may ignore or belittle contributions which don't fit their plan, or ask questions for which they have a Right answer in the mind. They may attempt to start a discussion at too advanced a level or at a pace too fast for most of the group, so that discussion is only possible if there are one or two students who are self-confident and familiar with the subject. Other students are left either to drift off or to try to guess the teacher's plan, rather than think about and articulate their own ideas.

- Teachers who don't know how to encourage participation may leave a group floundering because they fail to realise the need for a clearly-defined starting point for discussion. Or they may hover over a group — rushing in to break up any silences instead of allowing people to collect their thoughts, asking questions to which the answer is obvious, or answering questions so conclusively that further discussion is pointless.

All the tutors say, you know, do ask a question if you don't understand me, but if you really have no idea of what on earth they're going on about you can't very well say 'Well, would you start again at the beginning'. You can't ask a question because you just don't know what to ask it about.

A student

How can a group cope with a teacher's authority? Start with the assumption that it's the responsibility of the whole group, not only the teacher, to make a group work and ask yourself if you have contributed as fully as possible. A teacher who takes a deliberately dominant role may appear to determine a group's character, but she or he can only dominate if the rest of the group allow this to happen — if for example, you seldom address comments or questions directly to each other. As a group, work out clearly what you expect and want from the discussions. Keep in mind that if you aren't prepared to take action, you can't expect the situation to change.

- What aims would you each like the group to have?

- What do members have to offer each other in discussions, and what skills and knowledge does the teacher have which are valuable to the group?

- If you find the teacher difficult, can you work out why and together decide on ways to handle the problem?

- What activities could the group undertake which would help each person participate fully?

- If you think that assessment of contributions to the group is preventing full discussion, can you suggest alternatives?

- If you don't understand an aspect of the discussion, are you each willing to ask about it?

- If the discussion seems aimless, are you each willing to say so, explain why, and suggest a definite direction the discussion might take?

- Are you each prepared to renew the discussion after a silence?

You may want to talk about these and other questions during or outside group meetings. If at all possible, talk directly with the teacher concerned about any problems rather than suffering in silence or grumbling and doing nothing. Teachers who are concerned about their students and their teaching know that they can often learn from students and welcome well-thought-out suggestions. Such a direct discussion may require considerable courage if a teacher is authoritarian and more than a little tact if a teacher is well-meaning but unskilled. It's usually easier to talk to a teacher if you've met on a one-to-one basis early in the course, so that you see each other more as individuals with particular interests in a course rather than as a 'Teacher' and a 'Student'.

After a group

After a group meeting, **review the discussion** to think about how it relates to you, your learning and the course. To help you remember what was discussed, as soon as possible, make a brief summary and follow up anything you haven't understood. If you gave a paper, think back over your presentation and the ensuing discussion. If required, see the group leader to evaluate your paper. Make sure that you know what the next topic for discussion will be and precisely what you're expected to prepare.

Another way to learn more from a formal discussion is to get together afterwards with one or two other students to **talk informally about the topic**. You can sort out points you didn't understand, make some of those comments which were lost in the larger group, and consolidate and build on what you did understand. The moral support that such discussions can give is invaluable, particularly for less confident students.

> . . . all my confidence diminished as I was to hear someone talk of *The Plague* all the time referring to the Germans in France during the War. What in heaven's name was she talking about? I had also read *The Plague* and found it a most interesting story of a town infested by bubonic plague, but it never entered my head that these things were all symbols. From that moment I was frightened to open my mouth. At coffee break, however, I was to learn a couple of others felt the same reaction to this piece of news.
>
> Brian's Wife Jenny's Mum

You may have **persistent problems in a group** and feel dissatisfied or unhappy. If you've contributed as fully as you can, you may want to discuss your feelings privately with the group leader. You could sound out the other group members to see if they share your feelings and if so, arrange to devote some of the formal discussion time to dealing with the problem. You may be able to change to another group if these attempts to deal with the problem don't succeed. Such a change often only involves asking the teachers concerned and is preferable to wasting your time.

* * *

Do you usually enjoy discussion groups? Most students feel confident and interested in some groups, and uncertain and bored in others. Perhaps the most important thing about groups is that for no apparent reason some groups work and some don't, and that even good groups have their off days. The success of a group as a whole depends on every member assuming responsibility for it; the success of a group for you as an individual member depends on your willingness to participate both by speaking and listening.

Further reading

Pfeiffer, J. William and Jones, John E. *A Handbook of Structured Experiences for Human Relations Training.* Vols. I–IV, University Associates Press, Iowa, 1972.

Nuffield Foundation, The. *Small Group Teaching: Selected Papers.* Group for Research and Innovation in Higher Education, London, 1976.

Rogers, Carl. *Encounter Groups.* Penguin Books, Middlesex, England, 1973.

Rudduck, Jean. *Learning Through Small Group Discussion.* The Society for Research into Higher Education, University of Surrey, Guildford, England, 1978.

1 Developing Your Own Writing Voice

> ...becoming a writer is all a question of learning to trust yourself, to trust your own voice.
>
> Katherine Anne Porter, quoted by Erica Jong

If writing is one way you often express yourself and communicate, you probably have a strong sense of your unique writing voice, and your formal academic writing will be enriched by your experience with the craft. In tertiary institutions, written expression is emphasised, and learning is assessed primarily through writing of examinations, essays and reports. You may have opportunities to take an oral exam, to deliver a paper orally, to present an assignment in film, on tape, as a collection of photographs or drawings, or by writing a play, a short story or a poem. Don't overlook these. However, the reality is that to pass courses in tertiary institutions you must be able to write prose.

You're usually expected to write formal essays and reports in tertiary institutions, and only students in creative writing courses have the opportunity to experiment with other forms of writing. However your writing should improve if you practise writing regularly in any form and try to locate your particular writing strengths as you do so.

Do you think that 'academic writing' demands a particular style? If so, you're partly right. You may be expected to understand a particular theory well enough to write about your topic using the terms and concepts of the theory [see 'The Subject Area', Ch. 8]. You're usually required to present your ideas in formats such as essays, reports or reviews, and there are conventions to follow for matters

such as bibliographies, methods of footnoting and use of colloquial-
isms. A certain dispassionate restraint in language is often expected.
But if you think that an 'academic' style necessarily uses long technical words — forget it.

Sometimes you do need to make use of particular terminology to
convey a precise meaning, but such terminology can easily degener-
ate into jargon if used carelessly or only to impress. When in doubt,
opt for simplicity. The main aim of academic writing is to communicate what you want to say to someone, and the basic need to
be lucid and direct applies as much to scholarly writing as to any
other. When writing assignments, express your honest, carefully
considered response rather than paraphrasing or plagiarising other
people's words and opinions, or indulging your prejudices [see
Appendix 'Discrimination'].

You have your own way of using words when you speak and,
while you may not be a Shakespeare, you probably have your own
style of writing. Use it in your academic writing. If your style includes irony, metaphor, an occasional flash of wit, or cartoons and
drawings, use them unless they meet with strong disapproval from
the people who assess your work.

> From time to time I feel a need, sharp as thirst in summer, to note and
> to describe. And then I take up my pen again and attempt the perilous
> and elusive task of seizing and pinning down, under its flexible double-
> pointed nib, the many-hued, fugitive, thrilling adjective...The attack
> does not last long; it is but the itching of an old scar.
>
> Colette

The **process of writing** involves thinking, dreaming and imagining
as much as putting words on paper. And writing isn't merely transcribing words from inside your head according to a plan; it stimu-
lates new thoughts and directions to which you have to respond as
you write. Sometimes the process of writing flows easily, while at
other times the words just will not come. Experienced writers often
sit for hours over a page of work, or write several drafts and edit
ruthlessly before producing the final one. Rarely is a writer entirely
satisfied with even that final version.

Unless you're writing purely for yourself, writing is communicating. This involves thinking about the person or people who read
your writing. You're trying not only to express your thoughts fluently, accurately and creatively, but to do so in a way that your reader
will understand. To do this you must be clear about what you want
to say and why, and you'll draw on any language, experiences and
beliefs that you and your readers share.

> Find a subject you care about and which you in your heart feel others
> should care about. It is this genuine caring, and not your games with

language, which will be the most compelling and seductive element in your style.

Kurt Vonnegut

Does writing usually come easily to you? Do you enjoy putting ideas, thoughts, feelings on paper? Do you enjoy playing with different writing styles?

Do you have specific problems with writing which hamper your ability to say what you want, or do you freeze up if asked to put pen to paper? You perhaps sit for hours over one sentence or paragraph, or write draft after draft of an assignment. You may have difficulty with writing because you think that what you write falls short of the standards expected by a teacher. Perhaps your vocabulary is limited, or you find it difficult to decide where to start writing on a topic, or you feel that each sentence you write must be perfect. Problems also arise if your confidence in your ability to write has been undermined by severe criticism.

Developing your writing style is a continuing process, as your style changes with time and according to your subject and purpose for writing. If you're not aware that you have a distinctive writing voice, you *can* discover it. If you're unhappy with the way you write you *can* develop a style that suits you.

Whether you usually find writing easy or difficult, the suggestions offered in this chapter can help you explore, develop and have confidence in your own writing voice. The chapter suggests that you try different writing methods, that you write frequently, and that you share your writing.

Experiment with different writing methods

Structured writing

Sometimes you write according to a plan and edit your work as you write. This is the writing method usually taught and expected in formal education, and you're likely to use it when writing a report, an article for a paper or a business letter. Practice in editing and structuring writing is a valuable part of the writer's craft and is discussed in more detail in the next two chapters.

Free writing

When you are free write without a plan and without editing as you write, the process of writing is the stimulus that helps you discover the focus and approach of what you want to say and how you want to say it. Free writing can help bring out ideas which are lying dormant or jumbled in your head and give them coherence. This method is particularly valuable if you freeze up when you have to write or if you have a mental block when writing an assignment [see 'Free writing', Ch. 12].

> You are allowing yourself to proceed without a full plan — or allowing yourself to depart from whatever plan you have. You are trying to let the words, thoughts, feelings, and perceptions try to find some of their own order, logic, coherence. You're trying to get your material to do some of the steering instead of doing it all yourself.
>
> Peter Elbow

Sit quietly for 10–15 minutes while you write down the thoughts that flow through your mind. Don't stop to select, organise or edit what you're writing, and don't worry about details such as spelling and punctuation. If your mind suddenly flashes elsewhere, explore that sidetrack. Don't stop writing. If you can't think of anything to say, write 'I don't have anything to say' over and over until a thought hits you.

Practising this writing method can develop your writing voice in a new way — try free writing about your dreams or problems, about people or events. Incorporate this method into the initial stages of your assignment-writing [see 'Free writing', Ch. 12]. To help break the habit of always editing as you write, try free writing directly on a typewriter or speaking your thoughts into a tape recorder and then transcribing them.

Write often

> Learning to write again is...not a tightening up process. It is not a matter of learning lots of techniques. It is learning to relax one's muscles and one's brain.
>
> Brian's Wife Jenny's Mum

One of the most effective ways to improve your writing is to write, write, write — and then write some more. Write about everything and anything. Play with words and write in as many forms and styles as you can.

Letters, articles, poems and other forms

> I am not urging you to write a novel...although I would not be sorry if you wrote one, provided you genuinely cared about something. A petition to the mayor about a pothole in front of your house or a love letter to the girl next door will do.
>
> Kurt Vonnegut

Do you write letters to family and friends, turn out business letters and reports as part of your job, keep a journal, write an occasional poem or short story, or send 'letters to the editor'? Many people who write in these forms don't see themselves as able to write because they aren't producing a book or because writing isn't a major part of their job. But regular practice in a variety of writing forms can help you discover and develop your writing voice.

If you haven't thought of letters, articles or poems as part of your writing, try experimenting with:

— writing letters occasionally instead of 'phoning your friends, and keeping copies of your letters
— capturing an experience or playing with words in poems, lyrics, short stories or dialogue
— writing a letter to the editor of your local paper if you feel strongly about an issue, or
— writing an article for the newsletter of a community group in which you're active.

If you're accustomed to writing letters, poems, articles or dialogue you could occasionally use these familiar forms in your assignments. For example:

— an essay comparing Freud with Jung could take the form of an exchange of letters setting out the basis of the disagreement between the two men
— an assignment on evolution could be written as a dialogue between Bishop Samuel Wilberforce and Thomas Huxley, or
— a preface or introduction to an essay may be written as a poem or a personal letter.

Keeping a journal/diary/notebook

> I never travel without my diary. One should always have something sensational to read in the train.
>
> Oscar Wilde

If you've ever kept a diary, what did you record in it? As a teenager, did you record those major events in a small notebook that you kept hidden, or did your entries read something like, 'Got up early this morning. School was okay except I got into trouble on the way home. Watched TV.' When travelling, have you ever kept a diary as a record of places and events? During periods of emotional trauma, have you written pages and pages that you destroyed afterwards? For some people, the thought of keeping a diary or journal conjures up images of monotonously recording facts and details or pouring out secret feelings on paper. A journal can be these, but it can also be much more.

What is a journal?   A journal is a place where you write for yourself. As such, it's a place where you can be as honest as possible with yourself, where your thoughts and ideas won't be judged by others, where you collect what interests you, and where you're free to write as you like. You may use a journal to make an occasional entry, or write intensively for a couple of months and then let it lapse. You might write in a journal daily to describe the events, experience, feelings, people and ideas from each day.

Keeping The Daily Log

Think back to how you felt when you awakened in the morning. Describe the mood, the sensations — physical, mental.

Do you have the feeling that you were dreaming during the night? What was the general atmosphere of those dreams?

How much of them can you remember and write down?

What was your mood as the day started? How did the morning unfold?

What thoughts kept coming into your mind without your deliberately thinking them? Worries, hopes, fantasies? What emotions? Angers, loves?

What events took place with people, works, groups?

Did unusual situations occur, situations of intensity, crisis, joy?

How does the day proceed? Note the rhythms of the day as you move from the morning to the afternoon, into the evening. Does the quality of your feelings, your mood, your emotions change?

Recapitulate your experiences of the day — all the occurrences that you can perceive both within your mind and on the outside of your life.

Write these without judgement: nothing to be proud of, nothing to be ashamed of; no praise, no blame.

Now feel the day as a whole. Write a few adjectives and a metaphor for how the day feels to you.

Ira Progoff

A journal might be about yourself:

— your dreams, daydreams and fantasies, descriptions of the circumstances in your life that connect with these, and discussion of them
— your emotions
— how your body feels
— your reflections, thoughts and reminiscences on your past, and
— your ideas, theories or inspirations.

It might be about your world:

— descriptions of a particular situation or event
— observations about people, and
— comments on public happenings or issues.

It could include items such as:

— poems, short stories, song lyrics which you write or collect

— important letters to you or copies of letters from you
— clippings from newspapers or magazines and your comments on them, and
— notes on books, lectures, movies or television programmes.

If you write about your private life and thoughts in your journal, do you worry that other people might read it? You don't have to write about personal matters, but if you do, be careful not to leave your journal where it might be found. You can use symbols instead of names and places, or write as if describing a fantasy or a dream that makes sense only to you.

A format. You can keep your journal entries chronologically or organise them into sections. A looseleaf format enables you to organise or reshuffle your writing into sections, to easily remove pages you want to share, and to elaborate on entries started long ago. You can also carry a couple of pages in your pocket or bag, in the glove box of your car, or attached to your clipboard, and write when the impulse moves you.

Why keep a journal? In some courses you may be required to keep a working journal or log. If this is not required, recording your inspirations, thoughts and questions about your formal learning and about lectures, reading and discussions can help you understand who you are as a learner. Keeping a journal as part of your learning and writing can help you become aware of the experiences, enthusiasms and biases you bring to your learning. As keeping a journal also provides an opportunity to experiment with and explore different writing styles without being judged, it can have a positive impact on your formal writing.

If keeping a journal is not a part of your life and you think you'd find it valuable, set aside a regular time so that you can enjoy writing it. If you haven't already done so, read the diaries of some well-known diarists such as Anais Nin or Charles Darwin to enrich your own journal writing. If you're already an avid journal writer, you'll understand how Anais Nin feels about writing in her diary.

> Never have I seen as clearly as tonight that my diary-writing is a vice. ... I glided into my bedroom, closed the curtains, threw a log into the fire, lit a cigarette, pulled the diary out of its last hiding place under by dressing table, threw it on the ivory silk quilt, and prepared for bed. I had the feeling that this is the way an opium smoker prepares for his opium pipe. For this is the moment when I relive my life in terms of a dream, a myth, an endless story.
>
> Anais Nin

Share your writing

Who reads your writing?
Do you ever write solely for yourself, or for one or two close friends?
If you write letters, short stories or poems, do you share these with friends?

Writing alone is a traditional method of producing assignments, sitting for hours at your desk with the aid of innumerable cups of black coffee the night before the assignment is due. And usually only your teacher reads your formal assignment-writing, so you receive only one person's perception and evaluation of what and how you write.

Comments from others on your writing can be invaluable. Have one or two friends read your writing and respond to it, or tell your teachers that you want to improve your writing and ask for detailed feedback on your work. Perhaps you'd like to share what you write with a wider audience but feel unsure of the criticism you might receive. If you work on your writing with a group of people who feel as you do, sharing your work and actually writing in their company is likely to give you confidence in developing your writing style.

> The apprentices do each other a further mutual service which no older and sounder critic could do. They read each other's manuscripts....a fellow apprentice has two great virtues as a critic. When he reads your poem, he may grossly overestimate it, but if he does, he really believes what he is saying; he never flatters or praises merely to encourage. Secondly, he reads your poem with that passionate attention which grown-up critics only give to masterpieces and grown-up poets only to themselves. When he finds fault, his criticisms are intended to help you to improve.
>
> W.H. Auden

Why join a writing group?

1 Actually writing in the same place as other people who share a common writing purpose can provide a new stimulus for what to write about and how to write.

2 If other people read or listen to what you've written and each comments on it immediately, you receive a variety of feedback which you can question and discuss. If this feedback is positive and is accompanied by useful suggestions, you won't be devastated by criticism and you'll have some ideas on how to change your writing.

3 As each member of the group will have his or her own writing voice, listening to or reading other people's work gives you access to a variety of different styles and approaches to each subject.

4 After some time, giving feedback on other people's work and receiving comments on your writing can help you evolve your own writing objectives and standards.

Setting up a writing group

1 Find people with whom you share a purpose in writing, such as making journal entries, writing an assignment or putting together a student magazine.

2 Keep the group small enough for each person to take part, yet have sufficient people to provide variety and depth in feedback.

3 Attend regularly, and after the first few meetings don't admit new members. People who get to know each other feel more comfortable about sharing their writing.

4 Agree on the length and frequency of meetings according to the size and purpose of the group.

5 Between meetings, do any necessary rewriting or preparation for the next meeting.

6 If group members bring a piece of writing to be discussed, provide copies for everyone to make discussion easier.

7 Every member of the group should actually write for a short time during each meeting. You might:

— free write (as described earlier in this chapter)
— practise a particular style (such as, discursive or satirical) or form (such as, dialogue or a scientific report), or
— focus on a specific subject, such as an apple, a piece of music, the theory of evolution.

8 While there should be no compulsion for people to share their writing, allow each member the opportunity to present his or her work. In some sessions the group might discuss everyone's work, while in others it may centre on the writing of one or two people.

9 Allow time for each piece of work to be read with care, perhaps both silently and aloud.

10 Feedback should be constructive, emphasising strengths rather than weaknesses. Initially negative criticism which points out weaknesses should be avoided because it can undermine a beginning writer's confidence which the group is aiming to build. Destructive criticism is always taboo. When negative criticism is given, suggest how to make changes. Give feedback by responding to the piece spontaneously, or according to agreed-upon criteria such as those set out in the next two chapters or those below which are recommended by Peter Elbow.

- Pointing — indicate which words are loud, prominent, energetic, piercing, or memorable.

- Summarising — quickly and briefly say what struck you as the main point, the main feelings, the centres of gravity.

- Telling — tell what happened to you as you read or listen to the words; for example, 'First this happened to me, then I noticed that, then I thought about such and such, and so on and so on'.

- Showing — through metaphors or fantasies, reveal to the writer perceptions of his or her words which you can't otherwise articulate.[1]

Whether you write on your own or with other people depends on your purpose and subject.. You could make journal entries with a group of other journal writers, write a report with one other person, or write poetry by yourself. Trying alternatives to find out which ones you enjoy is one way of discovering and exploring your writing voice.

*   *   *

A writer does not just sit down and instantly write a great book. She spends time practising the craft of writing and puts in many hours on the individual book. Writing has become part of her daily life as well as a talent which delights readers. You may not be a world-famous author, but writing frequently and experimenting with a variety of forms and styles can help you develop your own writing voice and give you an appreciation of writing as a craft. It can also improve your skill and your pleasure as a writer. And as a great writer refines her skills and thrives on the response of both her fellow writers and her readers, so can you polish and enjoy your writing if you share it with others.

Further reading

Darwin, Charles. *The Voyage of the Beagle*. Bantam Books, New York, 1972.

Elbow, Peter. *Writing Without Teachers*. Oxford University Press, New York, 1973.

---

[1] Peter Elbow, *Writing Without Teachers*, Oxford University Press, New York, 1973, pp. 85–92.

Macrorie, Ken. *Writing to be Read*. Hayden Book Company, New York, 1968.

Progoff, Ira. *At A Journal Workshop: The Basic Text and Guide for Using the Intensive Journal*. Dialogue House Library, New York, 1975.

Stuhlmann, Gunther (ed.) *The Journals of Anais Nin*. Vols. I–IV, Quartet Books, London, 1974.

2 Writing Assignments

> ...I always try to write on the principle of the iceberg. There is seven-eights of it under water for every part that shows.
>
> Ernest Hemingway

Writing an assignment is more than putting words on paper — defining your purpose and topic, and carrying out your research are integral to what and how you write. Each activity requires careful and creative thought as you integrate your purpose with what's expected of you, and your ideas with the information you find. Each activity can also have its own pleasures — discovering new information, turning ideas on a topic over in your mind, talking about them with other people or trying them out in different combinations and sequences. When you have more or less defined and researched a topic you can begin to focus on the task of writing the assignment as a whole.

This chapter looks at the processes involved in producing an assignment and at alternative writing methods. Although primarily concerned with writing assignments, the ideas in the chapter can also be used in producing oral or audiovisual work, as these often rely on a written outline or script.

The processes outlined are intended as a framework from which you can develop your assignment writing. This framework can help you understand written comments on your work, or can be used as a basis for discussing your assignments with a teacher or a group of students. When writing an assignment you may use the entire chapter, or you might prefer to use parts of it to help with specific problems such as planning an assignment or writing coherent paragraphs.

However, the framework offered is useful only if you write frequently and if you receive a lot of feedback from others. Each assignment is not an isolated end in itself — what you learn from writing one can help you with the next, even if the content and format of each differ. Improving your writing takes time and practice and your writing may seem worse before you notice any improvement — it takes time to change old habits and develop and refine new skills. Saying exactly what you want and in the style you want is easier if you have confidence in your writing abilities [see Ch. 11].

Before you start writing

As a result of your thinking and research, perhaps you've written sentences or paragraphs which capture thoughts you want to use. You should also have notes and a written definition which reflects the purpose and theme of your assignment.

Your definition of the topic

An assignment develops from your definition of the topic which you arrive at as a result of research [see 'Your revised definition', Ch. 6]. This definition should do the following.

- Make clear your purposes for the assignment. Ask yourself, 'Why am I writing an assignment in the first place?' 'For what purpose was this assignment set?' 'What is my purpose for writing this particular assignment, and for choosing this topic?'

- State the theme/thesis/argument of your assignment. Ask yourself, 'What position will I take on the topic? On what will I focus?'

- Indicate the overall content and the main points in your definition of the topic. Ask 'Exactly what is my topic?' 'Do I have a clear title for it?' 'What are my main points in the topic?' 'In what depth and breadth will I write about the topic?' 'How many of my own ideas will I include?' 'What information or reasons or examples will I use to support my theme, thesis or argument?'

- Indicate the approach you will take.

Your readers

Now before you start writing the whole assignment, think about your readers. Is your teacher the only one who'll read your assignment? Are you writing a paper to be read or listened to by a group of students? Is there a possibility your paper will be published in a collection of student work or elsewhere?

To communicate effectively:

— have clear in your mind something you think is worth saying
— keep in mind your purpose for saying it
— be aware that you're communicating with someone
— take care to say exactly what you want to, and
— say it simply and succinctly.

I wish thee as much pleasure in the reading, as I had in the writing.

Francis Quarles

Writing your rough draft

We would be given an assignment. I would take one look at it and think, "That's the end of that. I won't be there next week so I won't have to worry about it." After two harrowing days, when I kept thinking, "Will I, won't I?" I'd sit down to look at it.

Brian's Wife Jenny's Mum

For each assignment you write, start with a rough draft, or more than one if your definition of the topic changes as you write and if you have the time. Your final draft will then be a matter of editing your last draft.

When you write the rough draft of an assignment, your main concern should be the *structure* or framework of your topic and the *clear expression* of your ideas. You may be expected to fit your material into a particular format [see Ch. 13], but even so, you'll still need to organise the material within the sections of that format and to express yourself clearly.

Whether or not you're using a set format, concentrate on saying what you want, in the order you want, and as accurately as you can. Don't worry about niceties of style or about having the precise word. And don't become bogged down with concerns about perfect spelling or being absolutely correct and detailed in conventions such as footnoting. Be as precise and detailed as you need to be to express your ideas clearly and fully, and leave the perfecting formalities to your final draft.

Most professional writers produce several drafts of a work before arriving at a final version. Many students, however, sit down with pen and paper and expect to start writing the first sentence and to write straight through to the end, producing a more or less complete assignment in one draft. This is not the way to produce a satisfactory assignment — any method of writing relies on thoughtful research and time to mull over the topic before writing, and any method should lead you to a rough draft which has three clear sections, an introduction, a body and a conclusion. How these sections should be organised and written is outlined in 'Writing to a plan'. To ensure that you've included these necessary points use the checklist of questions in 'Working with your rough draft'.

Working from your definition of the topic, you can produce your rough draft by free writing, working from a detailed plan, or a combination of these two methods. Any of these methods can be effective.

Free writing

In free writing you use the act of writing to clarify your thoughts without editing them as you write [see 'Free writing', Ch. 11].

If you have a mental block when writing assignments, particularly when starting to write, it may be because you don't feel confident about your writing or about your knowledge of a topic, or because you're anxious about your study, or have other pressures in your life [see 'Emotional energy', Ch. 1]. If you do block, but you have to or want to write, sit down with lots of paper and a pen or pencil. Don't worry about notes or plans or references. Start writing *anything* on your topic that comes to mind and write *continuously* for about ten minutes. If you can't think of what to write, write about why you can't think of what to write, or about the thoughts which are coming between you and the topic. When the time is up, look over what you've written. Some of it may be useful later or may stimulate new thoughts. This free writing activity is often enough to shift a mental block, but if it doesn't you may need to leave your work for a few hours or days, or longer if possible. And remember that even for skilled writers, sometimes writing refuses to flow easily.

> The writer wandered to the water cooler, washed his hands, looked up the weather report, made some unnecessary phone calls, looked at his tongue in the mirror for symptoms of fatal disease and, when he had at last exhausted methods of killing time, went to his typewriter.
>
> Russell Baker

You can also use free writing *to produce an entire assignment* in draft form. Review your ideas and notes on the topic but don't plan what to write. Write a first draft of all or part of the assignment *without editing as you write*. Then look at what you've written and quickly sum up the themes of your writing in one statement. Write a second version, again without editing and repeat the looking over and summing up process. If your topic is still unclear in your mind, write a third draft. When you have a draft that pleases you, use it as the basis for your final one, and so proceed with your editing. Be prepared, however, to throw away much of what you've written. Using this process may sound time consuming but it isn't. Allow the same time as you usually would for writing an assignment.

Writing to a plan

When writing in this way you edit as you write so that you keep more or less to a plan. The plan gives more structure to your definition and includes:

— your purpose
— your theme/thesis/argument
— your approach
— an introduction and conclusion
— the order of your main points and how you intend to link these
— the balance between each of your main points, and
— your supporting points.

The introduction

This outlines *what you are going to say*. It should make clear your definition of the topic and make your reader want to read on. You might:

— ask a question you'll attempt to answer
— state a case you'll argue
— pose a hypothesis you'll test and report on
— outline your reasons for focusing on specific aspects of a general topic
— give selected data to establish an issue as worth writing about, or
— use a quote which conveys the key ideas you'll discuss.

Any terms or words which are central to your topic should be defined in the introduction or early on in the body of the assignment.

The body of your assignment

Here you *say what you want to*. You should order your main points effectively and make this order clear to your reader, present each main point as fully and accurately as necessary and write coherent paragraphs, and you need to keep a balance between your main points.

1 *Ordering main points.*   After the introduction, your theme/thesis/argument should be developed clearly and logically throughout the assignment and restated in the conclusion. The following suggestions may help you decide on the order in which to develop material.

Table 12.1   A sample essay plan

You're writing on the topic 'Examine the theory that the moon is made of green cheese'. After thought and research you decide it is likely that the moon *is* made of green cheese. You think that the most important and interesting aspects of the topic are the beliefs for and against the question, scientists' attitudes to the relevant theories and evidence, and popular myths about the green cheesiness or otherwise of the moon. You define the topic accordingly. The following model is a basic one you could use to structure your assignment.

Topic: Examine the theory that the moon is made of green cheese.

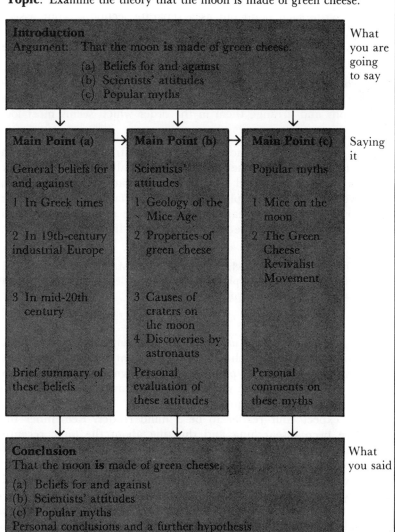

Introduction
Argument: That the moon **is** made of green cheese.

      (a) Beliefs for and against
      (b) Scientists' attitudes
      (c) Popular myths

What you are going to say

Main Point (a)

General beliefs for and against

1 In Greek times

2 In 19th-century industrial Europe

3 In mid-20th century

Brief summary of these beliefs

Main Point (b)

Scientists' attitudes

1 Geology of the Mice Age

2 Properties of green cheese

3 Causes of craters on the moon
4 Discoveries by astronauts

Personal evaluation of these attitudes

Main Point (c)

Popular myths

1 Mice on the moon

2 The Green Cheese Revivalist Movement

Personal comments on these myths

Saying it

Conclusion
That the moon **is** made of green cheese.

(a) Beliefs for and against
(b) Scientists' attitudes
(c) Popular myths
Personal conclusions and a further hypothesis

What you said

- Refer back to your purposes and definition
- If you've decided on your main points ask yourself why you chose these and how they are connected to each other. In the moon topic, shown in Table 12.1, you might have chosen the three points because they reflect significantly different aspects of the topic. Does an understanding of one point depend on explaining another point first? In the moon example you might have decided to put the point about general beliefs first as a background for scientific theories and popular myths.
- If you have several main points from which you'll choose as you write, write each point out as a separate section of your assignment. See what links emerge from what you've written and rewrite your final points as necessary to clarify the links and develop an ordered whole.
- As you write, use a separate page for each paragraph. When you come to order your whole assignment, you can add or delete paragraphs and arrange them in the order which seems most logical.

Your reader needs to know how you have structured your assignment. To convey this, use subheadings (if allowed) and pointers such as 'Having discussed idea X, I now want to examine...' or 'However...'. Include a plan or a detailed table of contents. Remember that to make clear the order of the main points in your assignment and to indicate the links between them, they need to be clear in your mind.

> "Then you should say what you mean," the March Hare went on.
> "I do," Alice hastily replied; "at least — at least I mean what I say — that's the same thing, you know."
>
> Lewis Carroll

2 Presenting main points fully and accurately.   Saying what you want to also entails presenting each of your main points fully and accurately. To support the major points of your assignment you might explain a point further, give reasons for a statement, cite statistics or facts, or use examples or quotes.

Don't expect your reader to be a mind reader. Remember that you have been researching and thinking about the topic recently, so a sentence you write which conveys a whole collection of ideas to you may not do so to your reader. Don't skim over points which need explanation. Don't assume that your reader automatically knows who or what Alcibiades is, or precisely what you mean when you use terms such as 'instinct', 'good' or 'Western society'. When you make general statements, support them with reasons or examples.

Even if your teacher is the only person to read your finished work, check if you're expected to write without assuming his or her knowledge of the topic so that you demonstrate your own knowledge fully. If you're in doubt about the level of writing to aim at, imagine that you're writing for a reasonably intelligent student just about to begin the course and with an interest in your topic. This helps to avoid pitfalls such as writing on the implications of Hegel's ideas without actually describing the ideas because you assume that your teacher knows what they are.

Each main point should consist of one or more **paragraphs**.[1] Each paragraph should contain one idea or cover one aspect relevant to the main point. This idea or aspect is frequently set out in a key sentence, which may come anywhere in a paragraph or may be implied by the total content of the paragraph rather than stated explicitly. Each of the other **sentences** in the paragraph should explain or illustrate the point which the paragraph is making, but each should also have a purpose of its own.

Stop for a moment and think about what you just read. Now look at the next paragraph. What is its main point? Is there an explicit key sentence? How does each of the sentences in the paragraph relate to the point of the paragraph?

A paragraph should be coherent, so that your reader is led smoothly from one sentence to another and understands the connection between them. For example, if the paragraph uses a central metaphor, each sentence may echo and expand that metaphor. Words and phrases such as 'similarly', 'because', 'besides', 'in contrast', 'meanwhile', 'therefore' or 'for instance' help to indicate the links between sentences [see Table 12.2]. If a paragraph is not coherent, your reader will be faced with bewildering jumps of thought, events out of sequence, or facts illogically arranged.

> Just as the sentence contains one idea in all its fullness, so the paragraph should embrace a distinct episode; and as sentences should follow one another in harmonious sequence, so paragraphs must fit into one another like the automatic couplings of railway carriages.
>
> Winston Churchill

---

[1] A paragraph may vary in length from one sentence to many (and such variety makes more interesting reading). As a *very approximate* rule of thumb for assignments, each paragraph averages about 100 words. Thus in a 2000-word assignment, you would have approximately twenty paragraphs, which you might divide up with two each for an introduction and conclusion, and an average of four or five paragraphs to make points which support each of three or four main points. Thinking of your assignment in this way can help you understand how many main points you can make fully and clearly.

Table 12.2   Transitional Words and Phrases

These are words and phrases which show relationships between two ideas of facts. They indicate:

Addition

in addition, again, also, and, besides, finally, first, further, last, moreover, second, too, next

Cause and effect

accordingly, as a result, consequently, hence, otherwise, therefore, thus

Comparison

similarly, likewise

Contrast

in contrast, although, and yet, but, however, nevertheless, on the other hand, on the contrary

Examples or special features

for example, for instance, in other words, in illustration, in this case, in particular, specifically

Summary

in brief, in conclusion, in short, on the whole, to conclude, to summarise, to sum up

Connections in time

after a short time, afterwards, as long as, as soon as, at last, at length, at that time, at the same time, before, earlier, of late, immediately, in the meantime, lately, later, meanwhile, presently, shortly, since, soon, temporarily, thereafter, until, when, while

3 *Balancing main points.*   Decide if all your main points should have equal weighting within the assignment. In the moon topic [Table 12.1], you might decide to look more closely at the scientists' attitudes and research, or you might devote more space to the popular myths because they are controversial.

Even with the most careful planning, as you actually write you may find that you need to devote more of the total assignment to a point to explain it fully, to give less emphasis to a point, or to delete a point which no longer seems essential to your approach.

Some assignments have a strict word length requirement. What do you do if you discover part-way through your assignment that it will be too long if you present all the points you've planned to cover? You may need to reduce the number of points you cover, or to eliminate repetitive sections. Conversely, does your assignment look as though it will fall short of the length required? If so, check that your plan hasn't been too skimpy on the number of points you cover, and check that you've supported each of your main points thoroughly.

When in doubt about whether or not to include or omit material, refer back to your purposes for the assignment and your definition of the topic, and ask yourself if the material fits with these. Learning to discard material is an essential but often difficult part of writing — you may have to force yourself to do it.

> Have the guts to cut ... If a sentence, no matter how excellent, does not illuminate your subject in some new and useful way, scratch it out.
>
> Kurt Vonnegut

The conclusion

This draws together *what you've said* in the body of your assignment. It should sum up and reflect your main points and your approach to the topic, and should be related to the introduction. You might suggest a question or hypothesis which arose directly from your conclusions, but you shouldn't introduce a main point or a statement which needs detailed explanation. As well as drawing together what you've said the conclusion serves to round off your assignment — don't make it so abrupt that your reader is surprised that the assignment is finished.

> There are two things I am confident I can do very well; one is an introduction to any literary work, stating what it is to contain, and how it should be executed in the most perfect manner; the other is a conclusion, shewing from various causes why the execution has not been equal to what the author promised to himself and to the public.
>
> Samuel Johnson

* * *

Don't be surprised if you don't follow your plan exactly. As you write, the process of expressing your ideas can stimulate new thoughts and directions and lead you to see familiar ones in new ways. Actually expressing your ideas clearly involves searching for and choosing words, phrases and sentences, so part of the structuring can only be done as you write. Integrating new ideas into your plan and making choices as you write can further clarify what you want to say and can lead you to revise your plan. Hopefully, such revisions will only be minor at this stage of your work.

Alternative writing methods

Two extreme ways of producing the rough draft of an assignment are completely free writing it from your definition, but without a plan, or writing exactly to a detailed plan. Between these two lie many alternatives of which the following are a few.

- Use a plan and with your notes and references in front of you edit your thoughts and words as you write and occasionally use free writing when you are stuck. You could:
  - begin with the introduction and write in the order you planned, right through to the conclusion, or
  - write the body of the assignment first, and then the introduction and conclusion, or
  - begin writing the section where your ideas are clearest and proceed section by section until you've written the one which is least clear to you.
- Make a plan. Then with your notes and references put aside, free write your rough draft. If you don't understand a section well enough to write about it or if you need a quote or item of information, turn to your notes and references to refresh your memory — and then close them before you start writing again. When you finish writing your draft, check your work against your notes for completeness and for references you could cite.

It took me two hours to write this. I bit my finger-nails, cut my toenails, had a snack, crunched an apple and generally procrastinated. But I did it!

Brian's Wife Jenny's Mum

Working with your rough draft

Working with your rough draft is essentially a checking and rewriting stage, since by now you should have a clear idea of the purposes, content, structure and basic writing style of your assignment. Part of your work with the rough draft will probably be remedying oversights. For example, you may need to find full details for bibliography entries, or check on the precise wording of a quote or exact data for part of a graph. What else do you check for at this stage?

Purposes

Does the assignment reflect your purposes in:

- undertaking an assignment in the first place
- doing this particular assignment
- choosing this particular topic, and
- selecting your theme and focus within the topic?

Content

- Is your topic clearly defined?
- Does your definition fit with your topic?
- Is all your material relevant to your definition?
- Do you have too much or too little material for the length of your assignment? Have you repeated yourself often?
- Does the material chosen reflect your approach to the topic?
- Have you been too biased or subjective in your selection of material?
- Have you incorporated your own ideas, if allowed, and supported these?
- What are the main points of your assignment?
- Have you included reasons or evidence or examples to support your main points?
- Are quotations and examples which you have used integral to your assignment?
- Have you clearly defined any central terms?

Structure

- What is the structure of your assignment?
- Does your structure logically and effectively develop your theme and definition of the topic?
- Have you clearly indicated to your reader the stages by which you develop your theme/thesis/argument?
- Does your introduction accurately outline your definition of the topic, and seduce your reader?
- Are your main points presented as clearly and fully as necessary?
- Is there a balance between your main points?
- Have you linked your main points clearly?
- Does each paragraph contain only one main idea?
- Have you clearly connected your paragraphs?
- Does your conclusion:
  — reflect the material and theme presented in the assignment
  — relate to your introduction
  — finish smoothly, and
  — suggest any further areas or questions to be followed up without introducing any major new ideas?

- If you're expected to organise your material within a particular format, have you done so?

Style

- Have you expressed your ideas clearly and simply?
- Is your writing style your own?
- Have you incorporated any formal style requirements into your writing?

> Reheating a piece of writing after it has cooled, tempering it, and sharpening it is enjoyable — if you know how. Otherwise it may turn out worse, brittle and misshapen.
>
> Ken Macrorie

If you've thoughtfully researched, planned and written your assignment, you're less likely to have to make major revisions in your rough draft. However, sometimes when you re-read your draft you're struck with a new idea about the structure or content, or you suddenly see a major flaw in what you've written. If you have sufficient time, you may want to substantially rework an initial rough draft. Be prepared for this, but realise that at some stage you have to stop working on your assignment and let it stand as it is, warts and all. If you're writing your assignment at the last minute, you're unlikely to have the time for detailed rewriting. In this case, the amount of work depends on how clearly you really knew what you wanted to say before you started writing.

When you've finished writing and working on your rough draft, you've done most of the work on your assignment. Wherever possible, write a rough draft, work on it and put it aside for at least a few days before you write the final one. You might discuss it with others, or have someone else read it and comment. You may want to change a phrase, add a word, rewrite a sentence or a paragraph. In any case, give yourself time to stand back from what you've written, time to reflect on your whole assignment before you finally sit down and edit it.

Editing your final draft

In the final draft, you edit what you've written to polish your writing style and to complete details of formalities such as punctuation or footnotes.

- Often a good assignment is difficult to read because of inadequate **proofreading**. Chapter 14 is designed to help you check details such as presentation, writing conventions and spelling.

- Improving your **writing style** involves imagination as well as hard work [see Ch. 11]. When polishing your writing in an assignment, check carefully for points such as unnecessary repetition, inaccurate use of words of whose meaning you're uncertain, and ambiguous use of 'it', 'this', 'they', 'them'. Reading your assignment aloud (particularly to someone else) is an effective way of checking for these items.

Evaluating your assignment

Ask yourself:
What were my purposes for the assignment?
How well have I achieved these?
How would I change what I researched, planned and wrote if I repeated the assignment? Why?
Has working on my assignment led me to any ideas or questions I might follow up?

You should be the first person to evaluate the strengths and weaknesses of what you write. You'll provide your readers with a basis for constructive criticism if you include your written evaluation (as well as your plan or detailed table of contents) with your assignment.

The next page is up to **your readers**. If your assignments are usually read only by your teacher and the teacher provides helpful feedback, you'll be encouraged to write more even if you have difficulties to overcome. If your teacher provides only curt or cursory comments on your writing, find one or more other people who'll spend time and care commenting on your work. If such help is not possible, you can discover a new perspective in your writing by reading your work aloud to a tape recorder and listening to it. Even if you have comments from other people, learning to evaluate your own work is part of the craft of writing.

The more useful the feedback you receive on an assignment, the more you can evolve your own style and craft as a writer. Think carefully about any comments you're given and discuss them with your reader to learn more about your strengths and weaknesses as a writer. Remember that for your writing, yours is the final evaluation [see Chapter 15 for more on evaluating your own work].

* * *

Hopefully, writing an assignment is not a postscript to research, or a duty that you scribble through at the last minute. If you think of assignment-writing as a craft to be practised and as part of all the writing you do, you'll understand that it can reward you for the time, care and imagination you put into it in ways which are more satisfying than achieving a good grade.

Further reading

Bate, Douglas. *Essay Method and English Expression.* Harcourt Brace Jovanovich, Australia, 1979.

Clanchy, John and Ballard, Brigette. *Essay Writing for Students.* Longman Cheshire, Melbourne, 1981.

3 Writing Scientific Reports

Some of the worst [articles in scientific journals] are produced by the kind of author who consciously pretends to a "scientific scholarly" style. He takes what should be lively, inspiring and beautiful, and in an attempt to make it seem dignified, chokes it to death with stately abstract nouns; next, in the name of scientific impartiality, he fits it with a complete set of passive constructions to drain away any remaining life's blood or excitement; then he embalms the remains in molasses of polysyllable, wraps the corpse in an impenetrable veil of vogue words, and buries the stiff old mummy with such pomp and circumstance in the most distinguished journal that will take it. Considered either as a piece of scholarly work or as a vehicle of communication, the product is appalling. The question is, does it matter?

F. Peter Woodford

Yes, it does matter — whether your report is published in a scientific journal or is a course requirement. Communicating your findings and observations in a report is an integral part of science, and communicating clearly is interwoven with thinking clearly. Unless your reports are clearly thought out and written, your practical work — no matter how good — is of limited value.

What do you bring to an experiment or field trip which affects the quality of your written report? Your knowledge of a subject — of underlying theory and specific detail — is obviously important and can be improved with preliminary reading. Your care in observation [see 'Observation', Ch. 7], your practical skills, and your expertise in using research techniques also affect the standard of your scientific work and writing.

Your purposes.   Another facet which is basic to good research and report writing is an awareness of your purposes. Some of your purposes are very specific — to test a particular hypothesis, to observe a certain phenomenon. However, you also need to think about why you are doing the research in the first place. And as one of your purposes is to communicate your findings, think about who will read the report. You might:

— write a report on a routine laboratory session for your teacher, where both carrying out the practical work and writing about it are exercises in using a meticulous scientific method, or

— write a public report for a government department or the popular press or as part of your work in an interdisciplinary course; readers of such reports need emphasis on general ideas without too much scientific detail or too many bland descriptions.

Each individual research project and its report has a different purpose. Keeping your purposes and your readers in mind when researching gives you a basic framework for clear report writing.

This chapter looks at basic principles of writing highly structured reports. It's mostly concerned with reports based on gathering primary data from laboratory experiments and fieldwork and less concerned with reporting on secondary data gathered from reports of other people's research [see 'Identifying primary and secondary sources', Ch. 7].

How you use the chapter depends on the detail in your laboratory manuals, and on the number of practical sessions you have each week, and on the extent to which you design your research. For example:

— if your laboratory manual describes in great detail the experiments you're to carry out, focus on planning the experiment and use each section of the chapter as you write your report

— if you have to write up three laboratory sessions each week, you could use this chapter to help you write any difficult sections, and

— if your research is substantially your own, the sections on writing styles and conventions may be particularly valuable.

Beginning a report

Is 'writing up' something you see as a task to be done after the 'real work' of an experiment or fieldwork is over? In practice, the process of writing can help you to clarify your thoughts and stimulate new ideas, so write at all stages of laboratory and fieldwork rather than leaving this activity to the end.

Your laboratory or field notebook

> ...a lab notebook. Everything gets written down, formally, so that you know at all times where you are, where you've been, where you're going and where you want to get. In scientific work and electronics technology this is necessary because otherwise the problems get so complex you get lost in them and confused and forget what you know and what you don't know and have to give up...Sometimes just the act of writing down the problems straightens out your head as to what they really are.
> Robert M. Pirsig

Begin writing for a report during your practical work as you record methods and results, and immediately afterwards while the work is still fresh in your mind. This helps you think critically about what you're doing, and can lead you to repeat an experiment while it is still set up, or to fill in gaps in your field observations. Your notes should be a complete and chronological record of what you did and when, including calculations and diagrams of apparatus.

As you carry out and record research, your results are usually in the form of numbers. For example, if you're interested in how long it takes a one-celled animal to divide, you'd measure the time from one division to the next with a number of these animals and then derive the average time. The results would be a set of numbers called *data*. In the early stages of analysing data, ordering them in tables or graphs can help you see patterns emerging in your results. Include in your notebook a brief discussion of your main results or observations.

Write the name of each of the sections of your report on separate pages of your notebook and record your ideas, observations and results under the appropriate heading. Don't worry at this stage about your writing style or the order of material within a section — concentrate on putting ideas and information down as clearly and concisely as possible.

Planning your writing

Before you start writing your whole report plan *what* you're going to say and how you're going to say it — this is where your sheets of paper for the various sections are useful. Discussing your work with others — teachers, students, friends — gives you practice in explaining your ideas and results and helps clarify what you want to say and how. Consider also *how* you might write your report. You could tackle it in stages, so that you start by writing up Materials and Methods, drafting the Conclusions, and planning your Discussion, and you edit each section as it's written. Another method is to write the whole paper at once, concentrating on conveying your ideas and information accurately, and then editing what you've written. *When* you write your report probably depends on when it's due and your overall workload, but the earlier you begin writing, the more time you'll have to set your completed report aside and think about it [see 'Writing to a plan', Ch. 12].

As you write your report

A scientific or technical report usually follows a highly structured format, and is expected to follow certain conventions in data presentation and writing style.

Format

Think about your report as a whole, rather than as an assortment of sections. However, each section should by itself convey intelligible information to your reader.

When considering the sections which make up a report, it's important to realise that there's *more than one format* for reports. For example:

— biomedical reports often consist of an Introduction, Materials and Methods, Results and Discussion
— reports in descriptive field sciences are likely to include an Introduction, Materials and Methods, Geographical Context, Analysis of Data, Results, and
— more theoretical papers may consist of an Introduction, Theoretical Analysis, Applications, and Conclusions.

In a first-year student report, you're probably given a title, expected to write a one or two sentence introduction, and to describe the materials and methods as in the laboratory manual. Most of your own effort on the report is spent on your results and discussion sections. Occasionally reports require a cover page, a table of contents or illustrations or preface, and they may include recommendations, appendices and acknowledgements. It's not unusual for two sections, such as the Results and Discussion, or the Conclusions and Recommendations, to be combined when this makes sense.

It's *the purpose of each section* of a report which is important. Even if you're told which sections to use in your report, think about the function of each section in the whole report.

The following descriptions of report sections include some points which apply more to articles for publication than to conventional student reports. These points are mentioned because they relate to the purpose of a section, and as such need to be thought about early in your report-writing career.

1 The Title, or 'What's the specific problem or the specific question being asked?'

Your title should attract a potential reader and should be short and specific. For example, 'Resources and Environmental Management: Fundamental Concepts and Definitions', or 'Numerical Data Bases for Australian Science and Technology'.[1] Use a subtitle if a fuller description is necessary, and for the sake of brevity omit words such as 'a', 'the', and 'on' where possible.

The title should state the problem posed or the question asked and indicate how this problem or questions was approached; but a title is not a summary of your report. On the page headed 'Title' in your notebook, list key words and write the title before you write your full report. Check it for accuracy afterwards and ask yourself, 'Do the results and discussions actually answer the particular question or problem set out in the title?'

2 The synopsis or abstract, or 'What's the summary of my main findings?'

Your synopsis or abstract is a precis of the content of your report, and is meant to be read in conjunction with the title. A synopsis should enable your reader to decide whether to read the whole report, so it should be intelligible by itself and shouldn't be full of technical jargon. To help you clarify your ideas and plan your material, it may be useful to write the synopsis before the rest of your report. After the whole report is written, revise the synopsis to ensure that it presents the essential content of your report in a balanced manner.

A synopsis differs from a *summary*, the latter being a review included at the end of a report to help your readers understand your conclusions or recommendations. Such a summary includes more detail than a synopsis and may contain tables and figures.

3 The introduction, or 'What did I do, and why?'

In Part One of formal scientific method, which is the statement of the problem, the main skill is in stating absolutely no more than you are positive you know. It is much better to enter a statement "Solve Problem:

---

[1] *Search*, 9, 12, December, 1978.

Why doesn't cycle work?" which sounds dumb but is correct, than it is to enter a statement "Solve Problem: What is wrong with the electrical system?" when you don't absolutely *know* the trouble is *in* the electrical system. What you should state is "Solve Problem: What is wrong with cycle?" and *then* state as the first entry of Part Two: "Hypothesis Number One: The trouble is in the electrical system".

Robert M. Pirsig

The introduction should state the specific problem or question under consideration, perhaps as an enlargement of the title.

- State clearly the purpose and scope of your work. If you're testing an hypothesis, introduce the relevant theoretical background.

- Discuss selected research studies which, when taken together, show that your work is logical and worthwhile within its field. Don't cite a large number of studies in the introduction. Either refer to any papers which review the relevant research literature or, if you want to discuss a large body of research literature, add a separate section after the introduction or a review which is separate from your report.

- Explain any unusual or complicated theoretical aspects of the subject which aren't covered by the literature, particularly if your readers include people without a strong background in the field.

- State the assumptions and limitations of your work, and define any technical terms as you introduce them.

- Paraphrase your conclusions if necessary, but without attempting to provide a review of these or of your results.

4 *The materials and methods, or 'How did I go about what I did?'*

This section describes what you did in the order in which you did it, *so that a reader with experience in the same field could repeat the experiment or observations*. Strike a balance between being concise and giving sufficient detail. To this end, a diagram of apparatus used can be preferable to a long written description of the same apparatus.

- Broadly outline the overall experimental design or theoretical approach of your research, unless this is obvious from your introduction.

- Describe the subjects used (where applicable).

- List the apparatus used.

- Refer to any preliminary experiments and any changes of techniques you have made.

- State the conditions and procedures of the experiment and observations.

- Describe sampling and control devices used.
- Describe measurement techniques used.
- Include your reasons for choosing a particular method if there were alternatives.

5 *The results, or 'What did I observe or find?'*

The purpose of this section is to present in a logical order a statement of your findings and observations. These should be supplemented with tables or graphs derived from an analysis of data recorded [see 'Data presentation']. Your results are usually presented in relation to your hypothesis, and provide the building material for the discussion and conclusions.

If you can fully report the results in a few words or figures or in a simple table or graph, the Results section should be coherent on its own. If your results led to further experiments which produced further results (and so on), you might want to combine your results and discussion sections.

- Any raw data, or data to more decimal places than appropriate for the summaries in your results, should be placed in an appendix.
- State the number of results obtained, and your reasons for omitting any of these from this section.
- Select the results which support your conclusions (or lack thereof), but be careful that your selection doesn't distort the results in order to reach a particular conclusion.

6 *The discussion, or 'How have I interpreted the results and what are my answers to the specific question asked?'*

> I am appalled by the frequent publication of papers that describe most minutely what experiments were done, and how, but with no hint of why, or what they mean. Cast thy data upon the waters, the authors seem to think, and they will come back interpreted.
>
> F. Peter Woodford

The discussion is the heart of your report and the section where you have the greatest opportunity for creative analysis. Your aim here is to interpret your results, show their significance, explain how they add to what's already known, and discuss your work in relation to the theory underlying similar studies. Refer back to the introduction and evaluate your results to show whether your hypothesis is tenable or whether you've answered the question asked.

- Discuss the precision of your results. Refer to or take them as read, rather than summarising them.

- Explain any irregularities, shortcomings or unexpected results. Note that these discrepancies, rather than being a problem, can often alert you to significant findings.

- Compare your results with the findings of studies that you mentioned in your introduction. To do this satisfactorily, check the original studies to find out exactly what other researchers did, how they did it, and the conclusions they drew, then report these findings accurately.

- Give theoretical explanations for the data discussed.

- Avoid any obvious subjective judgements, such as talking about 'excellent results' or 'highly useful data'.

The points in your discussion should be logically argued and developed, but the section should not be too discursive. Use subheadings to help your reader follow the stages of your argument unless your discussion is brief. The reader should be able to judge the validity of your conclusions from the information in the discussion.

7 *The conclusions, or 'What conclusions can justifiably be drawn?'*

> The TV scientist who mutters sadly, "The experiment is a failure; we have failed to achieve what we had hoped for," is suffering mainly from a bad scriptwriter. The experiment is never a failure solely because it fails to achieve predicted results. An experiment is a failure only when it also fails adequately to test the hypothesis in question, when the data it produces don't prove anything one way or another.
>
> Robert M. Pirsig

State succinctly the conclusions which are justifiably be drawn from your work, and indicate their significance. If your results are inconclusive, say so, give reasons for this, and suggest improvements or further work to be done. Don't present another summary of your results.

8 *The references, or 'Which studies did I cite?'*

Your list of references should be in alphabetical order, and should consist only of reports or studies cited in your report, not literature consulted. When citing from references which report on other people's experiments, each reference should be checked if possible to ensure that any errors in citing the original experiment are not repeated [see 'Conventions'].

* * *

Many student reports are intended to teach a scientific method and subject material as well as to provide an exercise in writing. In this case you'll be faced with the often-conflicting aims of showing your teacher how much you know about a subject, while including only necessary detail as expected in a professional report. When confronted with these dilemmas, don't rehash textbook material on basic theory, and don't bury your discussion and conclusions under a mass of detail. Do talk about the problem with your teacher for suggestions on how the different aims can be reconciled or to which one to give priority. When deciding what to include and what to omit, remember that in professional reports the readers usually know less about the subject than the author, while the reverse is presumably true of the readers and writers of student reports. However don't assume that because your teacher knows a subject you shouldn't explain it fully and clearly. Your teacher needs to know that you understand the basic principles of a subject.

Data presentation

Your data must be ordered, presented in a clear format, and interpreted, or your readers won't be able to make sense of them. How you order and present your data depends on a host of factors, but the guiding principle is always clarity. To achieve clarity, data are usually presented in tables and graphs, accompanied by an explanatory text.

Why use tables or graphs?

Use tables or graphs if they enable your reader to understand the data more clearly. Use them if, for example, they present data more concisely than words could, if they enable your reader to visualise the relationships within your data, or if you use them at the beginning and end of your analysis of results to show the relationship between variables in a graphic form. Don't use tables or graphs simply for the sake of having them in the report.

How will you present data?

This depends on the information you have to convey. For example, don't use graphs if you've data for an insufficient number of points. Think about whether the relationships within your data can be displayed more effectively in a graph or in a table. Consider which form of presentation might be appropriate for your data when it's simple and when it's complex, when it's new and when it's repetitive.

Ordering data. There's more than one way of ordering your data within a table or graph. If your reader has sufficient knowledge of the type of data you're presenting, you can arrange your information so that the patterns and exceptions are easily seen. If you can't assume your reader has this knowledge, supply a sentence or two interpreting the information presented. The patterns and exceptions should then be clear after your reader has read the interpretation. To achieve this clarity, think carefully about the ordering of your data, rather than putting it down in the first format which comes to mind. For example, when presenting tables the following are some points to consider.

- Decide to what degree of accuracy you'll present your figures. Depending on the purpose of your tables and the precision of your experiment, you may be able to round off your figures without losing any vital information. Your reader may do this anyhow to understand your table easily.

- Consider whether to present your data primarily in columns so that your reader's eye is led down the page, or in rows across the page. Which form makes it easier to see the patterns and exceptions in the data presented?

- Decide whether to include aids such as averages, columns or rows, totals, maxima or minima, or percentages to help your reader interpret your data.

- Think about how to set out and space your material, for example, where and how to divide columns of figures from each other.

Amount of information. There's a limit to the amount of information you can convey in one table or graph. Often it's better to opt for several small tables or graphs rather than for a large complex one. This allows you to place each one close to the relevant text, and helps your reader focus on one or two aspects of your data at a time.

Labelling. To label your graphs or tables:

— number them in consecutive order
— give each one a title which is precise but concise, and a legend to explain the elements it contains.
— specify the units used in the headings for columns and rows, so that each entry in the column or row need be a number only, and
— indicate units and magnitudes clearly on the axes of a graph.

* * *

Presenting data in tables and graphs is an integral part of com-

Table 13.1   A sample table

	Private Sector		Education		Public Sector	
	1972	1976	1972	1976	1972	1976
Arts & Social Sciences	35.1	31.2	38.3	41.5	26.5	27.2
Science	23.2	29.1	42.2	38.1	34.6	32.8
Engineering	42.6	58.2	5.0	4.4	52.5	37.4

First full-time employment of new graduates by subject and sector (Graduate Careers Council): as % of all those in subject group securing full-time employment.[1]

[1] Graduate Careers Council of Australia (1972–76), *First Destinations of University Graduates* cited by Stuart Macdonald, 'Unemployed Among Qualified Scientists and Engineers in Australia', in *Search*, 10, 6, June 1979, p. 227.

Note that the author has:
— given figures to one decimal place
— presented the data as percentages rather than as raw data
— arranged the data primarily in columns
— presented the 'sector' headings at the top of the table and the 'subject' headings at the side
— arranged the data into three 'sectors' rather than putting together all the 1972 figures and all the 1976 figures, and
— given an explanatory title for the table.

municating your findings from practical work. In student practical sessions you may have little latitude to opt for different forms of data presentation. But when you design experiments yourself, have someone who knows your subject look at your initial data presentation to see what it conveys to them, and try different formats and ordering of your data to see which one conveys most precisely what you want to say. Data presentation is a complex skill, and this section touches on only a few of the basic points. To learn how to convey information as concisely and unambiguously as possible, find people who are skilled in the use of data presentation techniques, and work with them on the results of your own experiments.

Writing styles and conventions

> ...execrable writing...is the product of shoddy thinking, or careless condescension, or of pretentiousness.
>
> F. Peter Woodford

Your writing style in scientific and technical reports is likely to be shaped by conventions about what 'scientific' thinking is. For example, you're usually expected to avoid using 'I' or 'we' when describing what you did or found because scientists are supposed to be impartial observers. Become familiar with the range of techniques available and practise these often so that they become part of your writing repertoire. Whatever conventions and style you choose, use them to help you report your findings more clearly, rather than to impress your reader or hide ignorance. The principles which underlie all successful communication also apply to scientific writing. Be lucid and unambiguous, and ask yourself:

— 'Exactly what do I want to say?'
— 'Why do I want to say it?'
— 'How can I say it most effectively?', and
— 'To whom am I saying it?'

Style. Reports should describe concisely what happened in an experiment or in field work — they shouldn't be written in a narrative or story-telling style. Events are usually presented in chronological order, and arguments should develop logically, step by step. Write most of your report in prose, and be careful of over-using formulae and other abbreviations when the information they convey could easily be expressed in words.

Language. The language you use shouldn't be too technical or too elementary. Your level of writing should be aimed at whoever will read your report and you should:

— define any new words or mathematical symbols when you first use them
— use technical terms accurately, for example, 'constantly' and 'efficient', and avoid careless use of words which can have a technical meaning, such as 'parameter' or 'factor'
— use chemical and pharmacological names rather than unfamiliar trade names
— write scientific names, proper names, numerical data, equations and formulae correctly, and
— opt for familiar, short or concrete words rather than unfamiliar, long or abstract ones.

I am a Bear of Very Little Brain, and long words Bother me.

A.A. Milne

Conventions. Check with your teacher which conventions you're expected to follow in a report.

● Are you expected to use passive tense rather than active? For example, are you expected to write 'pH4 is needed by enzyme' (passive) instead of 'the enzyme needed pH4' (active)? Using the passive tense doesn't in itself make your writing more scholarly, and active tenses generally make your writing more direct.

- Are you required to use past tense when describing your methods and reporting your results? Are you expected to use the present tense when stating facts which are generally agreed upon?

- Are some numbers to be written in words and some in figures? How are times and dates to be recorded?

- Will you number your report sections and sub-sections consecutively as in '2.1.1.', '2.1.2.', '2.1.3' etc.?

To cite **references**, it's customary to use the author's name and the year of publication in the body of your text, rather than using footnotes. For example:

'According to Brown (1959)...
'Recent studies (Black, 1975; White, 1976) show that...'
'After a thorough training. "The student can no longer write; he pontificates" (Woodford, 1967).'

For references you cite but have not seen in the original:

'The mouse ran up the clock (Green, cited by Blue, 1971)...'

If you refer frequently to other research literature, the text may become so cluttered with bracketed references that it's difficult to read. In this case list all references at the end of the text (alphabetically or in order of appearance) and number each item. To cite one of these references, quote the number of that reference in your text. For example:

'The mouse ran up the clock'[31]

or,

'The mouse ran up the clock' (31)

Grammar, spelling, punctuation. If poor grammar, spelling and punctuation prevent you communicating clearly, work on these with the help of a good reference text on the subject [see Further reading for this chapter, and 'Grammar, spelling and punctuation', Ch. 14]. Find a patient friend who's proficient in these skills and willing to proofread your work.

Sentences and paragraphs. Keep your sentences short and simple if in doubt about their length. Construct your paragraphs so that each one contains one idea [see 'The body of your assignment', Ch. 13]. If you have trouble writing coherent sentences and paragraphs, work with someone who'll help you improve these skills. Read and analyse plenty of well-written articles to get the feel of effective writing — *Science* and *Nature* are good sources of these.

* * *

When your report is finished, set it aside if you have the time so that you can come back to it with something of the approach of a person reading it for the first time. While it's set aside, think about what you've written and make occasional corrections — but allow yourself some distance from it before you prepare your final version.

Editing the report

Check through the **contents** of your report. If some of your report seems irrelevant or too detailed, prune it ruthlessly. See if you've covered all the points in 'As you write'. For example, have you:

— recorded all experimental information such as strength of solutions, ambient temperature, specification of instruments?
— put units against all your measurements and results?
— defined all symbols?
— checked your calculations?
— compared your results with expected or established results, and
— dated your work?

Look at your **writing style**. Be prepared to replace an inappropriate word and to rewrite a clumsy sentence or paragraph. Proofread your report for mistakes or omissions in details such as spelling, grammar and punctuation, or ask someone else to read your work to point out incorrect details and to suggest ways in which you can polish your writing style. When you've edited the content and style of your report, write or type a clean, legible copy [see 'Presentation', Ch. 13].

Writing a scientific report involves putting words on paper, but it also involves thinking about and planning what you want to say as you take notes during an experiment or fieldwork, as you begin to draft your whole report, and when working on your final draft. As you try to express exactly what you want to say, the process of writing itself can set off new ideas and make you look again at old ones. And remember, writing is you communicating about your work to your reader.

Questions and mistakes

Many students see experiments and practical work as exercises to be gone through to find the Right answers. Yet any real learning for you as an individual follows from the questions *you* ask, because you want to know. Following procedures laid down by someone else to answer a question asked by someone else inevitably leads to someone else's answers. You *can* learn from someone else's answers — but only if their answers have a connection with your questions [see Ch. 4].

You interpret the results of an experiment according to the hypothesis being tested, and according to what you expected to find. The way a question is asked, a problem stated or an hypothesis worded influences the results you're likely to come up with. Even researchers who start with the same hypothesis and arrive at similar results can and do interpret those results to reach considerably different conclusions. Their results and conclusions are then interpreted by other researchers in the light of their own hypotheses and findings and opinions. To discover how scientific research has developed in an area, and just how shaky 'facts' can be, take a paper on a specific topic, and read through the originals of any studies cited in that paper. Read these original studies carefully, and compare their actual findings with the way in which these findings have been cited in the later paper. It's not uncommon to find noticeable discrepancies between the two.

> School books even more rarely tell us how thinkers of the past have gone about trying to answer their own questions, and still more rarely, what mistakes they made along the way. A graduate student in Psychology suggested one day to a noted professor in that field that there should be a publication in which psychologists would write about their mistakes, the hunches that had not worked out, the experiments that had not proved what they meant to prove; or didn't prove anything. The professor agreed that such a publication would teach students a great deal about the doing of psychology. But, he said, there was no use even thinking about such a publication, because no-one with a reputation to defend would ever put anything in it. So we find it hard to find most of our mistakes because we are so rarely told how the do-ers of the past came to make and later find theirs.
>
> John Holt

If, at the end of an experiment or fieldwork, you haven't found the answers you expected, if your results are inconclusive or point to other answers, don't automatically think you've failed. Think about what you did and try to discover *why* your results were inconclusive or unexpected. If you made a mistake, acknowledge it. If your work could be improved, suggest how this might be done. If you discover related questions, or areas to be explored for a more complete answer, suggest these as part of your report. Don't try to hide your unexpected or inconclusive results, or distort them to produce the Right answers. You can learn much by analysing your mistakes.

* * *

You can learn as much from writing a report of observations made in the laboratory or field as you can from doing the practical work about which you write. The challenge of trying to describe your work accurately, logically and lucidly for someone else to read and understand should make you think about what you actually did. In serious research, describing your work helps you think about how to design and conduct experiments or a set of observations, and about the nature of the disciplines in which you're working and writing. What do you think science is all about? Or technology? Your answers to these questions will shape and he shaped by the reports you write about your scientific and technical work.

Further reading

Barrass, Robert. *Scientists Must Write: A Guide to Better Writing for Scientists, Engineers and Students.* Chapman and Hall, London, 1978.

Booth, Vernon. *Writing a Scientific Paper.* 4th edn. The Biochemical Society, London, 1979.

Cooper, Bruce M. *Writing Technical Reports.* Penguin Books, Harmondsworth, 1964.

Ehrenberg, A.S.C. 'Rudiments of Numeracy', *J.R. Statist. Soc. A.* 140, Part 3, 1977, pp. 277–297

O'Connor, M. and Woodford, F.P. *Writing Scientific Papers in English: An ELSE-Ciba Foundation Guide for Authors.* Pitman Medical, London, 1978.

Royal Society, The. *General Notes on the Preparation of Scientific Papers.* 3rd edn. Royal Society, London, 1974.

Ulman, Joseph N., Jr. and Gould, Jay R. *Technical Reporting.* 3rd edn. Holt, Rinehart and Winston, New York, 1971.

Woodford, F. Peter. 'Sounder Thinking Through Clearer Writing' *Science* 156, 3776, May 1967, pp. 743–745.

4 Using Conventions

"... besides that's not a regular rule; you invented it just now."
"It's the oldest rule in the book," said the King.
"Then it ought to be Number One," said Alice.

Lewis Carroll

When using conventions it's useful to understand their purposes rather than simply following rules. The standard conventions used by most Western publishers serve as a shorthand to make writing and reading easier. Much of this shorthand has its origins in the reporting of scientific research where the reader needs to be able to follow up references to fully understand or evaluate a report.

If citing a reference or paraphrasing an idea in a piece of writing, acknowledge your source. It may seem unimportant and pedantic to give full details of the reference. For example:

Savage, Jo. *The Film 'Fangs'*. Wolf Publications, Alaska, 1979, p. 54.

However, if you omit any of this information (for example, if you refer only to 'Savage's book on the movie Fangs'), your reader has to ask for further information to know how recent the book is, exactly who the author is, where the book was published, and precisely where in the book to find the reference.

Individual academic disciplines and publications frequently adopt their own variations of the standard conventions. For example, the usual format for a bibliography entry in the social sciences is:

Walrus, A. and Carpenter, T.H.E. *The Oyster Orgy*. 3rd edn. Mornay Books, Sandwich, 1990.

In the physical sciences the same book would usually be entered as:

Walrus, A. and Carpenter, T.H.E. (*1990*) *The Oyster Orgy*. 3rd edn. Sandwich, Mornay Books

As you can see, the essential elements are the same but the conventions of the format used vary. Whichever format you use, be *consistent* and *accurate*. Check with a teacher about the conventions you're expected to follow in a discipline, programme, course or assignment, and find out the teacher's personal preferences in these matters.

> Either stick to tradition or see that your inventions be consistent.
>
> Horace

But don't let the punctilious observance of correct conventions become the focus of your writing. *Use* them as necessary to help you communicate more clearly — and if in doubt about which one to use or whether to use them at all, rely on your common sense to convey clearly and accurately to your reader what you want to say.

This chapter outlines why and how to use quotations, references and bibliographies according to the conventions set out in the Australian Government's Style Manual. *The chapter also looks at the question of plagiarism, and at some conventions for presenting an assignment.* All of the examples used are taken from material written about the sea, a place where human conventions are subservient to nature.

Quotations

> I might repeat to myself, slowly and soothingly, a list of quotations beautiful from minds profound; if I can remember any of the damn things.
>
> Dorothy Parker

Why use quotations?

Quotations can be useful:

— to express a thought or concept succinctly
— to illustrate a point you want to make
— to convey the flavour of a work, or
— to analyse the quotation in depth.

How to present quotations

Long quotations. These should be set apart from the main body of your writing so that they are easily identified. If a quote is longer than 25–30 words, identify it by using one or more of the following:

— miss a line above and below the quotation
— indent from the left
— introduce the quotation with a colon, or
— use single-spaced typescript when the rest of the text is double-spaced.

For example:

- …In his book *Sailing to the Reefs*, Bernard Moitessier discusses the motivation behind single-handed sailing:

   And it is, I believe, this need not simply for novelty, but for physical and spiritual cleanliness which drives the lone sailor towards other shores; there, his body and mind are freed from their terrestrial ties and bondage, and can regain their essence and integrity in the natural elements which the ancients deified.[1]

   This description captures the spirituality of the experience….

- A familiar childrens' poem describes an unusual sea voyage:

   The Owl and the Pussy-Cat went to sea
   In a beautiful pea-green boat,
   They took some honey, and plenty of money,
   Wrapped up in a five-pound note.[2]

Short quotations. These are usually part of your text and are enclosed by quotation marks. For example:

   Truly immersed in the experience, 'one forgets oneself, one forgets everything, seeing only the play of the boat with the sea, the play of the sea around the boat…'[3] as the present takes priority over all else.

If quoting more than one line of poetry within your text, indicate the division between the lines with an oblique. For example:

   The single-handed sailor knows the power of being 'Alone, alone, all, all, alone,/Alone on a wide, wide sea!'[4]

---

[1] Bernard Moitessier, *Sailing to the Reefs*, trans. by René Hague, Hollis and Carter, London, 1971, p. 83.

[2] Edward Lear, *Nonsense Omnibus*, Frederick Warne and Company, London, 1943, p. 251.

[3] Bernard Moitessier, *The Long Way*, trans. by William Rodarmor, Doubleday and Company, New York, 1975, p. 52.

[4] Ernest Hartley Coleridge (ed.), *The Poems of Samuel Taylor Coleridge*, Oxford University Press, London, 1912, p. 196.

Paraphrasing and plagiarism

With just enough of learning to misquote.

Lord Byron

When you paraphrase, you re-express another person's thoughts in your own words and acknowledge their source. You plagiarise if you take someone else's thoughts and writings and present them as your own. Plagiarism often results in an unsatisfactory piece of work because, for example, your writing style differs awkwardly from that of the plagiarised piece, or the section you've copied isn't exactly relevant to your overall theme. You may not know that it's unacceptable to copy from a source without acknowledgement, and may offhandedly include in your own work phrases, sentences or paragraphs from another source. More extreme forms of plagiarism occur when a student copies, with or without minor changes, an entire article or chapter, or another student's essay.

In most cases, a teacher is familiar with the relevant source material and easily diagnoses a case of plagiarism. Otherwise he or she may ask another teacher to read your work, make a serious search for the original source, or discuss the paper with you. If plagiarism is confirmed, there are several possible courses of action for a teacher. You may be asked to write another paper or the piece of work could be failed; or work completed out of class might be disregarded and you may be expected to sit for an exam. Sometimes official disciplinary action is taken. In any case, reading the work of a student who's plagiarised someone else's words and ideas is a disheartening experience for a teacher.

How to avoid plagiarising

- You may be tempted to plagiarise if you're not confident about your knowledge of a subject or your writing ability, or because you feel pressured by work. If so, talk about these difficulties with someone who can help you (and use any relevant sections of this book) rather than resorting to plagiarism and being confronted with the same problems later on.

- When taking notes from material, read a section, put the reference aside and express the idea in your own words [see 'Notetaking and underlining', Ch. 8]. If you want to use another writer's words or ideas, put anything you copy exactly in quotation marks (with the page numbers) and clearly identify the beginning and end of paraphrases.

- When writing, put quotes in quotation marks. For quotes or paraphrases, use footnotes, endnotes or adjacent references to acknowledge the source. You can indicate clearly where a paraphrase begins by acknowledging the author immediately before in your text, for example, 'Humphries says...'. If you take an opinion from someone else, don't disguise it by using the passive tense, such as 'It has been said that...'. If you use factual information, for example, bibliographical or quantitative information, acknowledge the source.

References

Why include references?

References are used:
— to give the source of a quotation or paraphrase
— to give the source of authority for a 'fact' which a reader might question as true, or
— to make a cross reference to another part of your text.

How to reference material

Adjacent references.   These enable a reader to continue reading your text smoothly, and may also be used with footnotes or endnotes which comment on your text. They are the accepted form of referencing in scientific reports [see 'Conventions', Ch. 13]. These references give the author's surname and the year of publication, and need to include page numbers for quotes or references to a specific item in a source. Following are two examples.

- Bernard Moitessier (1975, p. 4) describes sailboats as living creatures.
- Sailboats are sometimes described as living creatures (Moitessier, 1975, p. 4).

Adjacent references are brief so they are used to refer to a work already under discussion and they must be complemented by a thorough bibliography. If bibliography items are numbered, refer simply to the number of the item and the relevant pages in that item.

- Sometimes sailboats are described as living creatures (2:4).

If an author has more than one publication in a year, distinguish these with letters after the year, for example, 1978*a* and 1978*b*.

Footnotes.   These allow for more information about your source than

Table 14.1   Abbreviations

app.	— appendix
bk., bks.	— book(s)
c, ©	— copyright
c. (circa)	— about a certain date [as in 'c. 1901']
ch. chs (or chap., chaps)	— chapter(s)
col., cols	— column(s)
diss.	— dissertation
ed., eds	— editor(s)
edn	— edition
et al. (et alii)	— 'and others' [used when a book has several authors, as in 'P. March et al]
et seq. (et sequentes)	— 'and following' [as in 'pp. 64 et seq]
f., ff.	— 'and the following' [to refer to page numbers]
fascim.	— facsimile [that is, an exact copy of writing, printing, picture]
fol., fols	— folio(s)
front.	— frontispiece
ibid. (ibidem)	— 'in the same work' [as previously cited]
ill., ills	— illustrator(s)

is possible in an adjacent reference. As well as being used to acknowledge a source, a footnote may be a comment on what you've written.[5]

Footnotes appear on the same page as the reference. A number follows after the quotation or paraphrase you are referencing and is repeated at the foot of the page.[6] Footnotes may be numbered consecutively throughout your text or numbered separately for each page or chapter.

A footnote acknowledgement need not be as detailed as an entry in a bibliography. However, the first time you acknowledge a particular book in a footnote, give whichever of the following details are

---

[5] Lengthy footnotes suggest that your essay hasn't been planned with sufficient care. This footnote, for example, is too long and distracts you from the flow of the text. In such cases, ask yourself if the footnote information is really necessary. If it is, consider whether the information should be incorporated into the assignment or placed as an appendix to the text.

[6] The quotation or paraphrase may be a word or phrase, a sentence or a paragraph.

loc. cit. (loco citato)	— 'in the same place (already) cited' [that is, in the same passage referred to in a recent reference note]
ms., mss	— manuscript(s)
n., nn.	— note(s) [as 'p. 56, n. 3' or 'p. 56 n.']
n.d.	— no date (of publication)
n.p.	— no place (of publication)
op. cit. (opere citato)	— in a work (recently) cited
p., pp.	— page(s)
passim	— 'throughout the work' [rather than on specific pages]
q.v. (quod vide)	— 'which see' [used in cross referencing]
rev.	— revised (by), revision
[sic]	— 'thus so' [to guarantee exact quotation when the reader might doubt this]
trans., tr.	— translator, -ion, -ed
v., vv., vs., vss	— verse(s)
viz. (videlicet)	— 'namely', 'in other words' [usually after words or statements about to be elaborated]
vol., vols	— volume(s)

available:

— the author/editor's name (surname last)
— the title of the book (underlined or italicised)
— the translator/illustrator/reviser's name
— the publication details (edition, publisher, place, year), and
— the page reference.

Francis Chichester, *Gipsy Moth Circles The World*, Hodder and Stoughton, London, 1967, p. 67.

● For immediately consecutive footnotes referring to the same source use the author's surname and the page numbers. For example:

[1] David Lewis, *Children of Three Oceans*, Collins, London, 1969, p. 60.
[2] Lewis, p. 66.

● If there's more than one item by the same author, give the author's name in each case and follow it with the title and page numbers of the individual item.

● If there's more than one author with the same surname, give forenames also.

Endnotes. These serve the same purposes as footnotes. If too much space would be taken up in your text with numerous, lengthy or complicated footnotes, use endnotes. They can be easier for your reader to refer to and are easier to lay out in the final draft of an assignment, especially if this is being typed. However, as with footnotes, if you've too many endnotes in relation to the length of your assignment, consider whether the assignment is adequately planned.

When compiling endnotes, all reference notes that would have appeared as footnotes are collected at the end of your assignment. Number these references consecutively throughout your text, and apply the same rules of abbreviation to them as to footnotes. It's useful for your reader if endnotes can be detached from your text for easier reading, and if they are headed 'References' to distinguish them instantly from a bibliography.

Bibliographies

Prepare a bibliography for all assignments whether written, oral, taped or audiovisual.[7]

Why include a bibliography?

A bibliography is designed:
— to provide a complete or selected list of the sources you consulted in preparation for writing an assignment, and
— to provide annotations, that is, brief commentaries on your sources.

How to present a bibliography

Book entry.   The basic format for these entries in a bibliography is:
— author's surname, followed by forename or initials
— title (underlined, in italics or in capital letters)
— publication details (publisher, place, date).

   Colgate, Stephen. *Fundamentals of Sailing, Cruising and Racing*. W.W. Norton and Company, New York, 1978.

An article, chapter, or anthology item.   The basic format for such entries

---

[7] A bibliography can also be a self-contained work which gives an exhaustive list of works on a topic.

in a bibliography is:

— author/editor's surname, followed by forename or initials
— title of article, chapter or item, enclosed by inverted commas
— author/editor of the book in which the chapter or item is found
— title (underlined, italicised or capital letters) of the periodical, book, anthology or newspaper from which the item was taken
— publication details of periodical or book, and
— page numbers of article, chapter or item.

For example

> Burke, K.M. 'A Dream in Ice and Snow', *Cruising World*. Newport, Rhode Island, 5, 1, January 1979, pp 60–63.
> Crealock, W.I.B. 'Stainless Steel and Panties', *Cloud of Islands*. David McKay Company, New York, 1955.

Differences between bibliographies and reference notes

Bibliographies	Reference Notes
Surname followed by forename or initials	Surname follows the forename or initials
Alphabetical listing by surname of author/editor	Consecutive listing as the notes first appear in the text
Items need not be numbered	Each item numbered
Full publication details	Publication details included as necessary
Subtitle and series information given (where applicable)	Subtitle and series information often omitted
May be annotated	No annotation
Page reference for articles but not for entire books or journal issues	Page references for each item
Full stops used to separate the three main sections (author, title, publication details).	Commas used to separate the three main sections.

Additional points

● Publication details are as follows:

— periodical: place (if overseas), volume and issue number (if pages are numbered afresh for each issue), date
— book: edition, place, publisher, date.

Table 14.2   Bibliography entries

Books

One author
> Van Dorn, William G. *Oceanography and Seamanship*. Dodd, Mead and Company, New York, 1974.

Two authors
> Pardey, L. and Pardey, L. *Seraphyn's European Adventure*. W.W. Norton and Company, New York, 1979.

Three or more authors
> Pariser, E.L. et al. *Fish Protein Concentrate: Panacea for Protein Malnutrition?* M.I.T. Press, Boston, Mass., 1978.

Repeat entry by same author
> Letcher, John S. Jr. *Self Steering for Sailing Craft*. International Marine Publishing Company, Camden, Maine, 1974.
>
> *Self-Contained Celestial Navigation with H.O. 208*. International Marine Publishing Company, Camden, Maine, 1977.

Author (or editor) and translator
> Moitessier, Bernard. *The Long Way*. Trans. William Rodarmor. Doubleday and Company, New York, 1975.

Editor
> Kemp, Peter (ed.). *The Oxford Companion to Ships and the Sea*. Oxford University Press, London, 1976.

Unknown author
> *The Voyage of Governor Phillip to Botany Bay*. London, 1790.

Corporate author
> Naval Training Command. *A Navigational Compèndium*, 2nd edn, Government Printing Office, Washington, D.C., 1972.

Article (unsigned) from reference book
> 'Oceanography'. *Encyclopedia of the Sciences*. 2nd edn Eds W.B. Sill and N. Hoss. Grosset and Dunlop, New York, 1968.

Personal conversation
> Driscoll, John. Personal conversation with author, 4 February 1978.

- If there's more than one entry for an author, list these entries in chronological order of publication.
- Entries may be classified into groups according to topic or the nature of the material, for example:
  — 'Primary Sources' and 'Secondary Sources'

Interview
> Fletcher, Dorothy. Interviewed by Jim Macbeth, 9 September 1978.

Excerpt from book not read in original but seen reproduced in another book
> Robertson, Dougal. 'Sunk by a Whale' in *Survive the Savage Sea*. Elek Books, London, 1973, in Ralph Stevenson (ed.). *Small Boats and Big Seas: A Hundred Years of Yachting*. David McKay Company, New York, 1978.

Chapter of a book where both are by the same author
> Crealock, W.I.B. 'Stainless Steel and Panties', in *Cloud of Islands*. David McKay Company, New York, 1955.

Article from edited book (author and editor different)
> Fuller, R. Buckminster. 'Formula for a Floating City,' in M.J. Dunstan and P.J. Garlan (eds). *Worlds in the Making*. Prentice-Hall, New Jersey, 1970.

Journals, newspapers

Article from journal
> Lundberg, Madeleine. 'Eugenie Clark: Shark Tamer', *Ms*. VIII, 2, August 1979, pp. 12–21.

Article from newspaper
> Heydon, Neville. 'Right Port for Jan'. *The Mercury* Hobart, 14 February 1980, p. 1.

Oral information

Information from a lecture
> Macbeth, J.W. Participant Research: a Cruisers, a study of a deviant subculture. Lecture, Murdoch University, 4 June 1979.

Information from a television or radio programme
> 'Voyage to the Ice' Australian Broadcasting Commission, Sydney, 27 September 1978.

— 'Books' and 'Articles'
— 'Items from Newspapers' and 'Personal Conversations'.

• The heading of a bibliography should indicate its scope, for example, 'Selected Bibliography', 'Brief Annotated Bibliography' or 'A General Bibliography'.

The finishing touches

You're expected to present your work clearly and to use correct grammar, spelling and punctuation in writing assignments and reports. Check with a teacher and with reference books if you are uncertain about the conventions you're expected to follow in these matters.

Grammar, spelling and punctuation

> "He has got no good red blood in his body," said Sir James.
> "No. Somebody put a drop under a magnifying-glass, and it was all semi-colons and parentheses," said Mrs. Cadwallader.
>
> George Eliot

A sound knowledge of grammar helps you write more fluently and is an important part of the writer's craft. Your ideas have less impact on a reader if your grammar, spelling and punctuation are poor. To improve these skills, consult books and ask for help from other people. You may have to learn by heart the correct forms and usages, but if you can discover underlying reasons for a particular rule you'll remember the correct version more easily. Read your work aloud to yourself (possibly into a tape recorder) and check the grammar and punctuation of any sections which don't flow smoothly.

> "I struggle through the alphabet as if it had been a bramble bush; getting considerably worried and scratched by every letter."
>
> Charles Dickens

Presentation

The purpose of presenting work clearly is to help your reader.

- Legible writing saves your reader from eye strain and irritation. Assignments should be typed or clearly written in ink. Take care with details such as dotting your 'i's accurately or forming your 'r's clearly, as these make your writing surprisingly easier to read. If your handwriting is atrocious, persuade a friend to write or type your assignments for you, or learn to type yourself.

- Keep a carbon copy in case your reader happens to lose your assignment.

- A wide margin (at least 4 cm) enables your reader to comment fully.

- For easy identification, provide a cover sheet giving your name, the assignment title, course, teacher's name, and date on which the assignment is due. The cover sheet may also include an abstract or synopsis [see 'Synopsis', Ch. 13].

- Secure all pages firmly together. Any appendices which the reader will refer to frequently should be detachable, for example, endnotes or tables of results.

- To help your reader understand the structure of your assignment provide a contents page and include in the contents a list of any diagrams, graphs or appendices.

* * *

Use conventions to help you say what you want to as lucidly as possible. Don't worry about the correct form of academic conventions so much that they prevent you from writing effectively. Become familiar with the basic conventions and their purposes, check which forms to follow for a particular piece of work, and then rely on your common sense to convey what you want to say to a reader. If you have trouble with using any convention, find yourself an efficient proofreader and work at overcoming your difficulties.

Further reading

Australian Government Publishing Service. *Style Manual: For Authors, Editors and Printers of Australian Government Publications.* 3rd edn., revised by J. Pitson. Australian Government Printing Service, Canberra, 1978.

Bailey, R.F. *A Survival Kit for Writing English.* Longman Australia, Victoria, 1976.

Fowler, H.W. *Modern English Usage.* 2nd edn., revised by Sir Ernest Gowers. Clarendon Press, Oxford, 1965.

Modern Language Association of America. *The MLA Handbook for Writers of Research Papers, Theses, and Dissertations.* Modern Language Association of America, New York, 1977.

Roget, P.M. *Thesaurus of English Words and Phrases.* Revised by J.L. Roget and S.R. Roget. Penguin Books, Middlesex, England, 1953.

Strunk, Jr., William and White, E.B. *The Elements of Style.* 2nd edn. The Macmillan Co., New York, 1972.

Turabian, Kate L. *A Manual for Writers of Term Papers, Theses, and Dissertations.* 4th edn. The University of Chicago Press, Chicago, 1973.

Whitaker–Wilson, C. *Punctuation.* Sun Books, Melbourne, 1975.

5 Learning from Evaluation

If you want to learn to speak Italian, you learn more quickly if you live among Italians. You can evaluate your pronunciation constantly by comparing it with what you hear, and you receive instant responses when you practise what you learn.

If you want to take a more effective part in discussion groups, you need frequent practice in talking and listening in groups. At the same time, you need to think about your strengths and weaknesses as a group member, and why and how you want to improve. You can then evaluate your participation and make more use of any feedback you receive from other people in a group.

In both these instances, evaluation and responses are fundamental to your learning. Part of the evaluation you need to do for yourself — to compare your pronunciation or evaluate your group participation. You appraise your learning on the basis of what you want to learn so that your goals and your strengths and weaknesses emerge more clearly. You may discover, for example, that you want to learn more colloquial Italian so you can take part in day-to-day conversations, or you may decide that in discussion you need to practise listening carefully to other people. These discoveries provide you with further criteria for evaluating what you learn ... and so the learning process continues.

This chapter emphasises that evaluation — whether your own or other people's — should help rather than hinder the process of your learning. This chapter looks at the purposes of evaluation and at who evaluates your learning and how this is carried out by feedback and recorded assessment. In conclusion, we list some of the assumptions underlying the evaluation of your formal learning.

In your formal learning you both give and receive responses. If a friend gives you an essay to read and asks for helpful comments, what sort of comments might you make? You could respond with the first thoughts that come into your head. You might write down your reactions in detail, confine yourself to a few pithy statements at the end of the essay, or discuss your comments with your friend. If you do discuss your comments, you'll probably modify some of your criticisms as you understand more clearly what your friend was trying to achieve. And if you don't already realise it, you'll soon come to know that your responses are subjective — they come from your preferences and learning and beliefs. Do you believe that you know how 'good' essays should be written? If you judge your friend's work according to a particular model of what's desirable in essay-writing, you need to explain this model so that your friend can accept or reject it. Your comments will be more useful if you make it clear that you're giving personal reactions to the work.

When you're in a situation where your knowledge of a topic is to be assessed, how would you choose to prove what you know? Would you submit writing you've done, other people's comments on your work, or your own evaluation? Could this evidence adequately demonstrate what you have learnt? You might want to discuss what you know with the people assessing you, or to take an exam on the topic. What particular aspects of your learning would you want to be tested? Who do you think could best assess these? Answering these questions involves thinking about what you set out to learn, and considering why and how you went about learning it. These reflections in turn might lead you to ask if you wanted or needed someone else to assess your knowledge at all, to ask 'What are the purposes of evaluation?'

Why evaluation?

Learning further

One explicit purpose of formal evaluation is to help you learn further, to help you progress towards *your objectives*. You're likely to change your skills or behaviour or ideas according to the responses and evaluation you receive when you try to communicate and practise what you're learning. These changes may be slight, for instance, when you learn how to pronounce a word more accurately; or they may be a new cornerstone in your learning, for instance, if you gain a significant new insight into how people behave in groups. The feedback you've received then becomes an integral part of what you're learning, rather than an extra which is applied at the 'end' as is often the case when you sit for a final exam or hand in an assignment. However sometimes you don't have enough experience and knowledge to make use of the information in a response you're given, and at other times you reject feedback because it 'feels wrong' or doesn't fit with your knowledge or beliefs. Being able to use other people's responses to your learning depends on being ready for them.

Being able to ask for and use responses also requires that you think about your purposes for undertaking an assignment or a course, about *why* you want to learn. Think about your objectives or *what* you want to learn, and ask yourself *how* and *when* you want to learn. These questions are often too complex to answer fully, but unless you're content to follow the goals other people set for you, you need to consider them seriously. Your purposes will probably evolve further during your learning, so reformulate them and your objectives as this happens. If your purpose and objectives are clear, you can use them as criteria to evaluate whether you're learning, what you're learning and how well you're learning.

Proving your knowledge

> A schoolgirl answered the question 'In what countries are elephants found?' Elephants are very large and intelligent animals, and are seldom lost.
>
> James Agate

Another explicit purpose of formal evaluation is proving your knowledge to satisfy *other people's objectives*. These people are usually teachers, who directly assess your work, and include academic and administrative committees within a university or college, professional bodies, and prospective employers.

When you begin a programme, course, or assignment, the objectives your teachers have planned for it should be clearly formulated. These objectives should preferably be set down in writing so you can refer to them, and you should be able to discuss them with your teachers and other students. When teachers don't set out clear objectives, this may be because they are unaware of them beforehand or because they haven't thought them through in detail. Teachers may also choose to conceal their aims. For example, early in a course you may be given a written assignment to introduce you to a basic area of knowledge and at the same time to diagnose your writing problems; to test you more 'effectively' you may not be told about the second objective.

Like you, teachers often develop new objectives as a programme or course progresses, perhaps as implicit purposes become obvious or in response to the students taking the course. As new purposes emerge, they should be discussed with you. To decide whether or not you accept your teachers' objectives, be clear about your own.

Teachers often use their evaluation to judge if you're ready to move on to what they consider more difficult material. This use of evaluation is important in subjects which teach a sequence of physical skills, where mastery of the preliminary steps is necessary to cope with the more demanding ones. This sequential model is often applied to intellectual learning, and sequences are constructed according to a teacher's particular model of a body of knowledge. For example, unless you understand and can do what a teacher defines as elementary grammar, you're not permitted to move to more advanced language courses. These sequences are not essential for you to learn a subject — they are not inherent in the material. You *can* take structured courses in Italian which formally evaluate your learning at various stages; but you *can* learn Italian by living in Italy and immersing yourself in the language.

> ...reading, unlike dancing, is not a muscular act, and it is a serious mistake to treat it like one. The dance master must stretch and strengthen the student's muscles so that the student may make the next movement, and without injury. But one cannot injure onself with a difficult thought.
>
> John Holt

Who evaluates your learning?

> It is much more difficult to judge oneself than to judge others.
> A. de Saint-Exupéry

Who gives you feedback on your learning?
Who formally assesses your work?

You should be the first person to evaluate your work. Make your evaluation more than a passing reflection or a casual comment to a friend. Compare what you learn with your objectives and with the aims of a programme, course or assignment. You may not be the only person who can evaluate your learning — other people can help you. reach your objectives. However, you should know your objectives, abilities and previous learning best, so by these criteria you are the best person to decide how satisfactorily you're learning. If when you hand in an assignment you also submit a written evaluation or if you make an end-of-year evaluation of your learning, your teachers will be more able to comment usefully on your individual work.

A discussion or study group to which you belong can give you feedback on work such as on an essay plan or a seminar presentation [see 'Share Your Writing', Ch. 11]. The group may also formally assess your work. This alternative to more traditional assessment requires thorough planning to work well, but people in groups which undertake this collective responsibility gain a great deal from their involvement in each other's learning.

An adviser whom you seek out to be your sounding board can provide you with help ranging from correcting spelling errors in a report to giving a detailed critique of a major assignment. This adviser might be a sympathetic teacher, a learning skills counsellor, a student who's previously taken the course, or a friend.

A teacher with whom you work in a course is usually responsible for formally assessing your work, sometimes in collaboration with you or other teaching staff. And the amount of informal feedback teachers give you varies according to their teaching styles — and to your willingness to ask for comments.

> I wrote my name at the top of the page. I wrote down the number of the question '1'. After much reflection, I put a bracket around it thus '(1)'. But thereafter I could not think of anything connected with it that was either relevant or true.... It was from these slender indications of scholarship that Mr Welldon drew the conclusion that I was worthy to pass into Harrow. It is very much to his credit.
>
> Winston Churchill

Ideally the person who comments on your ideas and work should be someone you respect and find stimulating as a learner and teacher, and he or she should be easily accessible. Your official teacher may be difficult to find or talk to, or may give you little or no feedback on your work. Make an appointment, go with a clear question or idea to discuss, and ask for comments on particular aspects of your work. If your attempts don't change the situation, find another person or group of people with whom you can discuss your learning. If your teacher is the person who formally assesses your work, you still need to be prepared to approach her or him if you want to discuss or question an assessment you're given.

How is your learning evaluated?

Your evaluation

A written evaluation of your own work enables you to look at yourself in relation to what an assignment, course or programme has given you and what you have put into it. Of course your life can't be neatly segmented as if it was an orange, and in a self-evaluation you inevitably comment on parts of your life connected with the subject such as another course, your approach to studying, or personal experiences.

Sounds like a lot of writing? Self-evaluations can vary in length from a couple of handwritten pages to half-a-dozen typewritten pages or three months of diary entries. The guidelines in Table 15.1 were used by students preparing a written self-evaluation for a half-hour discussion with their teacher at the end of a course. They may suggest to you some ideas for evaluating your own learning.

Build up **a learning portfolio** during your formal education.

Table 15.1   A self evaluation

Imagine you're writing for someone you'll meet in the future. This unknown person wants to know about you and your work during the course.

- What were your goals when you started the course?
- What strengths did you feel you possessed?
- What were your weaknesses?
- How did you apply your strengths?
- How did you try to overcome your weaknesses?
- What work did you accomplish in quality and quantity (for example, in assignments or for tutorials)?
- How much recommended reading did you do for the course and for tutorials?
- What reading did you do beyond recommended readings (author, title and comment)?
- What ideas came from your 'outside' reading, and how did they relate to the course?
- What do you feel you learned:
  — about tutorials
  — about university
  — about yourself
  — about improving your ability to learn, and
  — about directions you want to pursue in future learning?

A self-evaluation shouldn't be a compilation of your real or imagined shortcomings, or a prosaic listing of the number of books read and lectures attended. Write about your strengths as well as your weaknesses. Evaluate your learning so that if you read the evaluation again in a couple of years' time it would tell you about this one aspect of yourself. Your evaluation is not a formal course assignment to be judged, and will be next-to-worthless if you're not honest with and about yourself.

This gives you a sense of how your learning develops, and can serve as a file from which to choose material when applying for entry to a particular course, an honours or postgraduate programme, or a future job.

What might you include in a learning portfolio?

• Put in items you've written about yourself as a learner — your aims, your questions, your enthusiasms [see 'Why keep a journal?', Ch. 11]. Your self-evaluations are an important part of this.

• Keep individual pieces of work you've completed, along with comments and assessments by yourself or others.

• Include any material connected with you as a learner, material such as drawings you've done in response to an idea, items of information you want to follow up, articles which have been particularly significant for you.

• Include descriptions of your involvement in a job or community work which is an important part of your learning.

His *'noteworthy contribution'* is an essential step demonstrating a student's readiness for a degree. This may be a work of art, a research finding, or a community service. It will be intended to show that the candidate for a degree is more than a consumer of what earlier scholars, creative artists, and social leaders have given to him.

University Without Walls

Other people's evaluations

Think about what you would do in one of the following situations, and discuss this with friends if you can.

• *If asked to record an assessment of a friend's essay in an official student file, on what would you base your assessment? How would you record it?*

• *You're in your first year at university or college, and don't have to enrol in a particular programme until you've completed several first-year courses. You're told that all first year courses will be assessed only on a Pass/Fail basis. How does this assessment method affect your choice of courses?*

• *You've spent two weeks carefully preparing and writing an assignment. When it's returned at the end of a tutorial, you skim through the pages and find the only comment on the final page — 'C+. Satisfactory work'. You'd like to ask the tutor for further comment but don't feel as if you know him well enough. What do you do?*

After some years it began to happen that I would find myself in the middle of writing a comment and begin to wonder whether it could really be trusted, whether it was really useful. Perhaps I was telling someone about his flowery and wordy diction. His diction was indeed wordy and would be called flowery. But I began to wonder if this was *why* I was complaining about it. I sometimes found myself suspecting it was something else I couldn't put my finger on that bothered me but floweriness was more available. If I were in a different mood or the paper were in a different place in the stack, perhaps I wouldn't have made the comment I did.

Peter Elbow

The two most common methods used by individual teachers when evaluating your learning are:
— giving you feedback in the form of comments which are not officially recorded, and
— making an assessment which is to be recorded on your official student file, usually as a percentage, a letter grade or a Pass/ Fail.

1 Unrecorded feedback

A person giving you feedback on your learning should comment on both the strengths and the weaknesses as they perceive them, rather than demonstrating your seeming inadequacies or rating your work according to 'objective' criteria. You may not be ready to understand and use all such feedback, but you should be able to find it when you need it and you should be able to decide how detailed any responses need be. Ask for the feedback you want — you can't expect a teacher to know this exactly. If possible ask for feedback from the person you think might give you the most useful responses for a specific piece of work.

What form might feedback and comments take? Ideally, this depends mostly on what you need. In formal education, the comments might be written or oral. They might be given ad hoc, or structured according to specific criteria or the requirements of situations such as a seminar. They might be part of a required one-to-one discussion with your teacher at the end of a course, or given when an assignment is returned to you.

Feedback needs to be *given in a way you understand*. For example, if you ask for an idea to be clarified, you need an explanation which gives you more information but doesn't overwhelm you with detail, and if you've used a word inaccurately, you need to see it in different contexts so that you understand its correct meaning.

Feedback is most useful if *given immediately or when you want it*. For example:

— if a friend shows you how to throw a frisbee after you've made several unsuccessful attempts
— if a teacher gives you comments when you attempt to remember the proof of a theorem, or

— if you ask for comments and discussion on a tutorial paper immediately after delivering it.

Your teacher should have set aside time when work is due; your responsibility is to hand in your work on time. Ask your teacher when your work will be available. If it hasn't been returned by this time, ask when you can expect it back. It's particularly important to ask for prompt comments if you need them to proceed with your next assignment, or if you're an external student for whom the return of work is already slow because of mailing time.

2 Recorded assessment

> For most of the students, the competitive grade has come to be the essence. The naive teacher points to the beauty of the subject and the ingenuity of the research; the shrewd student asks if he is responsible for that on the final exam.
>
> Paul Goodman

Assessment may include formal, structured comments, but more usually it consists of a letter grade, a percentage or a Pass/Fail mark. The effect of *grades and percentages* on students' learning is controversial. Some people argue that grades and percentages enable student performances to be ranked more efficiently and objectively. However, others argue that grading creates pressures which hinder learning, and that at least some aspects of student learning (such as tutorial participation or introductory courses) should not be graded. Some educational theorists question the validity of making *any* recorded assessment of a student's learning.

Recorded assessment may be based on *continuous* assessment and/ or on a major *final* paper or exam [see 'Exams', Ch. 5]. 'Continuous assessment' refers to frequent cumulative assessments of your learning by methods such as weekly tests, regular seminar papers, monthly assignments or a combination of these. It may be used on its own or in combination with a major final assessment.

Educators debate the value of both forms of assessment. Continuous assessment provides you with a variety of approaches and with regular feedback, but can limit your freedom to pursue topics in depth and in your own way. If your work is assessed only at the end of a course, you've no formal indication of your progress until then, and it's difficult to convey your total understanding of a subject in one final assessment.

Criteria and standards

When other people evaluate your learning, they usually do so in comparison with certain criteria. These include:

— your previous knowledge or work in an area
— the work of other students on a topic or subject area
— specific standards which have been decided on by one or more of
  the teachers involved in a course, and
— the educational models, theories and preferences of an individual
  teacher who directly assesses your work.

As well as academic standards, the evaluation of your work is shaped by administrative requirements. These may include demands for assessment methods which require minimum staff time or results which can be recorded in a particular computer format. They may reflect a desire to conform to practices in other institutions and the expectations of employers and professional organisations.

The criteria used may be widely accepted and may be clearly defined in an individual teacher's mind, but this doesn't make their use objective. In practice, the individual teacher adopts some of the guidelines used for evaluating learning in an area and combines these with a preference for certain academic conventions. And when applying these methods and criteria to your work, a teacher arrives at a result partly because of the feeling that your work evokes at the time.

The criteria used to arrive at a recorded assessment should reflect the objectives of an institution, a programme, a course and an assignment. For example, if you're expected to display knowledge about a particular topic or to write cogently, the assessment criteria should explicitly take account of this. Such criteria should be available to you so that you can check them against your objectives, so that you know what's expected of you, and so that you can plan your work schedule ahead of time.

For each programme, course or assignment, you need to know how you're to be assessed and the standard you're expected to reach to pass or achieve a particular grade or percentage.

You need to know:

— what work you're expected to complete, and when
— whether you must pass each assignment in a course (or each course in a programme), or whether you can fail one or two of the individual assignments/courses and still gain an overall pass
— whether results are given as a Pass/Fail, a grade, a percentage and/or comments
— who assesses your work
— what degree of choice *you* have in the four previous points
— whether you are able or expected to contribute to the assessment of your work, and
— whether you can appeal against or record a dissent from an assessment in your official file.

However, some evaluation criteria and standards are subjective, and subjective criteria cannot always be spelt out. Recorded assessment based on other people's aims inevitably means that you have to do a certain amount of guessing about what you're expected to learn. And as you're also required to compete with other students in your guessing, it's only fair that the rules of this guessing game are made as clear as possible.

This is particularly important where teachers have more than one criterion for assessment. For example, an assignment may be graded according to the content you select *and* your use of quotations *and* general writing style. If the result is recorded by a single letter— A, B, C, D, or E — the letter you're given can't tell you how well you've done on *each* of the criteria. Neither does it indicate how your teacher averaged or added up your performance for each criteria to arrive at a single grade. To learn from evaluation it's vital that you know *explicitly* why your teacher chose the particular letter grade, and that your receive comments or grades for each of the criteria involved. If recorded assessments are to mean anything useful to you, they must be accompanied by detailed comments. Hopefully, recorded assessments are formalities which follow on from the comments you're given, but this seems rarely to be the case. Why?

> ...students have to play an academic game to succeed. The rules of this game are determined by personal and organisational requirements of the course as they see them. These perceived requirements frequently conflict with aims explicitly stated by teachers. Teachers say they want students to have critical minds, but they feel threatened if they do. Teachers say they like students to write thoughtful answers in examinations, but they award marks on the basis on regurgitated 'facts'.
>
> Donald A. Bligh *et al*

Some underlying assumptions

Many students go through the process of being evaluated in their tertiary education without stopping to think about or question the process itself. However, underlying the purposes, methods and criteria of evaluation are assumptions which are often not made explicit. These assumptions are integral to the educational system, and as such it may not seem necessary or desirable for you to understand or question them. However, understanding the assumptions underlying evaluation can demystify the evaluation process; and questioning the assumptions can help you use evaluation for your learning purposes instead of blindly following someone else's. What are some of these assumptions?

Students should be evaluated by formal institutions

In our society, compulsory education in primary and secondary schools is seen as inevitable and desirable. As part of this belief, it's assumed that one of the purposes of formal education is to evaluate and grade students according to the knowledge they are judged to have acquired and the characteristics they are deemed to have displayed. Teachers, for example, may define a child as 'hyperactive', 'promising', 'lazy', 'a problem child', 'a tomboy', or 'too sensitive', or a child may be placed in stream A or stream E, in a 'professional' or 'manual' or 'commercial' class.

In universities and colleges, evaluation and grading is continued in a specialised way. Tertiary education is often seen in itself as desirable in terms of intellectual and social status, if not always in terms of usefulness. Where and what you study has a further effect on this status. Are you attending a technical college, a teachers' college, a college of advanced education, or a university? Are you training as a surgeon or a primary-school teacher or an accountant? Are you planning to do postgraduate work, or are you studying for a pass degree? Courses such as veterinary science or geology may be seen as 'relevant', or as 'mundane' and 'too job-oriented'. Subjects such as politics and literature are sometimes seen as 'real' and 'people-oriented', and sometimes as 'airy-fairy'. Your enrolment in these areas is often taken as an indicator of your status.

> "I've been to a day-school, too," said Alice. "You needn't be so proud as all that."
> "With extras?" asked the Mock Turtle, a little anxiously.
> "Yes," said Alice: "we learned French and music."
> "And washing?" said the Mock Turtle.
> "Certainly not!" said Alice indignantly.
> "Ah! Then yours wasn't a really good school," said the Mock Turtle in a tone of great relief.
>
> Lewis Carroll

Evaluation is best done by teachers

In universities and colleges, it's usually assumed that people who've researched and published in a subject can also teach that subject, whether or not they are trained as teachers. It's further assumed that they can and should evaluate students' learning in the subject. Correspondingly, any evaluation you as a student make of your own formal learning is usually seen as less satisfactory than a teacher's, or your evaluation is ignored altogether.

Students often assume that teachers decide what is worth learning and why and how this learning is evaluated. In reality these decisions are made by an individual teacher, a group of teachers, administrators, other educational institutions or — at a fundamental level — society in general. A teacher may decide if you deserve to pass a course which leads to your becoming a doctor; but he or she is mostly making that decision on behalf of other people. Those people may include a professional medical association which sets down standards for doctors, patients who expect certain skills in doctors, and government bodies which make decisions about the number of doctors needed.

Learning can be reliably graded

Along with the assumption that teachers are the best people to evaluate your learning goes the assumption that there are reliable methods which teachers can administer to grade learning, methods such as examinations and tests, essays and reports. Many people disagree about the value of these methods, but they are used frequently because they are familiar and because they produce 'results'. Too little consideration is given to whether the methods test what they are supposed to, or to alternatives such as self-evaluation or collective assessment. Very little thought is given to whether learning can or should be graded at all.

Evaluation can be objective

> Objectivity, in short, has the logical status of a myth: it builds up one sense of reality rather than others. It is a myth whose attainment and maintenance demands of its subjects a rigorous and continued asceticism ...
>
> Michael Novak

It's impossible for any human being to be completely objective, yet human beings make the decisions about the purposes, methods and criteria of evaluation and often assume that they are being objective. In practice their decisions are based on an array of beliefs and assumptions such as what 'education' can be, what a university or college should be, which knowledge is valuable, and whether such knowledge can or should be evaluated.

Sometimes the criteria by which your learning is evaluated appear to be objective. These criteria are often taken for granted, and most people who use them arrive at results they believe to be valid. These criteria appear even more objective when they are elaborated in a system of precedents and percentages, examinations and 'weighted averages', 'full-time equivalent students' and confidential files. How else, it is argued, is a teacher or employer to know the 'good' students unless students have mostly A's or firsts on an official record, unless a student has produced a thesis on an acceptable topic, or has completed all the work set for a course? It's easier and more economical to deal with the results of a system than with complex individuals. But problems arise when evaluation is claimed to be purely objective, or if the stated bases of evaluation differ from what students see as the real bases. As a student you need the opportunity to disagree with subjective assessments of your learning and to have an impact on these assessments.

Some teachers help with this because they acknowledge and attempt to spell out the assumptions, criteria, biases and beliefs by which they evaluate your learning. They don't assume that a practice which has 'always' been carried out, or which is used 'everywhere else' or is 'efficient' is thereby objective. These teachers don't attempt to judge your work by immutable standards of what Physics or History is all about. You as a student can then accept, reject or negotiate these teachers' decisions about your work according to your own reasons and needs for learning.

Academic failure implies personal failure

What if a piece of your knowledge is formally assessed and you are told that you don't know what you were expected to know — if you're given an E, or a Fail, or 45%? Many students assume there's little they can do. If you care about that particular area of knowledge, you'd probably try to find out what it is that you apparently don't know. You might ask yourself if you agree with the assessment. How would you decide? You could ask for the explicit criteria on which the assessment was based, but even then it would be difficult to decide if you agree unless you're dealing with a tangible physical skill like the ability to walk a straight line. What if you find that you disagree with the criteria? Do you challenge them?

Whatever you do, you will undoubtedly have to handle the implanted idea that you don't know. Do you fight it? Probably not, because teachers are people who know. Do you question a Fail on a university or college paper? Only if you have great confidence in your ability to write, to think and to understand, and if you are not overawed by authority of teachers and institutions. Can you learn from a Fail, apart from the unhappy fact that you have been classed as a failure? If you expected to pass or if you have to pass, you might try to find out why you failed and use this to help you pass. Otherwise you probably accept the verdict, and try again or drop out.

This is the power of evaluation in formal education — that even those who lose, accept that they deserve to lose. Why? Because all of us are taught from our first day at school that there are experts who know — doctors, judges, priests, scientists, football heroes and test pilots. And teachers are the experts who know when students should pass and should fail. We all know that we should learn and that we have to go to school to learn and then even to university or college if we want to learn some more. And teachers know what we should learn and when and how and why. As students, our job is to try to find our way through the maze of formal education, to discover the Right way to learn. We develop our own likes and dislikes among individual teachers and subjects, but we don't question the basic rules of the competition.

> School is...a training for later life not because it teaches the 3 Rs (more or less), but because it instills the essential cultural nightmare fear of failure, envy of success, and absurdity...
>
> Jules Henry

* * *

To have been accepted as a student in a tertiary educational institution means that you are accepted as a potential winner. The chances are high that as a new student you accepted most of the assumptions, purposes and criteria by which the decision was made. Whether you continue to accept any or all of them is one of the most fundamental decisions you can make as a tertiary student, and depends on how much you question and think about what learning is for you.

What are your assumptions about learning and formal education?
What do you want to learn?
How do you want to learn?
Why do you want to learn?

Further reading

Rowntree, Derek. *Assessing Students: How Shall We Know Them?* Harper and Row, London, 1977.

Appendix
Discrimination:
Sexist Language and Attitudes

The recent focus on discrimination has been concerned mostly with stereotypes based on sex, sexual preference or race. Some other stereotypes commonly perpetuated in our culture relate to a person's age, physical or mental handicap, religion, politics, economic circumstances and occupation. Using language which depicts people according to stereotypes is undesirable for a couple of reasons.

1 It shows a lack of awareness of our biases and prejudices. We can never be totally objective and it's essential to our learning and communicating that we're as honest as possible about our particular forms of subjectivity.

2 It reveals insufficient thought and care about what we're communicating. Some manifestations of the shoddy use of language are unsupported generalisations, terms which are not defined clearly, and cliches.

   • '*Australians are easy-going*'. Does this apply to all, most, many or a few? Has this general statement been supported and explained?

   • In '*a neurotic woman*' or '*the average Italian*', 'neurotic' and 'average' are both terms which have precise meanings in certain disciplines. Has their meaning been defined?

   • The phrase '*a career woman*' is sometimes used to describe a woman seriously interested in her work, or '*a dole bludger*' to describe someone who is unemployed. Why have these cliches been used?

In this appendix we look at sexist language and attitudes as an example of discrimination.

Avoiding sexist language

Sexist language is based on stereotypes which assume that being biologically male or female implies a whole range of associated characteristics. Occasionally it *is* relevant to describe a woman as petite or a man as husky, or to describe a female person as someone's wife or mother, but all too often adjectives such as these form part of a description in which they are irrelevant.

> 'Janet Smith, a petite brunette, has just become the first woman truck driver for the company.'

> 'Henry Jones, a husky ex-footballer, today graduated as a male nurse.'

One useful test for sexist language is to substitute mention of a woman where a man is mentioned and vice versa. Would you talk about a 'boy Friday' or write 'Fred Smith, a tall redhead who is married to a typist, was today awarded his second gold medal'? How do you react to reading 'The stockbroker should at all times protect her clients' interests'?

Pronouns — 'he'? 'him'? 'his'?

'He' is commonly used to refer to both females and males; for example, 'The best time to teach a child to do maths with little or no trouble is when he is about one or two years old'. This convention limits our view of reality. Studies have shown that children literally think of a male when they read or hear the word 'he', and many people who argue for the use of 'he' as a convenient shorthand to include both sexes object to the suggestion that 'she' might serve the same purpose.

The English language does not have a single pronoun which covers both 'he' and 'she' (or 'him' and 'her', or 'his' and 'her'), but there are alternatives to using only 'he', 'him', and 'his'.

- Replace the masculine pronoun with 'he or she', 'him or her', 'her or his', or with 'he/she', or 's/he', or with 'one' or 'you'.

- Alternate the use of 'he' and 'she':

> This monograph is for a teacher concerned with improving her communication with her students...the intention of the authors is to share experiences with the reader so that he may find some of them helpful in his own situations.

- Change from singular to plural:

> This monograph is for teachers concerned with improving their communication with their students...The intention of the authors is to share experiences with teachers who may find some of them helpful in their own situations.

- Re-word to eliminate unnecessary gender pronouns:

> This monograph is for a teacher concerned with improving communication with students...The intention of the authors is to share experiences so that a reader may find some of them helpful in teaching situations.

'Man'?

The word 'man' has a double usage — to refer to a male person and to describe humanity in general. As with the use of 'he', the word 'man' creates a male image for us. When we read of 'man the hunter' or 'the descent of man' we visualise a male person and forget about the women who are supposedly part of the total picture.

Instead of:	Consider:
Man or mankind	Humanity, human beings, people, the human race, men and women
Manpower	Human resources, human energy, workers, workforce
The man in the street	A typical person, the average person, lay person
Manmade	Synthetic, artificial, manufactured, constructed
Chairman	Chairperson, the chair, leader, co-ordinator, head.

Apples are apples and oranges are oranges; but apples *and* oranges are fruit.

Without Bias

'A man's job'? 'Woman's work'?

Our language is based on assumptions, frequently outdated about the occupations of women and men (for example, nurses are assumed to be female and doctors male). Men are often categorised according to their occupation and income. Women are categorised primarily as mothers and wives (despite the fact that over forty per cent of Australian women are in the paid workforce). We read newspaper headlines such as 'Rebel mum of three suicides in cell' to describe the prison death of a prominent political activist and journalist, or 'Dr Samuel Keep, a leading physician, and his wife Margaret' is used to introduce two doctors who are married. Women should be treated as people in their own right, and women in traditionally masculine fields (or men in traditionally feminine fields) should not be described as if they are freaks.

Instead of:	Consider:
'Anna Clarke, career girl' to describe a woman who takes her work seriously	Describing the woman's occupation 'Anna Clarke, teacher' or 'Anna Clarke, engineer'
Terms such as 'male secretary', 'lady executive' or 'woman doctor'	The terms 'secretary', 'executive' or 'doctor' to apply to both men and women
Workmen	Worker, labourer, employee or staff member
Author or authoress	Author
Waiter or waitress	Steward or attendant
The lady of the house, housewife	The consumer, home maker
Cleaning lady, cleaning women	Housekeeper, domestic help, cleaner.

Names

Different attitudes of men and women are reflected in the inconsistent use of forenames and surnames, for example, 'Peter Braithwaite and Miss Smith', 'Braithwaite and Janet Smith'. The use of titles also reveals attitudes, for example, 'Dr White and Alison Black' (instead of Dr Black). One of the most common examples of discrimination by title is that the title 'Mr refers to both married and single men, while the terms 'Mrs' and 'Miss' place emphasis on a woman's marital status (thus assuming marital status should be an important part of a woman's identity).

Instead of:	Consider:
Peter Braithwaite and Miss Smith	Mr Braithwaite and Ms Smith, or Peter Braithwaite and Janet Smith
'Dr Tom Jones and Ms Margot Thomas recently published a book on marine biology. Margot is now doing further research on this topic. Dr Jones is acting as her assistant.'	'Dr Tom Jones and Ms Margot Thomas recently published a book on marine biology. Ms Thomas is now doing further research on this topic. Dr Jones is acting as her assistant.'

Put-downs

Patronising descriptions of women are unnecessary and are often cliches.

Instead of:	Consider:
The girls, the ladies, the fair sex, the weaker sex	The women
The missus, the wife, the little lady, the better half	Wife (or refer to the woman concerned by her name)
Chicks, birds, girls	Girls (for the younger women), women
Bitch, shrew	Women, angry women
Libbers, bra burners	Feminists, liberationists

- Issues that seriously concern women should not be considered as trivial or funny, for example, the use of 'Ms' as a title, discrimination in employment, or rape.

- Jokes which are based on stereotypes of both women and men are offensive to many people, for example, jokes about nagging mothers-in-law, incompetent women drivers, frustrated spinsters, gossiping housewives, men-hating 'women's libbers', hysterical females, hen-pecked husbands, helpless house-husbands, playboys, effeminate males.

- Don't assume that women are always shorter, smaller and weaker than men.

- Referring to 'men and ladies' instead of 'men and women' or 'ladies and gentlemen' is discriminatory.

- Don't always refer to 'men and women' or 'he and she'; use 'women and men' or 'she and he' as well.

- Avoid talking about 'man and wife'; instead use 'partners', 'husband and wife', 'a man and a woman' or 'a couple'.

Identity

'Who's she?' they asked
and straight away
I answered back,
'She's Brian's wife'.
Why say it so?
Why not just say
'She's Josephine'?
A rose by any name
should smell as sweet.
But Josephine's a sweeter name
by far, than
'Brian's wife'
or 'Jenny's mum'
or 'Noelene's friend'.

Brian's Wife Jenny's Mum

Male and female characteristics

- Unless it's relevant to describe a woman's or man's physical or sexual attributes, omit them. Women are often described as blonde or brunette, curvaceous or slim, or men as tall, dark or handsome when such a description is unnecessary.

- Instead of assuming that only women can be gentle, compassionate, sensitive and only men can be decisive, logical, assertive, strong, or adventurous, think of these qualities as human rather than sex-based. Similarly, avoid the assumption that only women are passive, helpless or emotional and only men are insensitive, angry or ruthless.

- Women who don't comply with the stereotype of a passive female and men who don't conform to the image of an aggressive male are often described in a negative way.

Instead of:	Consider:
A pushy woman	A forceful woman
A gossiping woman	A talkative woman
An effeminate man	A gentle man
An hysterical woman	A woman who is upset
An aggressive woman	An assertive woman

Avoiding sexist attitudes

Sexist language is a subtly pervasive yet tangible way of perpetuating stereotypes. Sexist attitudes are equally pervasive and subtle. The following are some instances of sexist attitudes which you're likely to find in written material.

- **The 'invisible woman'** attitude occurs when women as part of a group or people or society are ignored or rarely included in writings about that group or society. For example:

  — in writings or human evolution, where only hunting societies and the activities of male homo sapiens are considered, with little or no reference to the female of the species
  — in sociology, where there has until recently been a dearth of studies of housework as work in itself, rather than as part of a woman's role as a wife/mother
  — in children's books, where the majority of characters in stories and illustrations are male, and

— in anthologies, where most or all of the writers represented are male.

- **The 'token woman'** position is seen when individual women are described because they are unusual but the majority of women are still ignored. For example:

  — in history texts, which include descriptions of the life of a woman who is prominent as a social reformer (such as Elizabeth Fry) or a pioneer in a traditionally male field (such as Elizabeth Blackwell), but which neglect the 'ordinary' female contemporaries of these women.

- **The 'patronised woman'** approach occurs when a special section is allocated to women without a corresponding section for men. For example:

  — in newspapers which have women's pages, with their implications that woman aren't interested in the rest of the paper, that men don't have gender-based interests, or that men don't share women's concerns.
  — a book index which has an entry under 'Women' but none under 'Men'.

- **Stereotypes** of women and men are common. For example:

  — in social studies texts, which assume that women are wives and mothers and that men are breadwinners.
  — in career information brochures, which assume that women are nurses and men are doctors, or that females have no serious work interests.

Instances of these attitudes can also be found when discrimination is based on grounds other than sex. For example, the 'invisible' ethnic group; the invisibility of people in poverty; the 'token' black or 'working-class' representative; the patronised handicapped person or religious sect; stereotypes of homosexuals or of elderly people or of 'socialists'.

* * *

In writing, reading and speaking, being aware of discriminatory attitudes or language in ourselves and in others requires that we question and evaluate what's communicated. The discriminatory habits of many academic disciplines need to be redressed, but these changes are not just exercises to be followed in the interests of scholarly 'objectivity'. They are changes which involve an awareness of the biases we bring to our learning, changes in who we are and how we see the other human beings with whom we live. Such changes can only be achieved by consistent and conscious effort because our discriminatory attitudes and language are part of who we have learned to be.

Further reading

Curriculum Development Centre. *Guidelines for Writers*. Curriculum Development Centre, Canberra, 1975.

International Association of Business Communicators. *Without Bias: A Guidebook for Nondiscriminatory Communication*. International Association of Business Communicators, San Francisco, 1977.

Lakoff, Robin. *Language and Woman's Place*. Harper and Row, New York, 1975.

McGraw-Hill Book Company. *Guidelines for Equal Treatment of the Sexes in McGraw-Hill Book Company Publications*. McGraw-Hill Book Co., New York, 1974.

Random House. *Random House Guidelines for Multi-Ethnic/Nonsexist Survey*. Random House, New York, 1976.

Notes

1 You

1   Bob Samples, *The Metaphoric Mind: A Celebration of Creative Consciousness*, Addison–Wesley Publishing Co., Reading, Massachusetts, 1976, p. 176.

2–3   Gay Gaer Luce, *Body Time: The Natural Rhythms of the Body*, Paladin, St. Albans, England, 1973, p. 177.

3   Evelyn Waugh, *Decline and Fall*, Chapman and Hall, London, 1928, p. 143.

4   Virginia Woolf, *A Room of One's Own*, A Harbinger Book, Harcourt, Brace and World, New York, 1929, p. 18.

5   Henry Ford (attributed), in J.M. and M.J. Cohen (eds.), *A Dictionary of Modern Quotations*, Penguin Books, Middlesex, England, 1971, p. 76.

6   Fred Morgan, *Here and Now II: An Approach to Writing Through Perception*, Harcourt, Brace, Jovanovich, New York, 1972, p. 3.

6   Liz Carpenter, in 'The All-American Complaint "If I Only Had the Time…"', *Ms*, January, 1977, p. 48.

         Lee Israel, in 'The All-American Complaint "If I Only Had the Time…"', p. 48.

8   Sidney B. Simon et al., *Values Clarification: A Handbook of Practical Strategies for Teachers and Students*, Hart Publishing Co., New York, 1972, pp. 13–14.

9   Eight-year old girl, in Hazel Edwards (ed.), *Women Returning to Study*, Primary Education, Richmond, Victoria, 1975, p. 43.

11   Margaret Norton, in Allan Hall (ed.), *Worse Verse* from the Look! pages of the Sunday Times, Times Newspapers, London, undated and not paginated.

12   Henry David Thoreau, *Walden and On the Duty of Civil Disobedience*, A Signet Classic, The New American Library, New York, 1960, p. 216.

2 Planning When and How You Study

13   Jerome K. Jerome, *The Idle Thoughts of an Idle Fellow*, J.W. Arrowsmith, Bristol, 1947, p. 51.

14   Proverb.

15–16	Norton Juster, *The Phantom Tollbooth*, William Collins Sons and Co., London, 1962, p. 24.
18	Edwin C. Bliss, *Getting Things Done: The ABC's of Time Management*, The Macmillan Co., Australia, 1977, pp. 32–3
18	Lewis Carroll, *The Annotated Alice: Alice's Adventures in Wonderland and Through the Looking-Glass*, revised edn., Penguin Books, Middlesex, England, 1970, p. 304.
19	Vivienne, in Hazel Edwards (ed.), *Women Returning to Study*, p. 26.
21	Lewis Carroll, p. 322.

3 Becoming an Independent Student

24	Thomas Carlyle, in *The Oxford Dictionary of Quotations*, 3rd edn., Oxford University Press, Oxford, 1979, p. 131.
25–6	Lewis Carroll, p. 88.
26	Michael Deakin, *The Children on the Hill: The Story of an Extraordinary Family*, Quartet Books, London, 1973, p. 27.
31	Gwen Wesson (ed.), *Brian's Wife Jenny's Mum*, Dove Communications, East Malvern, Victoria, 1975, pp. 164–5.

4 Asking Your Own Questions

36	John Holt, *Instead of Education: Ways to Help People Do Things Better*, Penguin Books, Middlesex, England, 1977, p. 20. © John Holt, 1976.
36	Donald Sutherland, *Gertrude Stein: A Biography of her Work*, Yale University Press, New Haven, 1951, p. 203.
37	Bertrand Russell quoted by G.M. Carstairs 'Concepts of Insanity in Different Cultures', in *The Listener*, LXXII, 1844, July 30, 1964, p. 160.
37	N.J Berrill, *Man's Emerging Mind*, Dennis Dobson, London, 1958, p. 158.
38	Kurt Vonnegut Jr., *Cat's Cradle*, Victor Gollancz, London, 1971, p. 150.
38	Jules Feiffer, *Crawling Arnold*, Dramatists Play Service, New York, 1963 in J.M. and M.J. Cohen (eds.), *A Dictionary of Modern Quotations*, p. 72.
39	Dylan Thomas, *Quite Early One Morning*, New Directions Publishing, New York, 1954, quoted in Daniel G. Kozlovsky, *An Ecological and Evolutionary Ethic*, Prentice–Hall, Englewood Cliffs, New Jersey, p. 7.
40	Lewis Carroll, p. 251.
41	John Holt, *Instead of Education*, pp. 87–88.
41	John Holt, *How Children Fail*, Penguin Books, Middlesex, England, 1969, p. 166.

5   Learning and Remembering

44   Ogden Nash, 'Who Did Which? or Who Indeed?' in *I Wouldn't Have Missed It: Selected Poems of Ogden Nash*, Little, Brown and Co., Boston, 1972, p. 224.

45   Lewis Carroll, pp. 137–88.

45   Sam Keen, *To a Dancing God*, Harper and Row, New York, 1970, p. 32.

47   Michel de Montaigne, 'On Liars', *Essays*, trans. by J.M. Cohen, Penguin Books, Middlesex, England, 1958, p. 30.

48   Lewis Carroll, p. 149.

50   Hermann Hesse, source unknown.

51   Lewis Carroll, pp. 247–8.

53   Jorge Luis Borges, 'Funes, the Memorious', *A Personal Anthology*, Picador, London, 1972, p. 33.

6   Defining and Researching a Topic

56   Lewis Carroll, p. 137.

61   Lewis Carroll, p. 269.

61   Robert M. Pirsig, *Zen and the Art of Motorcycle Maintenance*, Bantam Books, New York, 1975, p. 166. Originally published by The Bodley Head, London.

62   Marshall McLuhan, interviewed by Eric Norden 'Playboy Interview: Marshall McLuhan', *Playboy*, March, 1969, p. 54.

65   G.M. Trevelyan, *English Social History*, The Reprint Society, London, 1948, p. 588.

65   David Hawkins, 'What it Means to Teach' in *Teachers College Record*, 75, 1, September, 1973, p. 11.

68   Lewis Carroll, p. 86.

68   John Milton, in *The Oxford Dictionary of Quotations*, p. 352.

69   Idries Shah, 'Rahimi', *Thinkers of the East*, Penguin Books, Middlesex, England, 1974, p. 104.

70   Samuel Johnson, in *The Oxford Dictionary of Quotations*, p. 276.

7   Using Libraries and Other Information Sources

76   Edward Gibbon, in *The Oxford Dictionary of Quotations*, p. 224.

78   Sinclair Lewis, *Main Street*, Panther, London, 1961, p. 96.

79   *University Without Walls: First Report*, Antioch College, Yellow Spring, Ohio, undated, p. 32.

81   Werner Heisenberg, *Physics and Philosophy: The Revolution in Modern Science*, Allen and Unwin, London, 1959, p. 75.

83   John M. Culkin, S.J., 'A Schoolman's Guide to Marshall McLuhan', *Saturday Review*, L, March 18, 1967, p. 72.

84   Edmund Carpenter, 'The New Languages', in Edmund Carpenter and Marshall McLuhan (eds.), *Explorations in Communication: An Anthology*, Johnathan Cape, London, 1970, p. 163.

85   Marshall McLuhan, interviewed by Eric Norden, *Playboy Interview: Marshall McLuhan*, p. 54.

87   Ronald Firbank, 'The Flower Beneath the Foot', *The Complete Ronald Firbank*, Gerald Duckworth and Co., London, 1961, p. 500.

87   Marshall McLuhan, from the film 'This is Marshall McLuhan: The Medium is the Massage', USA, 1967.

8   Reading

91   W. Somerset Maugham, *The Summing Up*, William Heinemann, London, 1938, p. 92.

92   Doris Lessing, *Martha Quest*, A Plume Book, The New American Library, New York, 1970, p. 200.

96   John Holt, *Instead of Education*, pp. 74–75.

96–7   Doris Lessing, p. 28.

97   Lewis Carroll, p. 191

98   Francis Bacon, in *The Oxford Dictionary of Quotations*, p. 27.

100   Idries Shah, 'A Quality Must Have a Vehicle', *The Way of the Sufi*, Penguin Books, Middlesex, England, 1974, p. 61.

102   John M. Culkin, S.J., 'A Schoolman's Guide to Marshall McLuhan', p. 301.

104   Samuel Johnson, in *The Oxford Dictionary of Quotations*, p. 280.

106   Lewis Carroll, pp. 189–190.

107   Lewis Carroll, p. 25.

9   Listening to Lectures

110   Samuel Johnson, source unknown.

111   Donald A. Bligh, *What's the Use of Lectures?* Penguin Education, Penguin Books, Middlesex, England, 1972, p. 61.

112   Lewis Carroll, p. 122.

112   Lewis Carroll, p 146.

114   Anon, in *A Dictionary of Modern Quotations*, p. 5.

115   Enrico Fermi, quoted in Anthony Smith, *The Body*, Penguin Books, Middlesex, England, 1970, p. 16.

10 Participating in Tutorials and Seminars

119   Samuel Johnson, in *The Oxford Dictionary of Quotations*, p. 280.

123   Lewis Carroll, p. 235.

124   A student quoted in The Nuffield Foundation, *Small Group Teaching: Selected Papers*, Group for Research and Innovation in Higher Education, London, 1976, p. 123.

124   Ben Jonson quoted in Anthony Smith, *The Body*, p. 432.

125   Lewis Carroll, p. 158.

126   Cicero, source unknown.

127   Anon.

128   A student quoted in The Nuffield Foundation, pp. 122–23.

129   Gwen Wesson (ed.), *Brian's Wife Jenny's Mum*, pp. 79–80.

11 Developing Your Own Writing Voice

131   Erica Jong, 'The Artist as Housewife/The Housewife as Artist' in *Here Comes and Other Poems*, A Signet Book, The New American Library, New York, 1975, p. 255.

132–3   Kurt Vonnegut, 'How to Write With Style', advertisement in *Psychology Today*, September, 1980, p. 58.

134   Peter Elbow, *Writing Without Teachers*, Oxford University Press, London, 1973, pp. 31–32.

134   Gwen Wesson (ed.), *Brian's Wife Jenny's Mum*, p. 109.

134   Kurt Vonnegut, 'How to Write With Style', p. 58.

135   Oscar Wilde, 'The Importance of Being Earnest', *The Portable Oscar Wilde*, Richard Aldington (ed.), Penguin Books, Middlesex, England, 1977, p. 481.

136   Ira Progoff, Intensive Journal, unpublished handout from The Personal Growth and Creativity Program of Dialogue House Associates, 45 West Tenth St., New York, N.Y. 10011.

137   Anais Nin, *The Diary of Anais Nin 1931–1934*, Gunther Stuhlmann (ed.), A Harvest Book, New York, 1966, p. 89.

138   W.H. Auden, 'Making, Knowing and Judging', *The Dyer's Hand and Other Essays*, Faber and Faber, London, 1963, p. 40.

139   Colette, *The Vagabond*, trans. by Enid McLeod, Penguin Books, Middlesex, England, 1960, p. 13.

12 Writing Assignments

142   Ernest Hemingway interviewed by George Plimpton, *Writers at Work: The Paris Review Interviews*, Viking, New York, 1965. p. 235.

144   Francis Quarles in *The Oxford Dictionary of Quotations*, p. 403.
144   Gwen Wesson (ed.), *Brian's Wife Jenny's Mum*, p. 81.
145   Russell Baker, 'At Lunch' in Joseph Frank, *You*, Harcourt, Brace, Jovanovich, New York, 1972, p. 63.
148   Lewis Carroll, p. 95.
149   Winston Churchill, *My Early Life*, School edn., Andrew Scotland (ed.), Odhams Press, London, 1958, p. 143.
151   Kurt Vonnegut, 'How to Write With Style', p. 58.
151   Samuel Johnson, in *The Oxford Dictionary of Quotations*, p. 274.
152   Gwen Wesson (ed.), *Brian's Wife Jenny's Mum*, p. 120.
154   Ken Macrorie, *Writing to be Read*, Hayden Book Co., New York, 1968, p. 89.

13   Writing Scientific Reports

157   F. Peter Woodford, 'Sounder Thinking Through Clearer Writing', *Science*, 156, 3776, May 1967, p. 743.
159   Robert M. Pirsig, p. 100.
162   Robert M. Pirsig, p. 101.
163   F. Peter Woodford, p. 744.
164   Robert M. Pirsig, p. 102.
167   F. Peter Woodford, p. 744.
168   A.A. Milne, *Winnie-The-Pooh*, Methuen and Co., London, 1926, p. 48.
171   John Holt, *Instead of Education*, p. 99–100.

14   Using Conventions

173   Lewis Carroll, p. 156.
174   Horace, 'The Art of Poetry' transl. by Edward Henry Blackeney in *The Complete Works*, Casper J. Kraemer, Jr. (ed.), The Modern Library, New York, 1936, p. 401.
174   Dorothy Parker, 'The Little Hours, in *Here Lies: The Collected Stories of Dorothy Parker*, Longmans, Green and Co., London, 1939, pp. 209–210.
176   Lord Byron, 'English Bards and Scotch Reviewers', 1.66. in *The Poetical Works of Lord Byron*, Oxford University Press, London, 1945, p. 114.
184   George Eliot, *Middlemarch*, The Zodiac Press, London, 1950, p. 70.
184   Charles Dickens, *Great Expectations*, Chapman and Hall, London, undated, p. 50.

15 Learning from Evaluation

188	James Agate, *A Dictionary of Modern Quotations*, p. 2.
189	John Holt, *Instead of Education*, p. 61.
189	Antoine de Saint-Exupéry, *The Little Prince*, Harcourt, Brace and World, New York, 1943, p. 39.
190	Winston Churchill, pp. 21–22.
192	*University Without Walls, First Report*, p. 35.
192–3	Peter Elbow, p. 118.
194	Paul Goodman, *Compulsory Miseducation*, Penguin Education, Penguin Books, Middlesex, England, 1971, p. 106.
196	Donald A. Bligh, et. al., *Teaching Students*, A Exeter University Teaching Service Production, Devon, England, 1975, p. 91.
197	Lewis Carroll, p. 128.
198	Michael Novak, *The Experience of Nothingness*, Harper and Row, New York, 1970, p. 37.
200	Jules Henry, *Culture Against Man*, Penguin Books, Middlesex, England, 1972, p. 250.

Appendix
Discrimination:
Sexist Language and Attitudes

203	International Association of Business Communicators, *Without Bias: A Guidebook for Nondiscriminatory Communication*, International Association of Business Communicators, San Francisco, 1977, p. 22.
205	Gwen Wesson (ed.), *Brian's Wife Jenny's Mum*, p. 26.

Bibliography

How to study

Anderson, J. et. al. *Study Methods: A Practical Guide*. McGraw-Hill, Sydney, 1969.

Barnett, Kate. *How to Study*. Sun Books, Melbourne, 1978.

Burnett, J. *Successful Study: A Handbook for Students*. Teach Yourself Books, Hodder and Stoughton, London, 1979.

Buzan, T. *Use Your Head*. BBC Publications, London, 1974.

Cassie, W.F. and Constantine, T. *Student's Guide to Success*. Macmillan Press, London, 1977.

Maddox, Harry. *How to Study*. 2nd edn. Pan Books, London, 1967.

Morgan, Clifford T. and Deese, James. *How to Study*. 2nd edn. McGraw-Hill, New York, 1969.

Rowntree, Derek. *Learn How to Study*. 2nd edn, Macdonald General Books, London, 1976.

Teaching study skills

Entwistle, N. and Hounsell, D. 'How Students Learn' in *Readings in Higher Education*. 1, University of Lancaster, 1975.

Gibbs, G. 'Can Students be Taught How to Study?' in *Higher Education Bulletin*, 5, 2, 1977.

Gibbs, G. *Teaching Students to Learn: A Student-Centred Approach*. The Open University Press, 1981.

Gibbs, G. and Northedge, A. 'Helping Students to Understand Their Own Study Methods' in *British Journal of Guidance and Counselling*. 7, 1979.

Hills, P.J. (ed.) *Study Courses and Counselling: Problems and Possibilities*. The Society for Research into Higher Education, University of Surrey, Guildford, Surrey, 1979.

Main, Alex. *Encouraging Effective Learning: An Approach to Study Counselling*. Scottish Academic Press, Edinburgh, 1980.

Educational theory

Bligh, Donald A. et al. *Teaching Students*. Exeter University Teaching Services, Devon, England, 1975.

Goodman, Paul. *Compulsory Miseducation*. Penguin Education, Middlesex, England, 1962.

Holt, John. *How Children Fail*. Penguin Books, Middlesex, England, 1967.

Holt, John. *Instead of Education: Ways to Help People Do Things Better*. Penguin Books, Middlesex, England, 1977

Illich, Ivan. *Deschooling Society*. Penguin Education, Middlesex, England, 1971.

Reimer, Everett. *School is Dead: An Essay on Alternatives in Education*. Penguin Education, Middlesex, England, 1971.

Index